GONDOLIN PRESS

Angela Pellicciari

A HISTORY OF THE CHURCH

Popes and Saints,
Emperors and Kings,
Gnosis and Persecution

Foreword by Card. Robert Sarah

gondolin press

A HISTORY OF THE CHURCH — *Angela Pellicciari*

Original title: *Una storia della Chiesa* (2015)
© Edizioni Cantagalli (Italy)

Translator: Giuseppe Maria Gennarini

© **gondolin press**

1331 Red Cedar Cir
80524 Fort Collins CO

www.gondolinpress.com
info@gondolinpress.com

2020 © Gondolin Institute LLC

ISBN 978-1-945658-18-1 *(soft cover)*

All the literary and artistic rights are reserved. The rights for translation, electronic storage, copy and total or partial adaptation, by any equipment, (including microfilm and photostats) are reserved for all countries. The Editor remains at disposition for eventual holders of rights who have not been traced.

First U.S. edition: March 2020

to Kiko and Carmen

Foreword

by Cardinal Robert Sarah

Entering a church makes me feel at home. It is in in silence and discernment that I find my way. Yet my faith is not something confined to that moment of silence. It becomes concrete in life, coloring everything with a profound new meaning. It allows me to live in history while being outside of history. To be "in the world, but not of the world" (John 15:10-21).

That is why the great cathedrals – which arose in the hundreds across Europe according to a model people have sought to replicate throughout the world - tell a story.

It is a story of evangelization, above all. The story of bringing people to an encounter with Christ. The story of the moment that encounter truly takes place and overturns our lives so much that we are not only changed but become missionaries (Pope Francis, General Audience of August 31, 2017). And being missionaries means precisely that: being in History, and seeking to make mankind's history a History of the Love of Man.

The great cathedrals all testify to this. Angela Pellicciari writes: "The society that by the will of God went to Palestine to fight was the same one that, to give praise to God, built cathedrals and convents, the most beautiful cathedrals and the most beautiful convents, everywhere in Europe."

Cathedrals whose builders are the people. The author recounts history by rereading the words of Rodulfus Glaber, who speaks of the construction of churches as of "a competition between one people and another", so much so that "you would think the world, casting off its old rags, wanted to clothe itself everywhere in the white garments of new churches."

The people built the cathedrals and did so to speak of God. Romanic and gothic cathedrals, with their frescoes and stained-glass windows, are "a living Bible", "teaching those who cannot read, and reminding those who can, of the stories the Bible recounts."

This need to speak of God changes and shapes history. In the countryside, the towns grow around their churches, while the great cities grow around the cathedrals. The art, music, and architecture have didactic and liturgical purposes, and from Paris to Durham to Prague, all share the same structure. And in the meantime, the faith of the people also creates the great pilgrimages towards Compostela, Amiens, Jerusalem, Rome, Cologne, Rocamadour.

Before reaching the Middle Ages, the Church had a story that began in Palestine and spread from Rome to the world. Following the Middle Ages were the Protestant waves that still today put the Church in crisis, and then the ideologies of the Enlightenment and Masonry that are a constant threat.

For this reason, it is important to present a history, and for this reason *A History of the Church*, by Angela Pellicciari, is above all the story of a living encounter that manifests itself in History.

The path the Church travels, from Jerusalem to Athens and Rome, and from Rome to the whole world, is a rough road, one of trial and error, heresies and very human wars. Yet, despite the miseries and unexpected reversals of history, it is a true path of evangelization.

We cannot understand the Church's history without understanding its missionary impulse, to cross boundaries and borders. The Church is Catholic because it is universal, that is, the Gospel is valid at every moment and in every place. It is precisely this universality that has the power to shape the world.

The Church's history teaches us that a living faith remains always, continuing to give shape and substance to cities, ideas, and villages, creating humanity.

A reading of *A History of the Church* is important above all to place the topic of faith and reason back at the center of things, and at the same time answer those who, due to a dictatorship of an increasingly pervasive relativism, undervalue the Sacrament, the first and ultimate cause of our life.

This humanity that makes history is, after all, enlivened by the Eucharist, Christ become incarnate, the raison d'etre and faith of every Christian who looks to Christ, "the Way, the Truth, and the Life." A reason for living that was at the heart of daily life in the monasteries.

As Benedict XVI explained: "First and foremost, it must be frankly admitted straight away that it was not their intention to create a culture nor even to preserve a culture from the past. Their motivation was much more basic. Their goal was: *quaerere Deum,* to seek God. Amid the confusion of the times, in which nothing seemed permanent, they wanted to do the essential – to try to find what was perennially valid and lasting, Life itself. They were searching for God. They wanted to go from the inessential to the essential, to the only truly important and reliable thing there is" (Benedict XVI, *Meeting with Representatives from the World of Culture*, Collège des Bernardins, Paris, September 12, 2008).

The birth of this civilization thus derives from faith by "accident". Just as the deterioration of every civilization represents, deep down, a detachment from the faith.

It is no mystery – and it pains me greatly to say – that our modern world is currently distancing itself from God on a practical level, creating a void in people. Thus, all are called to seek something that might promise an absolute and discover along the way that nothing merely human can fill the heart completely.

Men have experienced this throughout in history. For this reason, it is important to go back into church, and understand the meaning of each sacrament, each gesture of the liturgy, and then return to the Church, rereading its history with the extraordinary reading key that is the desire to evangelize.

These are the thoughts that have come to me upon reading *A History of the Church*. And I conclude this reflection with an invitation to return to that original spirit of searching for God. It is only with faith that we can be bearers of civilization and makers of history.

Jerusalem

Holy city Jerusalem, city of the great king, heart's desire, city of peace, hope in the midst of affliction, place of God's manifestation. "Next year in Jerusalem!" This is how pious Jews greet each other. Throughout the history of the Jewish people, the most significant events all took place in Jerusalem: the sacrifice of Isaac, the kingdom of David, the Temple construction. Jerusalem remains the throbbing heart of Judaism for all ages.

Jerusalem is also the city where Jesus Christ, the long-awaited Messiah, fulfilled God's promises to the chosen people. Jesus died, rose again and ascended to heaven, all in Jerusalem. Also Pentecost took place in Jerusalem. Almost all the main events in the history of the world transpired in Jerusalem.

In the *Letter to the Hebrews* one reads that Christ took flesh, so "that through death he might destroy him who has the power of death, that is, the devil; and deliver all those who through fear of death were subject to lifelong bondage": the resurrection of Jesus is the event which changes history, because it frees people from the terror of death.

Witnesses to Jesus' resurrection, the apostles and disciples kept still until they were invaded by the strength of the Holy Spirit. Only then, were they empowered to leave the locked Cenacle and carry out what the Lord had commanded them: "Go into all the world and preach the gospel to the whole creation." The history of the Church is the recounting of the facts that occurred between Pentecost and the descent from heaven, from God, of the holy city, the New Jerusalem, "prepared as a bride adorned for her husband."

Certainly, during the time of this earthly pilgrimage, everyday faith is put to the test. Since the very first moment, the Church learned to deal with divisions, failures, and betrayals. However, the course had been already set: heaven. In the *Second Letter to Timothy*, Paul wrote: "I have fought the good fight, I have finished the race, I have kept the faith. Henceforth there is laid up for me the crown of righteousness, which the Lord, the righteous judge, will award to me on that Day."

In Jesus' age, the world was united under Rome's legal system, culture and power. Moved by the Holy Spirit, Peter and Paul, the first Pope and the apostle to the gentiles, took off for Rome and there concluded their earthly pilgrimage. "For here we have no lasting city, but we seek the city which is to come," is written in the *Letter to the Hebrews*. The Church was born in Jerusalem and though on earth it has no true dwelling place, it chose Rome as the seat for Peter's service.

Rome

> "A proud man was the Roman [Mark],
> His speech a single one,
> But his eyes were like an eagle's eyes
> That is staring at the sun." (V: 140-143)
> "Bear not my body home,
> For all the earth is Roman earth
> And I shall die in Rome." (V: 149-151)

This was written by Chesterton in *The Ballad of the White Horse*. The whole world is Roman earth, wrote the English poet at the turn of the 20th century. Chesterton identified in Rome the heart of the battle between light and darkness, order and chaos, life and death. The intuition of this connection to Rome articulates the common thread which accompanied Christian culture throughout the centuries.

"When the fullness of time had come, God sent his Son," wrote Paul to the Galatians. What does the phrase, "fullness of time" mean? The Fathers of the Church, for the most part, identified Rome and its empire with the fullness of time. Let's try to understand why.

Half a century before the birth of Christ, the Greek historian Diodorus Siculus described the essence of Rome with these words: "The whole world as if it were one city." The same words were used three centuries later by another Greek, the rhetorician Aelius Aristide, in his *Encomium of Rome*: "Everything is at everyone's disposal. No one is a foreigner anywhere"; at the turn of the 5th century the Latin poet Rutilius Namazianus sang: "You built one sole fatherland for different peoples; you shrunk the world to one city."

The whole world is one city; the whole world is Rome in the same way that the Christian announcement is catholic, which means universal. It is directed to the entire world and cannot be constricted by the boundaries of a single nation. "There is neither Jew nor Greek, there is neither slave nor free, there is neither male nor female, for you are all one in Christ Jesus," wrote Paul in the *Letter to the Galatians*; and in the *Letter to the Colossians*: "There is no longer Greek and Jew, circumcised and uncircumcised, Barbarian, Scythian, slave and free; but Christ is all in all!"

The universal dimension to which Rome aspires is fully embodied in the Church, as Leo the Great clearly stated: "That you, holy and chosen people, priestly and kingly city, would preside by divine religion more extensively than by earthly domination." This was precisely the reason for Peter's coming to Rome. In the words of Benedict XVI, this is "the permanent mission of Peter: that the Church never identify itself with only one nation, with only one culture or only one State; that it always be the Church of all; that it gather humanity into one beyond all frontiers and, in the midst of this world's divisions, make present the peace of God, the reconciling force of his love."

The Roman Empire at the peak of its expansion

It was for this reason that Christ's disciples insisted on their being roman. Tertullian defined it *ridicola dementia*, that is, a ridiculous folly, the thought that Christians were enemies to Rome. The enemies of Rome are rather those emperors who persecute Christians, wrote Lactantius. Ambrose thought that the Romans who remained pagan were barbarians while he exalted Christians as the true heirs of Camillus' *virtus* and Regulus' and Scipio's *militia*.

The history of the Church, of its persecutions, of its victories and of its defeats, coincides with the history of Rome.

The Virigin gives birth to a Child

"The virgin shall conceive and bear a child, who shall be called Emanuel." This is what Isaiah prophesied in the 8th century before Christ. Seven hundred years later in Rome, Virgil, the greatest poet in the time of Emperor Augustus Caesar, wrote in the IV Eclogue: "Now does the virgin return... a new humanity descends from the high heavens. A child is to be born and with him the iron peoples shall decline, a new golden people shall arise on the earth [...] He shall free the earth from the pangs of terror. He will partake of the life of the gods [...] immediately, my child, the earth, by no human work, shall bring forth its fruit, and our cattle shall no longer fear huge terrible lions."

Virgil wrote that flocks will no longer fear lions. Isaiah used similar expressions to describe the new creation brought about by the son of the virgin: "The wolf shall dwell with the lamb, the leopard shall lie down with the kid; the calf and the lion shall graze together, and a little child shall guide them. The cow and the bear shall graze together; their young shall lie down together. The lion shall eat straw like the ox. The nursing child shall play over the hole of the asp, and the weaned child shall put its hand in the adder's den."

Not by chance Dante chose Virgil as teacher and guide on his journey through hell and purgatory.

Inflexible and ruthless with its enemies yet careful not to break its agreements, Roman civilization was founded on respect for the law, *virtus*, and *pietas*. Rome became Rome because its will to power was sustained by a constant attention to familial and social virtues and duties. Worship of the gods and ancestors created a community which was conscious of its own duties and obligations because its identity was firmly anchored in its collective and family history.

Benedict XVI stressed how western culture is the synthesis between Roman law and the Gospel. *Unicuique suum*: "On the one hand was the great roman law, natural law, man's natural culture in the concrete form it took under roman culture, with its laws and sense of justice; on the other hand, was the Gospel." Pagan Rome and Christian Rome. Legend attributes the founding of Rome to the twin brothers Romulus and Remus. In the same way, the history and tradition of the Church identify the founding of Christian Rome with the two apostles Peter and Paul. "These are your holy fathers, your true shepherds, who in order to make you worthy of the kingdom of heaven, have built much better and more fittingly than those who worked to lay the first foundations of your walls," wrote Leo the Great.

Christians are accustomed to honor their history's greatest champions with feast days. The feast of Rome, the feast of its patrons Saints Peter and Paul is June 29. The same day unites the memory of Peter and Paul, a new brand of brothers, the two columns on whom the Church's capital was built.

The drunken woman

The universal and law-abiding Rome is not the only Rome. Next to her lives another Rome enslaved to power, violence and abuse.

In his *First Letter*, Peter wrote: "Your sister church in Babylon, chosen together with you, sends you greetings." While Christians identify themselves with the great roman tradition, at the same time, they viewed Rome as the Babylon of Jesus' times. Babylon was the place where the Jews had been deported and enslaved and the city's people were so cruel that they commanded the deported to sing songs of joy from Zion in their place of exile.

Probably as a precautionary measure, to avoid that his presence in Rome be noticed, Peter spoke to the community that "dwells in Babylon." Instead John, in the *Book of Revelation*, used a metaphor to allude to Rome. But his description is so precise that it cannot be mistaken for any other place: "The seven heads are seven mountains on which the woman is seated; also they are seven kings." With regard to the woman he said, "That woman was drunk with the blood of the saints and the blood of the witnesses to Jesus."

During the *pax romana*, the world saw an age united by culture: everywhere, the citizens of this immense empire lived in the same way. Throughout Europe, Africa and Asia, the archeological remains of cities and homes witness exhaustively to how roman culture was a unifying tissue which spread everywhere. Romans lived in the same luxurious, modern and splendid cities, planned according to a consolidated model; they lodged in homes built with the same criteria; their free time was cadenced by the same habits and pass-times. Besides the feasts, horse races, orgies, and thermal baths, there were also circus spectacles, games which pit life against death in a live show: Romans were passionate fans of gladiator combat and were greatly entertained by the sight of men caught up in a vain struggle to ward off the beasts they were served to as feed.

The "great whore", the "great city that rules over the kings of the earth," at the end will be devoured by the same beast on which she was seated, prophesied John in exultation: "Fallen, fallen is Babylon the great!" Without a doubt, Babylon is Rome. But it is not only Rome: the prophecy applies to every city that raises itself up as queen and master of the world. Against these cities, John prophesied Jesus' triumph and their complete annihilation together with the demonic beasts which enslaved them.

> "Hallelujah!
> Salvation and glory and power
> to our God;
> for his judgments are true and just;
> he has judged the great whore
> who corrupted the earth with her fornication,
> and he has avenged on her
> the blood of his servants!"

You, follow Me

The Book of Numbers says that, "the man Moses was very humble, more so than anyone else on the face of the earth." Simon was nothing less. Impulsive, impetuous, simple, in love with Jesus and by him called Peter. He denied the Master in the hour of trial. Forgiven, he mended his ways; he came to know himself and exercised the primacy by serving tirelessly and with all humility.

Verses 18 and 19 of chapter 16 in the Gospel of Matthew read as follows: "You are Peter and on this rock I will build my church, and the gates of Hell will not prevail against it. I will give you the keys of the kingdom of heaven, and whatever you bind on earth shall be bound in heaven, and whatever you lose on earth shall be loosed in heaven." Jesus wanted Peter to be the first and the apostles respected this assignment. Immediately after the effusion of the Holy Spirit, it was Peter who announced the victory of Christ over death; it was he who represented the Christian community; it was always Peter who spoke in John's presence – the same apostle whom Jesus loved and the only one who stood at the foot of the cross' torment. His person was so effective and so powerful, that his shadow was enough to heal the sick who thronged his path.

Though he was indeed the accepted leader, he was bitterly rebuked by apostles and disciples alike for entering the house of pagans and for eating with them (Jews referred to pagans as "dogs" and since they viewed them as impure, they were barred from having any contact with them). How did Simon-Peter react? With humility. He was neither irritated nor harsh in his reaction towards those brothers who spoke unwittingly; he limited himself to retelling the facts in all meekness and simplicity: I was praying, I had a vision, the Spirit told me to follow those who had come to find me without hesitation and I was lead to the house of the Centurion Cornelius; I had just started to speak when the Spirit descended on those who were there, just like at one time it descended upon us; "who was I that I could withstand God?" When they heard this, all rejoiced that the pagans converted. Yet, they had just put their leader on trial.

"I am coming to gather all nations and all tongues; and they shall come and shall see my glory": Israel had a hard time understanding that Isaiah's prophecy was fulfilled. Learning how to live together with pagans and how to accept them as brothers was no easy task for the chosen people. In fact, observant Jews view it as a scandal to entertain relations and eat with the uncircumcised. So the difficulties persisted. Sure. Peter had laid his hands on the gentiles. But, let's be reasonable here. We should still keep some kind of reserve, some distance: the new arrivals still have to learn how to submit to the demands of the law, to the laws of purity and, above all, to circumcision. Therefore, let them be circumcised.

What did Peter, the fisherman now fisher of men, do then? He hesitated. He waited for Paul and Barnabas. Newly arrived from Antioch and strongly opposed to the idea of forcing circumcision on the new converts, they fervently argued the issue against Jerusalem's elders, some of whom, for the most part Pharisees, were favorable. "After there had been much debate," the book of Acts details that "Peter rose" and resolved the issue: no, we must not impose anything on converted pagans: "God, who knows the heart, bore witness to them, giving them the Holy Spirit just as he did to us; and he made no distinction between us and them, but cleansed their hearts by faith."

This decision made history. The heart must be circumcised, not the flesh. It marked the passage from Judaism to Christianity.

Yet, the conflict didn't stop there. When Peter arrived in Antioch on a pastoral visit to the communities evangelized by Paul, the clash became public: "I opposed him face to face because he stood condemned," wrote Paul to the Galatians. In this case, the problem was the eating table: are Jews allowed to eat with pagans? Again, Peter hesitated: at first, he ate with them without a quibble. But then, "fearing the circumcision party," he "drew back and separated himself." Paul objected that if this was how things stood, then Christ's sacrifice was in vain: "If justification were through the law, then Christ died to no purpose." Peter understood that Paul was right, so he stopped acting "insincerely," and put an end to the hypocrisy and duplicity towards the gentiles. United to Peter, the whole Church accepted to grant full *status* of brothers to all pagan converts: "So then you are no longer strangers and sojourners, but you are fellow citizens with the saints and members of the household of God, built upon the foundation of the apostles and prophets, Christ Jesus himself being the cornerstone," wrote Paul to the Ephesians.

Jesus foretold with what kind of death, Peter would have glorified God in his old age: "Another will gird you and carry you where you do not wish to go." And what will become of John, asked the impulsive Peter after seeing the disciple Jesus loved following close by: "If it is my will that he remains until I come, what is it to you? You, follow me!" Peter really followed: crucified upside down in Nero's circus.

Many followed with Peter and in his footsteps. In the first three centuries, to be elected Pope was the same as signing a death warrant. Also more recent times, the last few centuries, showed how often, Christ has come back to say especially to the follower of the first among the apostles: you follow me.

The Age of Paul

A great historian of roman antiquity, Santo Mazzarino (1916-1987), a Marxist atheist, defined the 1st century after Christ as "the Age of Paul the apostle." Paul's personality, which "is not even remembered by contemporary historians," is the dominant personality: "The apostle Paul rises as the giant of his time."

It could not be better said. He was a Pharisee and a violent man, a persecutor of Christians on behalf of the Temple; an abortion, so he described himself. Upon his conversion, he became the most untiring witness of Jesus' resurrection: first to the Jews and then to the pagans. Persecuted everywhere by his fellow Jews, in the *Second Letter to the Corinthians* he wrote that, "five times I have received at the hands of the Jews the forty lashes less one; three times I have been beaten with rods; once I was stoned." After having done everything humanly possible to announce the Messiah's coming to the chosen people, he solemnly declared: "Your blood fall upon your head: I am innocent; from now on I will go to the pagans."

Nonetheless, also in Rome, while trying to convince people of his own blood that the salvation promised was fulfilled in Jesus Christ, at the same time, he exhorted the pagans not to swell up with pride if, for the time being, God had placed a veil on the heart of the Jewish people so that they would not convert: "A hardening has come upon part of Israel, until the full number of the Gentiles come in, and so all Israel will be saved." It was for the benefit of pagans that Jews were disobedient. It is in view "of the mercy shown to you." But the "gifts and the call of God are irrevocable" and Israel's election remains forever because "God has not rejected his people whom he foreknew." Paul reaffirms: "Through their trespass, salvation has come to the Gentiles." Israel is the good olive tree while the Gentiles are the wild olive shoots grafted onto the true olive tree.

Not by chance, Paul's doctrine about Israel is described with great detail in the *Letter to the Romans*, the reputation of which "is proclaimed in all the world." Still today, despite all the hardships faced during the second millennium, his doctrine remains the key point of reference for the Church's magisterium on the Jewish people.

Paul never tired of admonishing and writing to the communities he established in order to make the brothers become "perfect" in obedience to constituted authorities, in brotherly charity, in married life, in the education of children, in their relationship to slaves. Christian life is the life of the new man and Paul urged them to behave as he did: "I beg you, become as I am, for I also have become as you are," he wrote to the Galatians.

Paul was a giant in terms of his life's perfection, a giant in doctrine, a giant in outlining the structure of community life, a giant in his visions. But he was also a sign of contradiction. Therefore, throughout the centuries, he became a special target of the hatred shown by Jesus' enemies.

Peter and Paul, the Church's columns, were both public sinners: one was a traitor and the other was a murderous persecutor. It shall always be so for centuries to come: the heroism of one's love for God grows in proportion to the awareness of one's own sin. Just like it happened to Mary Magdalen, the woman from whom Jesus expelled seven demons. She loved much, so much that she merited receiving the risen Lord's first apparition.

Strive for perfection

"Blessed are you poor"; "Blessed are you when they shall insult you and persecute you, and utter all kinds of evil against you falsely on my account"; "for if you love those who love you, what reward do you have?"; "love your enemies": no man is able to carry out Jesus' will unless he is a man of heaven, someone transformed by the Holy Spirit into a Christian, that is to say, another Christ. How did the apostles behave in front of such high-minded teaching? Did they remain faithful to what was entrusted to them or did they give in to compromise?

Let's analyze the teaching of Peter and Paul in regard to marriage and slavery, two crucial aspects of civil life:

- Roman society made ample use of divorce and the Jews exercised repudiation. Jesus however forbade both: "For your hardness of heart Moses allowed you to divorce your wives"; "whoever repudiates his wife commits adultery." This teaching is so ludicrous for anyone, even for an apostle, that the disciples remarked: if this is the case then its better not to marry. But Jesus came to bring the Mosaic Law to fulfillment. So he clarified: "Everyone who looks at a woman lustfully has already committed adultery with her in his heart."
- After the death of Christ, Paul linked the indissolubility of marriage to Jesus' love for the Church as revealed on the cross: "This mystery is great, and I am saying that it refers to Christ and the Church," he wrote to the Ephesians; "As Christ loved the Church and gave himself up for her," likewise, "husbands should love their wives as their own bodies"; "Let the wife see to it that she respects her husband." Never before and in no society had women been placed in a position of such honor with respect to their husbands: husbands are called here to climb on the cross for them. Never before had human love known such extraordinary acclaim;
- in 71 B.C., the dramatic episode of the slave rebellion led by Spartacus concluded with an endless line of crucifixions. The Roman imperial economy was founded on slavery and even Jews admitted a certain type of temporary slavery, which ended each sabbatical year. What about the teaching of the apostles? In his first letter, Peter wrote the following: "Servants, be submissive to your masters with profound respect, not only to the kind and gentle but also to the overbearing. For it is a grace to you who know God when you endure pain while suffering unjustly": you well know how "Christ also suffered for you,

leaving you an example, so that you should follow in his steps." Also Paul exhorted Christians to behave as if their own masters were the Lord and to obey them if they were Jesus himself: "Slaves, be obedient to those who are your earthly masters, with fear and trembling, in singleness of heart, as to Christ," he wrote to the Ephesians. With regard to masters he says, "do the same to them, and forbear threatening, knowing that he who is both their Master and yours is in heaven, and that there is no partiality with him."

While these were the general guidelines, there is another guideline which is much more particular but extremely significant. Paul expressed it in one of his last and most moving letters. It was addressed to Philemon, his friend and the owner of a slave who after escaping had become Paul's disciple. The author at this point was old and in chains: "Though I am at full liberty in Christ to command you to do what is required, yet for love's sake I prefer to appeal to you – I, Paul, an ambassador and now a prisoner also for Christ Jesus." Paul sent Onesimus back. He sent the fugitive slave, back to his master. At the same time, he asked the master to show charity towards "my child […] whose father I have become in my imprisonment": "I am sending him back to you, sending my very heart"; "I preferred to do nothing without your consent in order that your goodness might not be by compulsion but of your own free will."

The *Letter to Philemon* is among the most vivid examples of how Christian freedom, founded on charity, can and does in fact transform a society and a people's customs from within. It needs no use of violence by Christians, no claims beyond that of a sincere affection. After three centuries of persecution, Roman society changed how it viewed the Gospel because the love by which Christians loved each other overcame their hardness of hearts. Again, we go back to Ratzinger's words: Christianity "had the power to convince because of the bond between faith and reason, and because action was guided beyond all social differences towards *charitas*, the loving care of the suffering, the poor and the weak."

The primitive Church

Besides Judas, the traitor who died committing suicide, and John, who died naturally of an extremely old age, all the apostles glorified God through cruel and violent deaths. In no way does this mean that in the primitive Church all displayed a heroic kind of holiness. It's enough to read St. Paul's letters. In the *First Letter to the Corinthians*, for example, St. Paul said: "It is acutely reported that there is immorality among you, and of a kind that is not found even among the pagans; for a man is living with his father's wife"; to the Galatians he wrote: "If you bite and devour one another take heed at least that you are not all consumed by one another!"

It is the eternal struggle between the good wheat and the weeds, the parable told by Jesus and recounted by Matthew: an enemy sowed weed among the wheat of a field and the servants wanted to rip them out. But the master forbade them from doing so "for in gathering the weeds you would uproot the wheat along with them." The harvest will take place at the end of times, and only then will God command his harvesters to gather the weeds, bind them in bundles and burn them.

Over time – Luther is only the most apparent case – the Church was subjected to schisms, violence, divisions, and irreconcilable hatreds in the name of a return to Christian life's perfection of the early days. It is an unmistakable fact that invoking the Church's golden age bears no good fruits because God is God, his arm does not shorten ("Is the Lord's hand shortened?" answers God to an incredulous Moses in the Book of Numbers) and because in every generation Christians can once again say the same Paul wrote in the *Letter to the Philippians*: "I can do all things through Him who strengthens me."

What are Christian communities? A well-organized body founded on charity. When Paul spoke of community in the First Letter to the Corinthians, it seems that he recalled the apology pronounced by Menenius Agrippa at the turn of the 5th century B.C. to make peace among opposite factions of the roman populace. There is one fundamental difference: Menenius made use of the body metaphor alluding to society as a whole; Paul instead uses the body metaphor in reference to a spiritual body: "Now you are the body of Christ and individually members of it." In the body of Christ there are many members, each one necessary, each in service to the others. After listing the charisms which belong to the Christian assembly, Paul exhorted the brothers to aim for the greatest charism: charity; because charity is God.

Together with envies, jealousies, divisions, thirst for power and riches, the temptation to use the gifts of God for one's own benefit, Christians of all ages competed in charity because they aimed high. They aimed to do everything possible so as to be like God: "Do you not know that in a race all the runners compete, but only one receives the prize? So run that you may obtain it!" wrote Paul in his first letter to the Corinthians.

Preceisely this heroic emulation, together with fruits of eternal life, always had an extraordinary effect in the social, cultural and economic life of various nations. Ignatius of Loyola, while restricted to his sickbed, read the lives of the saints and became inflamed with zeal: "Saint Dominique did this, therefore I must do it; Saint Francis did this, therefore, I must do it also," he wrote in his *Autobiography*. The "desire to imitate the saints, without giving importance to anything other than promising himself, with the grace of God, to do as they had done."

Just barely past her adolescence, Theresa of Lisieux, patron saint of missions, asked herself what God had in mind for her and discovered that nothing was greater than charity. So, she decided to follow a way of heroic and universal love from the hidden corner of a convent. In *History of a Soul* she wrote: I have always desired to be a saint and "the good God would never inspire me with desires which cannot be realized, therefore, in spite of my littleness, I can aspire to be a saint"; "I will look for some means of going to heaven by a little way which is very straight and very short, a little way that is quite new"; "It is your arms, Jesus, which are the lift to carry me to heaven. That is why there is no need for me to grow up. In fact, just the opposite: I must stay little and become less and less."

If they persecuted me, they will persecute you

Jesus prepared his disciples for persecution. The clash with those in power, with the prince of this world, is inevitable because the world rejects what is not its own. The world eliminates all those who, by behaving differently, indirectly challenge the legitimacy and goodness of selfishness, abjection, brutality. To live differently is possible. This is a scandal to the peace of mind of those in power.

Give back to Caesar that which is Caesar's, taught Jesus. Paul, writing to the Romans, established the Church's magisterium with respect to governing authorities: obedience is due to them because all authority comes from God. These are his words: "Let every person be subject to the governing authorities. For there is no authority except from God, and those that exist have been instituted by God. Therefore he who resists the authorities resists what God has appointed." *Unicuique suum*, said the Romans. Paul took the teaching up again: "Pay all of them their dues: taxes to whom taxes are due, revenue to whom revenue is due, respect to whom respect is due, honor to whom honor is due."

To further justify what he wrote, Paul added: "For rulers are not a terror to good conduct, but to bad conduct." Likewise, Peter expressed an analogous concept in his first letter: "Be subject for the Lord's sake to every human institution, whether it be to the emperor as supreme, or to governors as sent by him to punish those who do wrong and to praise those who do right."

The point is: if governments do evil, what must Christians do? Paul's letters were written in Nero's reign, the emperor who unleashed an abominable persecution in which the same Peter and Paul died. Though he well knew the stuff emperors were made of, Paul wrote in their defense. To clarify this key point of Christian doctrine, we must turn to Benedict XVI and his catechesis on Clement I. Towards the end of Domitian's persecution, in the last few years of the 1st century, Clement wrote a letter to the Corinthians which is considered "the first exercise of the Primacy of Rome." The letter ends in a prayer and, in this prayer, Clement pleas in favor of political institutions. Ratzinger explains: "The persecution had barely come to an end but Christians, well aware that persecutions would have continued, never stopped praying for those same authorities that had unjustly condemned them. The reason for this is first and foremost Christological: we need to pray for those who persecute us as did Jesus on the cross. But this prayer also contains a teaching which throughout the centuries has guided the attitude of Christians towards politics and the State. By praying for established authorities, Clement recognized the legitimacy of political institutions in the order established by God; at the same time, he expressed concern that these authorities should remain docile to God and that they 'exercise the power given to them by God in peace, meekness and piety (61, 2). Caesar is not everything. An alternative sovereignty emerges, whose origin and essence are not of this world but "of above': Truth, who boasts the right to be heard even by the State."

Since the very beginning, in all its heroism, Christian doctrine concerning power is crystal clear: obedience to authority but, first and foremost, obedience to God. If the authorities mandate what is contrary to the will of God, Christians must not obey but rather make opposition and resist, if necessary, even to the point of martyrdom. Over one thousand years later, in a completely different context but nonetheless in full theological continuity, Thomas Aquinas justified this disobedience by arguing that if the law opposes right reason, it is not law but rather a corruption of the law: when "a law is in contrast with reason, it is called a wicked law; in this case, however, it ceases to be a law and rather becomes an act of violence."

Tolerant paganism?

In the *Annals*, Tacitus recounts the first anti-Christian persecution unleashed by Nero in 64 A.C.: countless Christians were condemned "and on the way to their death, a mockery was made of them: after they were made to wear animal skins, they were attacked by dogs, or nailed to crosses, or they set on fire so that they might blaze after sunset like nocturnal torches. For this spectacle, Nero offered his gardens and would personally celebrate the games in the circus mingling with the crowd dressed as a charioteer or would take part in the races standing on a chariot. That is why, though Christians were viewed as guilty criminals who merited punishments unprecedented for their severity, a sense of pity was kindled: they died to satisfy one man's cruelty and not for the common good."

In more recent times, not only has Nero been rehabilitated, but it is fashionable again to believe the myth of tolerant polytheism and of a violent monotheism (as if no difference existed between Christian and Islamic monotheism). This belief was shared by Hitler who, in his *Table Talks*, depicted Romans as the prototype of tolerance: "The ancient world had its gods and served them. But priests, placed between gods and men, were servants of the State, because the gods protected the city. All things considered, they were the emanation of a power which the people had created. The idea of a unique god was unthinkable for those people. In this field, Romans were tolerance personified. For them, the idea of one universal god could not but seem a sweet folly."

The truth is that the Roman polytheist world unleashed a persecution of unprecedented ferocity against the helpless army of Christians. Just like ten plagues were sent against Egypt, ten great persecutions were unleashed against Christians: Nero, Domitian, Trajan, Antoninus, Severus, Maximinus, Decius, Valerian, Aurelian, Diocletian and Maximinus Daia. Augustine is the author of this list and he was not so sure, as some thought, that there would be no more persecutions before that dreadful onslaught unleashed by the antichrist at the end of time. In reality, the number ten is symbolic. Until the Edict of Milan in 313 not even one emperor let Christians live in peace.

Before Nero's persecution, some of the faithful had already been martyred by the Jews: Stephen, the very first martyr, James the elder, the brother of John. The Jews persecuted Christians because they considered them to be blasphemers: in fact, it was unimaginable for them that Jesus could be God, as it was unimaginable for them that the Messiah could rule through the "scandal of the cross." Moreover, those who profited economically from paganism soon became enemies of Christianity. The *Acts of the Apostles* recounts how "a man named Demetrius, a silversmith, who made silver shrines of Artemis, brought no little business to the craftsmen," and when Paul put Artemis' credibility in jeopardy, and therefore also his earnings, Demetrius riled up a crowd of fellow citizens against Paul. In fact, "there is danger that the temple of the great goddess Artemis may count for nothing, and that she may even be deposed from her magnificence, she whom all Asia and the world worship." The danger was very real because Paul's preaching in Ephesus had convinced "a considerable company of people" from the vanity of idols built by human hands. Understandably, at the shout of "Great is Artemis of the Ephesians!" Paul and his own were cast out of the city.

The Jews persecution of Christians stemmed from certain features of a particular religion linked to a people. The pagans persecuted them for local economic reasons. In Rome, the issue is different and more complex because Rome and its government identified with the law. They identified, therefore, with motivations that, at least in principle, claimed to be universal and applied to all citizens without distinction.

They slander tou as evildoers

After Jesus' crucifixion and Stephen's stoning in 37 A.C., Rome removed Pilate and deposed Caiaphas: in his excessive lenience towards the Jews, Pilate did not follow the law. Up until 62 A.C., though Christians enjoyed a time of relative peace, certain horrible calumnies were spread about them. Tacitus was the only historian who identified the cause behind the first persecution as Nero's attempt to blame others for his setting Rome on fire. But even he spoke of Christianity as an *exitiabilis superstitio*, he depicted Christians as those who hate mankind and recalled the scorn felt towards them because of their crimes (*flagitia*).

Why are Christians despised to the point of being called "those who hate mankind"?

In his *First Letter*, Peter identified the refusal to conform to widespread immorality as the cause for the accusations: "They are surprised that you no longer join them in the same excesses of dissipation, and so they blaspheme." The *Book of Wisdom* gives the same explanation for the persecution unleashed against the just: "Let us lie in wait for the righteous man, because he is inconvenient to us and opposes our actions; he reproaches us for sins against the law [...] He became to us a reproof of our thoughts; the very sight of him is a burden to us, because his manner of life is unlike that of others."

After Nero died by committing suicide, in 66 an anti-roman rebellion spread throughout Palestine. Christians did not participate. The rebellion warranted Rome's military intervention which put a decisive end to periodic Jewish uprisings by destroying Jerusalem and the Temple in 70 A.C.

Christianity spread everywhere and took a firm hold even within the same imperial family. In fact, the second persecution unleashed by Domitian in 95, struck first at the Christian components of the high aristocracy. These included the emperor's cousin, Flavius Clement who was killed, his wife Flavia Domitilla who was deported and the consul Glabrio who was also killed. In this instance, the cause for this persecution is, at least apparently, incomprehensible: Christians were accused of atheism. In what sense can people be viewed as atheists if their faith was so firm that they were willing to face torments and even death only to remain faithful to the Lord? The bottom line is that Christians refused to worship the emperor and the pagan gods. The pagans would have liked them to offer incense to deities who were believed to have made Rome great. They refused to do so. They were deemed atheists and therefore also impious because they attracted divine wrath on the homeland. The accusation was of utmost gravity, the crime they were accused of was religious and targeted singular individuals, not the Church as a community; anti-Christian violence spread throughout the empire.

Domitian's persecution fixed the main features for all future persecutions, although the manner of their enactment, in over two hundred years before the Edict of Milan was issued in 313, underwent significant variations.

He went off to make war on the rest of her offspring

By obeying the teachings of Jesus and the doctrine of the apostles, Christians are model citizens. They pay taxes, they respect the law, and they obey the authorities. Why then were they persecuted? What were the accusations that brought death upon them? It was becoming increasingly clear over time, that the crimes they were accused of (incest, because they called each other brothers; and infanticide, because they feasted on human flesh) were completely false. So? What were magistrates to do? Sentence them to death only for their *nomen*, simply because they were Christians and members of a criminal sect, or try them only for crimes actually committed? Should they actively hunt them down as dangerous or should they wait until someone actually filed an accusation? Should the accusers be granted anonymity, and so avoid private vendettas from getting the upper hand on the principles of justice and right, or should they be required to come out into the open and be held responsible for substantiating their accusations?

Anti-Christian persecution was such an impious issue that magistrates tried in vain to find a clear and univocal rule that would reconcile the punishments inflicted with the integrity of the great Roman legal tradition. The real point of the issue was not juridical but political: the state could not relinquish its demands for absolute obedience above all else, even when it drafted religious norms. After all, in Rome, also religion was political in so far as it was needed to secure the gods' protection and therefore, the empire's good fortunes. Not by chance, the highest political and religious authority coincided in one person: the emperor, *Pontifex Maximus*.

Under Trajan (98-117), one scrupulous governor from Bithynia, Pliny the Younger, asked the emperor for a further explanation: what must I do with the Christians? Pliny listed his misgivings: "I cannot even understand the legal basis for filing an accusation," I do not know if young and old should be treated in the same way nor if the name itself, Christians, is prosecutable as criminal or if criminal acts are required to warrant condemning Christians. "Is it the name itself 'Christian' that is to be punished, even without criminal offenses, or the lawlessness is inevitably connected to the name itself?"

And further: "An anonymous writing was circulated containing the names of many authoritative individuals" and I required, in order to dismiss the accusations against them, that "they recited after me an invocation to the gods and made offerings of wine and incense to your statue." Above all, I imposed on them that they should formally "curse Christ, something which I have understood, a real Christian cannot be forced to do." In the letter, Pliny invited Trajan to not underestimate the problem because it regarded "numerous persons of every age and every social class, men and women," and also because "the contagion of this superstition has spread not only to the cities but also to the villages and countryside."

Trajan applauded the governor's diligence and responded by clarifying:

- It is not possible to construct a universal principle or a specific formula for such a delicate issue;
- Christians "are not to be hunted down";
- Anonymous accusations shall not be introduced into the legal proceedings because they "set an awful precedent and are not in the spirit of our age."

The lack of clarity and of legal certainty in this imperial rescript and in all anti-Christian legislation is obvious. For example, if Christians posed a danger so great that it warranted their death, why legal authorities were excused from having to hunt them down is truly puzzling.

Trajan wrote the letter in 111\113. But about ten years later, already there was need for a second imperial pronouncement: Adrian's Rescript established that the burden to submit substantiating evidence fell on the accuser and that slanderers were subject to punishment. A few decades later, with Marcus Aurelius and Commodus, the decision was made to actively hunt down Christians. Midway through the 3rd century, with Valerian, Rome did not limit itself to punishing single individuals, but for the first time it targeted the Church as an organization and struck at its hierarchy. During the last wave of persecutions, that of Diocletian, Galerius and Maximinus Daia, especially in the East, the persecution aimed not only to kill, but mainly to induce Christians into committing apostasy. In this way roman authorities hoped to increase the persecution's effectiveness.

At the close of the 3rd century, the greatest novelty was that, in general, after so much ruthless violence, the population sided with the Christians.

Many Antichrists have appeared

Adam and Eve, made in the image and likeness of God, lived in God's presence in a splendid garden. Yet, Eve heeded Satan who suggested that God, her creator, envied her. Something unimaginable, incomprehensible! It is so incomprehensible, that the Church defines the problem of evil as a mystery: *misterium iniquitatis*. The tragedy of human history, including the suffering and death which accompany it, is described in the book of *Genesis*, but it comes back to repeat itself everyday in mankind's induvial and collective history. Satan invites us to clumsily mimic God and decide by ourselves the difference between good and evil. "For God knows," he said to Eve, "that when you eat of it [he is referring to the tree of the knowledge of good and evil, the fruit of which God had forbidden them to eat otherwise they would die], your eyes will be opened and you will be like God, knowing good and evil."

In the New Testament, all sacred authors repeatedly warn the brothers against heeding to the tales concocted by those whom Jesus in the gospel of Matthew defines as "ravenous wolves": "Beware of false prophets who come to you in sheep's clothing but inwardly are ravenous wolves"; in the *Acts of the Apostles*, Paul warned the Ephesians: "Some even from your own group will teach perverse doctrines in order to entice disciples to follow them"; in his *Second Letter*, Peter cautions: "there will be false teachers among you, who will secretly introduce pernicious heresies. They will deny the Lord their redeemer and bring a swift destruction upon themselves. Even so, many will follow their licentious ways and because of these teachers the way of truth will be maligned."

"You do the works of your father", Jesus said in the Gospel of John to those trying to kill him. You cannot hear the truth that I am because "You are from your father the devil and you choose to follow your father's desires. He was a murderer from the beginning and did not persevere in the truth, because there is no truth in him. When he lies, he speaks from himself, for he is a liar and the father of lies."

The father of all heresies in history is the devil, murderer and liar since the very beginning. Satan hates man: he wants man enslaved and dead. And yet, Satan, deceit personified, deceives him in the name of liberty. The Gnostics do the same. Gnostics – which according to the word's etymology means, "those who know" – believe they are able to define what is good and what is evil on their own. This presumption is the source of boundless violence, suffering and injustice. In the *Book of Revelation*, John wrote that Satan, after trying in vain to devour the newly born child and to swallow up the woman who had just given birth, "went off to make war on the rest of her children, against those who keep the commandments of God and hold the testimony of Jesus."

It could seem strange that the Church, from its very beginning, when it was still very small, fiercely persecuted and powerless, attracted people who lead a double life and who followed false doctrine. Peter referred to this in his *First Letter* when he invited the brothers to be watchful.: "Like a roaring lion, your enemy, the devil, prowls around, looking for someone to devour." The fact is that Jesus Christ is in the Church. The fact is that Satan hates Christ and therefore, no matter how big or small, Satan can never stop persecuting the Church. *Revelation* continues: "Then the dragon took his stand on the sand of the seashore." Satan battles the Church on two fronts: he intimidates her with the ghost of persecution – this is what the dragon does; he stands firm on the seashore, trying to prevent Christians from confronting the waters of death like Jesus, with the certainty of his victory – and attacks Peter's magisterium trying to corrupt true doctrine.

Historians believe that at the beginning of the 3rd century, the Church had already won the battle against Gnosticism. But Gnosticism advances in tandem with the history of the Church and contingent with the times assumes greater or lesser visibility, different forms and expressions. In 1907, in an exemplary clear and precise encyclical, the *Pascendi Dominici Gregis*, Pius X condemned modernism as the "synthesis of all heresies." Modernism is simply a distillation of Gnosticism.

They will forbid marriage

"What some call the deep things of Satan": with these words, the *Book of Revelation* describes the key features of gnostic belief. John, Peter and Paul, invited the faithful to be watchful against the deceits of the devil: the brothers must not go "beyond" the teachings of Christ transmitted by the apostles; they must not follow doctrines that supposedly have been revealed to some and hidden to the many; they must not give in to the deceit of the antichrist. In his *Second Letter* John says: for "Many deceivers have appeared in the world, those who do not recognize that Jesus has come in the flesh. Behold, such is the deceiver and the antichrist! Be on guard over yourself."; "Everyone who does not hold to the teaching of Christ, but goes beyond it, does not have God." In his *First Letter*, John had already written a warning. Be careful because "as you have heard that the antichrist is coming, so now many antichrists have already come": "They went out from us, but they did not belong to us."

In his two letters to Timothy, Paul prophesied the coming of false teachers. In the first: "Now the Spirit expressly declares that in the last days some will renounce the faith by heeding to deceitful spirits and diabolic doctrines, seduced by the hypocrisy of imposters whose consciences are seared with a hot iron. These will forbid marriage"; in the second he emphasized: the day will come "when people will not put up with sound doctrine, but having itching ears to hear something, they will surround themselves with teachers to suit their own desires, refusing to hear the truth so as to wander away to myths."

Justin, Irenaeus, Hippolytus and with them also Eusebius of Caesarea (263-339), the first historian of the Church, identified Simon the magician as the first follower of Gnosticism. He tried to infiltrate the Church by "simulating faith in Christ," because he was attracted by the miracles the disciples worked. In fact, as a magician, he had succeeded in making others adore him like God. Peter launched an anathema against Simon. In later centuries, Popes and bishops will do the same to defend the flock entrusted to them from the greed for power, money and lust of ravenous wolves.

The world of Gnosticism is extremely diverse. Each group, each founder is certain to be smarter than the others and therefore to possess the truth that the others do not know. Putting aside the infinite array of differences, gnostic sects have various points in common: dualism (there exist two principles, two deities, one good and one evil), contempt for matter (followed often by anomie, and the consequent orgiastic practices and ritual homicides), contempt for the common people, esoterism, magic, faith in the divine virtues of those who founded the different schools.

The antichrist does not acknowledge Jesus come in the flesh and forbids marriage. Despite the explicit assertion in the book of *Genesis* about the goodness of creation and about the increasing goodness of man, contempt for creation, the exaltation of the spirit at the expense of and against matter, are the most typical features of the Gnostic attack on Christ, son of God incarnate and son of the Virgin. Man's reason which lays down laws without and against God, without and against revelation, is unable to accept that God took flesh. Likewise, it cannot accept the goodness of matter and of the body because their features seem to limit the free world of the spirit. The free world of those perverse fantasies which they call spirit. Followers of Gnosticism condemn the flesh and often, in opposition and as a sign of triumph over it, abuse the flesh and its pleasures, culminating in a condemnation of both marriage and reproduction.

Revealed doctrine is the exact contrary of the gnostic creed: "Be fruitful and multiply", God said to Adam and Eve right after creating them. Marriage is a sacrament. Sexual life outside the sacrament blessed by God and open to life is a practice which alters man. Created to be temple of the Holy Spirit it transforms him into the temple of Satan. The Church blesses marriage but also exalts virginity. Hence the endless ranks of men and women consecrated to God who, within one of the infinite number of charisms inspired by the Holy Spirit in every age, lived a life here on earth which anticipated that of the heavenly Jerusalem.

Truth is in Rome

Time passing and the progressive branching out of gnostic temptations, the Church, besides leaning on the help of preaching and Scripture, equipped herself to confute point by point the presence of heresy within. Christians of all epochs cannot neglect to fight this battle for truth. In fact, though their substance is always the same, new insidious attacks always besiege the brothers. The first champion in the battle against Gnosticism and heresy was Irenaeus of Lyon (135-203?), disciple of Polycarp, who in turn was a disciple of John: *On the Detection and Overthrow of the False Gnosis*, this is the title of his key work. How to shield oneself against false lambs, false saints, and haughty men who threaten the Church? What to do in order to discern true from false, catholic from gnostic doctrine? What to do in order to be perfect and not become, as Paul wrote to the Ephesians, "children, tossed to and fro by the waves and blown about by every wind of doctrine, according to people's deceit, with that shrewdness which leads to error"?

Irenaeus fixed the distinguishing criteria: one must not heed those who are on the hunt for novelties which turn their followers into leaves blown by the wind; rather one must follow the apostolic tradition transmitted by bishops, successors of the apostles, and not turn aside either to the right or to the left. The apostolic tradition is public, pneumatic, and unique. It is public, meaning it is not secret. It is not esoteric. It is not destined to the few; it is for everyone. It was not revealed by Jesus only to some disciples in particular, something the followers of Gnosticism claimed because they wanted to justify their own thirst for power and the supposed superiority of their knowledge. Tradition is pneumatic and therefore guided by the Holy Spirit: it neither depends on culture nor on human ability. Tradition is unique because it does not vary from place to place. In fact, it conforms to will of Jesus who established unity as the distinctive feature of the Church. Irenaeus wrote: "The churches founded in Germany have neither received nor do they transmit a different faith; neither do the churches founded in Spain, or among the Celts, or in the eastern regions, or in Egypt, or in Libya, or in the center of the world." The Church is one and universal. The Church has nothing to do with nationalisms. The Church is Roman. The canon, tradition and apostolic succession, are the most reliable guarantees against heresy.

The word "heresy" is derived from a Greek verb which means to select, to choose, to privilege one single aspect over others within a doctrinal body, in the attempt to make the overall edifice more acceptable from a rational point of view: less scandalous to reason; more easily adaptable to our ability to comprehend and to our desires; in two words, less divine. A few decades after Irenaeus, the efforts spent to confute heresies were gathered by Hippolytus and then by an uninterrupted series of Popes, bishops, monks and lay people. In the modern age, the papal magisterium played a providential role: it enlightened the dangers and highlighted the contradictions and grave errors hidden in gnostic thought, which underlie the order of Freemasons and the Enlightenment. In our days and age, the magisterium of Pope Wojtyla and Pope Ratzinger warned against the totalitarian implications of nihilist relativism.

Come over to Macedonia and help us

From the moment Paul, in a dream, received a Macedonian's plea to come by his region to help them ("Come over to Macedonia and help us!"); from the moment when in the Aeropagus he responded to the Athenian philosophers who crowded about him and asked him for explanations about his faith by announcing Jesus' resurrection starting from rational considerations, Christianity, stated cardinal Ratzinger in 1999 during a conference held at the Sorbonne, introduced itself purporting to be the true *religio*. This implies that "Christian faith is neither based on poetry nor politics, these two great sources of religion; it is based on knowledge." Christianity found "both its forerunner and its preparation in philosophic rationality; not in religions." It has nothing to do with myth or the political exploitation it is normally subject to. Rationality "became religion and ceased to be its adversary" because Christianity is a universal religion. Likewise, the rational arguments it puts forth are also universal. Formed by studying Saint Augustine, Ratzinger quotes his teacher who placed Christianity within the scope of philosophical rationality. By so doing Augustine was "in perfect continuity with the very first theologians of Christianity, the apologists of the 2nd century."

During the 2nd century, the Church made a great effort not only to defend herself from her internal enemies, that is, heretics, but also to reply to false and vilifying accusations which were used as pretexts to unleash persecution. The first apologist whose work was preserved was Justin (100-162?), philosopher and martyr. While searching in vain various philosophical schools for the truth, Justin understood that the only way to solve the unsolvable problems of philosophical speculation is through revealed religion. Therefore, he believed Christians have all the right to call themselves philosophers. To fully grasp how credible Justin's considerations are, it is enough to think that no Greek, no matter how great a genius he may have been, neither Plato nor Aristotle, ever arrived to formulate the concept of creation – a fundamental notion to grasp the reality we are part of – instead, the very first verse of Scripture starts there: "In the beginning God created the heavens and the earth."

In the first centuries, the Church waged a battle without quarters against the idolatrous and magic world of myth, the world of paganism. It found an ally in philosophical reason: on the one hand, the Old Testament; on the other, Greek philosophy. They were like the two roads that both lead to the *Logos*, both lead to Christ, claimed Justin. This belief was pronounced in Rome where Justin taught. The prestigious school of Alexandria moved along the same wavelength. Midway through the 2nd century, Clement of Alexandria (159-215?), who directed the school, taught that there was only one New Testament while there were two old: Jewish law and Greek philosophy. He believed that philosophy was to pagans the equivalent of what the law was to Jews. In *Fides et Ratio*, John Paul II reminds us that, according to Clement, philosophy "is a teaching which prepares the Christian faith." The Church always started from the same assumption: before studying theology, one must first study philosophy, defined by Thomas *ancilla theologiae*.

In the last few decades, both the philosopher Pope, Wojtyla, and the theologian Pope, Ratzinger, standing before a world cast into a whirlwind of scientific irrationalism, with rigor and strength defended human dignity, defended man made in the image and likeness of God, and defended the power of man's reason to attain the truth. In 2006, during the *Lectio magistralis* held in Regensburg, Benedict XVI claimed that, "by modifying the first verse of *Genesis*, the very first verse in the whole of Sacred Scripture, John began the prologue to his gospel with the words: In the beginning there was the λόγος [...] *Logos* means both reason and word – precisely reason which is creator and able to communicate itself as reason"; the Greek heritage "purified critically, is an integral part of Christian faith."

Though any compromise in Christianity is inadmissible from a doctrinal standpoint – no culture may add or modify anything substantial because it is God who established the features of the Church – Christianity incorporated the Greek philosophical world within itself and once it was "critically purified," it became its constitutive heritage. Not by chance, the whole of the New Testament is written in Greek.

Anthony the Great

"If you wish to be perfect, go, sell your goods, and give the money to the poor, and you will have a treasure in heaven; then come, follow me," Jesus said. Anthony entered a Church while these words of Matthew's gospel were being proclaimed. He heard them and put them into practice to the letter. This made his hundred-year long life (251-356) a masterpiece. When someone puts the Word of God into practice since glossa, the most unforeseeable things occur; these produces lasting changes which have the capacity to influence the life of a society in all its aspects, including the economical.

The Egyptian desert is not only an anonymous and boundless expanse of sand. It is also a mountainous, rocky and granitic place. It has the most varied forms and the most intense and diverse colors which vary with the hours of day. It is a place where one can begin to fathom how ranks of hermits and monks followed Anthony in order to find God. It is a place where life is battle. It is not a solitary refuge where one can spend his days in peace and quiet far away from the hardships of communal living, as is told by many anti-Christian legends. It is the kind of place where one's choice, to live alone in order to serve and search for God is questioned day by day and moment by moment, because the conditions of this type of existence are extreme, tragic. The life of a hermit like Anthony or of a cenobite like Pacomius (292-348) was full of God. But it was also full of his adversary: the devil. Even in a physical sense: Anthony had to confront the devil who did not limit himself to tempting him, but challenged him also physically. He was often beat up. An extremely harsh experience which happened only to a few giants of Christian life: Catherine of Siena and Father Pius, just to mention a few.

Anthony spent twenty years alone. Afterwards he became a 'father' for all those who, attracted by the road he found, were in search of God. Pacomius is the 'father' of cenobitic life, in which monks obey a rule and live together in small cells bounded by small surrounding walls. The ways in which men and women decided to live alone with God are full of imagination and often quite bizarre. In the mid-5th century, for example, near Aleppo in Syria, Simeon Stylites decides to move to a shack built on top of a column: he spent the last thirty years of his life in this way, surrounded by great veneration, with men and women who went to his column asking for prayers, comfort, counsel and the emperor Theodosius II himself, who involved him when he attempted to reconcile opposing political factions.

Monasticism founded by Basil the Great (329-378), bishop of Caesarea in Cappadocia was radically different. A saint who came from a family of saints, he recalled the importance of the role his grandmother played in his life: "For all my life, I will never forget the strong stimuli that my still tender heart received from the speeches and examples of this most pious woman." After having spent time with monks from all different regions of the empire and opposed to the life of hermitage which he believed contradicted human nature's basic instincts, Basil founded a kind monasticism which exerted a great influence also on western Benedictine monasticism. The followers of Basil lived in urban centers, they livened local community life, played a leading role in the evangelization and in liturgical life, lived constantly occupied with a network of works of mercy ranging from schools, to hospitals, to leper colonies, to hospices.

In our days we witness a limited but extraordinary flowering of monastic life. With new forms, new rules, or by returning to the stricter observance of the founding fathers, again the daily battle against the devil in solitude and privation is being staged; also today there are some who become recluses out of love for Jesus and to defend sinners. It's true, Judas was one of the twelve, but the others were saints. *Corruptio optimi pessima*: people often speak about how in the Church there are apostates, robbers, degenerates and traitors, how these are a scandal and therefore cause much harm. But the Church has a countless army of saints and martyrs who, often without anyone ever becoming aware of their existence, over the course of their whole life live out their faith *sine glossa*.

Flavius Valerius Aurelius Constantinus

Constantine (272-337) was the emperor who after three hundred years of persecution gave the Church religious freedom. He made Christianity a *religio licita*. That is why the Orthodox Church venerates him as a saint. Did Constantine really convert? Or did he exploit the Church's strength to achieve his own political ends? Both points of view have supporting arguments. Rather than entering into the details of the emperor's personal convictions, here, we prefer to list some facts. There is no doubt that Constantine was an emperor which marked the course of history: under his watch the empire's life, newly unified after Diocletian's decision to divide it, underwent an enormous change. Likewise, Church life also was deeply transformed.

Constantine was roman emperor. Today, it is only with great effort that one can grasp the enormity of the power wielded by this universal authority. Moreover, while the emperor was still alive, his authority was often worshipped as divine. Without reaching the madness of Caligula who to slight the senate assigned a seat on the senate to his horse, imperial authority always carried a boundless power. Often, this universal power's decisions were ruthless. Constantine had his wife and son murdered. Yes, indeed. However, per se, these crimes do not speak for or against Constantine's pagan beliefs since his actions could have been motivated by political considerations; something that also in the Christian court of Byzantium will often happen.

Eusebius of Caesarea, great cantor of the Constantinian epoch, recounts that, fearful of his adversary Maxentius' magical power, in the battle of Ponte Milvio in 312, Constantine was defended by the cruciform insignia. Eusebius reported: "When the sun was beginning to set, with his own eyes, Constantine saw in heaven, above the sun, the trophy of a cross of light on which were written the words *In Hoc Signo Vinces* [with this sign you shall win]. He was taken by great amazement and with him his whole army." Constantine believed the vision, changed his army's insignia by substituting the eagle with the cross, won the battle, and the day after, avoided going to the Capitol to thank Zeus, Optimus Maximus. By so doing, he broke the most ancient of Roman traditions. Moreover, this tradition was a foundational element of imperial identity in which the highest political and religious authority coincided. Constantine stopped serving in the role as pagan High priest. In 313, he issued the Edict of Milan wherein he declared that Christianity was legal and invoked God's protection on the empire: "Whatever deity there may be in heaven, let it be appeased and favorable to us and to all those who are placed under our power."

From that day onwards, up to his death in 337, multiple legal provisions show that Christian piety had profoundly altered the Roman social tissue.

Among other things, the emperor:

- forbade face branding of those condemned to forced labor on the basis that it was not lecit to profane the human face since it is made in the image and likeness of God;
- removed fines imposed by Augustus on people who were celibate or who had no children; in this way he recognized the goodness of monastic or virginal life;
- approved the "Sunday law" setting Sunday aside as a day of rest;
- made divorce rather difficult, forbade marriage infidelity, forbade separating families of slaves, forbade gladiatorial games and crucifixion.

The first Christian emperor, Philip the Arab (244-249), implicated in the assassination of his predecessor Gordian III, in 244, was obliged by bishop Babila of Antioch to make penance in a form as public as the crime committed: could precedent set by Philip's case have inclined Emperor Constantine to refrain from being baptized in order to avoid making a commitment that would have seriously affected his handling of government matters? Constantine received baptism only on Easter night of the year 337, the same year of his death. He died on the day of Pentecost and until that moment dressed only in white. This is what Eusebius recounted.

What does Constantine say of himself?

Constantine's mortal remains were laid to rest in the Basilica of the Twelve Apostles because the Emperor was convinced to be equal to the apostles (isapostle). Constantine called himself "bishop of those outside" (*episkopos ton ektòs*), bishop of the non-Christians. He did in fact serve as universal bishop and therefore his service was superior to that of single bishops. Furthermore, he acted as arbiter in their controversies. He acted in order to avoid compromising his own personal salvation (to avoid facing God's judgment) but also to guarantee unity and peace in the empire, his foremost concern. Under his rule, Roman Imperial ceremonial custom, which required kneeling before the emperor, was kept in Constantinople and extended to all western courts, including that of the Pope.

For over 30 years as emperor, the laws he issued in favor of Christians were numerous:

- freeing slaves before a bishop was made valid;
- by request of the relevant parties, bishops could act as judges in civil lawsuits;
- haruspicy, a pagan practice, was strictly forbidden on pain of severe punishment: a first limitation of pagan worship;
- donations to the Church were legal;
- the clergy was guaranteed immunity;
- Christians were the preferred choice for appointments to public offices;
- pagan temples were deprived of their income and, Aphrodite's temple which was built on Christ's burial grounds was destroyed;
- the quite substantial assets seized from pagan temples were assigned to the bishop of Rome;
- Constantinople, second Rome and new capital, had distinct Christian features: churches, Christian monuments in the squares, crosses on the imperial palace's rooftops;
- throughout the empire, a grandiose construction plan was set in motion for the construction of basilicas; these buildings' finest details, even the furnishings, were cared for by the emperor himself;

Right after victory over Maxentius, Constantine started to handle the Church's internal conflicts himself: in the West there was the Donatist controversy while in the east there was the Arian. Rome had just finished condemning Donatus (*Roma locuta causa soluta*: when Rome has spoken, the case is closed), that the emperor advocated reopening the controversy. In 314, he convoked a Synod in Arles which did not resolve the issue. Though Constantine resorted to force, exiled bishops and confiscated churches, the schism continued. On the opposite front, in the east, to resolve the Arian controversy,

Constantine convoked the first Ecumenical Council of Nicea in 325: he did so without asking the Pope's opinion, took up all costs and started the council's work in the imperial palace; he burned all anonymous letters addressed to him and reproached bishops for resorting to such petty behavior; at the close of the council he offered every bishop a gift and gave a banquet which Eusebius compared to the eschatological banquet. Unanimity against Arius was reached thanks to the emperor's political influence.

Jerome wrote that, "from when the Church acquired Christian emperors, it has certainly grown in power and riches, but its moral strength has diminished." The Constantinian revolution implied significant novelties: the Church was no longer persecuted but rather privileged; the Church began to attract those individuals who aimed primarily at the advantages which derive from religious affiliation; covered in gifts, goods and honor, clergymen compete to become bishops and consequently often, the most career oriented were the ones who prevailed.

Claiming to be invested with those titles that convey spiritual authority – isapostle and bishop – which no temporal authority can ever legitimately demand to have, Constantine took an active role in the Church's organization and management. Whether or not Constantine was really Christian the consequences brought about by this claim were cause for endless conflicts, lacerations and problems.

Is the Pope infallible?

In his last years of life, Constantine changed his position and espoused Arianism. At first, between 328 and 378, the empire was Arian; then, during the brief reign of Julian, also known as the Apostate (361-363), it became pagan again; and then finally Arian once again. Constantine II, the son of Constantine, decreed: "What I want must have force of law in the Church." The empire sought after Arius, a brilliant, very learned and ascetic priest from Libya. We must admit, that the Trinity, though it is clearly stated in the New Testament (in the Gospel of Matthew, Jesus Christ says, "Go therefore and make disciples of all nations baptizing them in the name of the Father and of the Son and of the Holy Spirit"), is quite difficult as a concept: is there one sole God or are there three? Reason demands clarity. Arius brought clarity in the sense that he adjusted revealed truth to his personal reason. With regard to Jesus, he wrote that, "There was a time when Jesus was not": Jesus is not co-eternal with the Father. Jesus is a creature. Therefore, he is not God in the proper and full sense of the word. The Father is the only true origin.

Why did the empire side with Arius? Let's suggest a hypothesis. In Constantinople-Byzantium, the emperor was viewed as god's highest representative on earth. Admittedly, a political move of such cultural and religious significance was facilitated by having only one, unique and unopposed God: only one God in heaven; only one emperor on earth. If the only God is One and Triune, then it becomes a little more complicated. In fact, the exclusiveness of the emperor's claim to being the only divine representative is harder to make also because one must admit, at least from a logical standpoint, that not all that is God's is Caesar's. If Caesar incarnates the powers of God the Father on earth, then who incarnates the powers of the Son? We are forced to acknowledge the autonomy of the spiritual power. Faith in a God who is One and Triune expedites the separation of powers: "Give back to Caesar that which is Caesar's and to God that which is God's."

"When people say, 'there is peace and security,' then sudden destruction will come upon them as travail comes upon a woman with child, and there will be no escape," wrote Paul in the *First Letter to the Thessalonians*. This is exactly what happened in the years which followed 328: the persecution, which never seemed to end, ultimately finished and as soon as everyone began to sigh in relief, behold all of a sudden, unforeseen the persecution began again. Bishops were not prepared for this new drama and gave in to the Arian imperial will. All of them. In the East, all but one: Athanasius, bishop of Alexandria was repeatedly condemned, slandered and exiled. In the west, all but three and the Pope: Eusebius of Vercelli, Lucifer of Cagliari, Dionysius of Milan, Pope Liberius. The imperial pressure put on them was unbearable. An Arian bishop was forced on Milan; in Rome, Liberius was kidnapped in the dead of night, taken to Milan and from there exiled to Thrace while a new Pope was installed by force. This is how Eusebius of Vercelli described the situation in a letter to his community: I beg you, "remember us always, so that the

Lord may deign to grant freedom to his Church who is now oppressed over all the earth." Two years later, the Pope returned to Rome. Why was Liberius freed? There are two contrasting theories: according to the first, the Pope caved in under the persecution's duress and bowed down to Arianism; according to the second, quite the opposite, it was Constantine who caved in under the faith of the Roman people who never acknowledged the antipope and demanded the return of the legitimate one. The issue is quite complex, and historians have conflicting views. However, one thing is certain: Athanasius (295-373), the great fugitive, and Jerome (347-420), father of the Church and author of the Vulgatae, two decidedly authoritative figures, both spoke about how Liberius somehow broke down. Athanasius wrote that, "Liberius, returned after being exiled for two years and fearing the death he was threatened with, signed"; Jerome held the same opinion and claimed that it was out of fear that Liberius signed a heretical document.

If this is how the matter stands, if Liberius did in fact yielded in fear and under the suffering inflicted, would the solemn promise Jesus gave to Peter guaranteeing infallibity then default? No. For a very simple reason: all decisions made in a state of duress, that is, with constricted freedom, have no juridical value. If Liberius did fall, and this is still not certain, only his own moral strength and faith would be compromised. Not the pontifical magisterium.

Christianity, official religion

In the speech delivered at the Sorbonne in 1999, Ratzinger stated that Christianity is announced in the whole world "not as a specific religion which represses all others by virtue of some kind of religious imperialism, but rather as the truth which makes all appearance superfluous." From the moment when, at the end of the 4th century Christianity became the official religion, and from the moment when it became the empire's duty to defend Christ's Church from enemies both internal (heretics) and external (barbarians), everything became more complex. On the one hand, the emperor almost always overstepped the boundaries and crossed over into the spiritual arena. This is what Constantine and Constantine II did since the very beginning. On the other hand, only in some very isolated circumstances, a local Christian community violently rose up against those who practiced pagan cults.

Here is the text of *Cunctos Populos* which was enforced throughout the empire in 380 by edict of the emperors Gratian, Valentinian and Theodosius:

"It is our desire that all nations subject to our clemency and moderation should remain faithful to this religion which was transmitted by God to the apostle Peter, and which he transmitted personally to the Romans, and that obviously (this religion) is maintained by Pope Damasus and by Peter, Bishop of Alexandria, a man of apostolic holiness. According to the apostolic teaching and the doctrine of the Gospel, let us believe in the unity of the divine nature of the Father, the Son, and the Holy Spirit, equal in majesty and in a Holy Trinity. We demand that the title "Catholic Christians" be given only to those who do not violate the claims contained in this law. As for the others, we deem them to be unreasonable fools, decree that they be condemned to infamy[1] as heretics, and they shall not presume to give their gatherings the name of churches. In the first place, they must be condemned to suffer divine retribution. Then, the punishment we have been authorized to inflict in accordance with the will of Heaven."

Upon Theodosius' death in 395, the bishop of Milan Ambrose (337-397) wove the emperor's praises. The Christian emperor's praises. One episode in particular motivated Ambrose: Theodosius ordered the massacre of Thessalonica's population as Roman customary punishment for the killing of an imperial official; repenting for the cruelty of his order, he sent the counter-order but the slaughter had already taken place; Ambrose courageously barred him from entering into church without first doing public penance; an extraordinary event took place because Theodosius, the Roman Emperor, undressed of his imperial insignias and actually did public penance in the Cathedral of Milan. The Christian descended from his imperial station and made himself small. The emperor is in the church and does not have license to neglect neither the Decalogue nor the

---

[1] In general, to condemn a person to infamy means to strip that person of their civil rights.

bishop's decisions. This is the teaching left to us by Theodosius. However, he is an exception because in the East, the custom is to give to Caesar even what is God's. "Caesaropapism"; that's what they'll call it.

In 494 there was an attempt to clearly and neatly define the boundaries of their spheres of influence. Pope Gelasius established them by writing to emperor Anastasius during a falling-out between east and west when the emperor supported the Monophysite heresy. In the letter *Two are the highest authorities in this world*, the Pope wrote: "In all truth, there are two [powers], august Emperor, by which this world is chiefly ruled, namely, the sacred authority of the pontiffs and the royal power." Consequently, while the emperor should submit to the Pope in the spiritual field, in the temporal, the opposite is true: the Pope should submit to the emperor. The empire is one; the highest authorities are two; each holds a sword; the sword held in the right hand – the chief hand – is held by the pontiff because eternal life is more important than this earthly life. Gelasius' position, which went down in history as the "Theory of the two swords," though clear as day in its wording, was insufficient neither to heal the ongoing schism nor to halt the conflicts which ensued between the papacy and the empire. After all, the interests at stake were too substantial.

Recently, Pope Ratzinger quoted the two swords theory to commend the distinctive features of the State-Church relationship in the USA. In 2004, in a speech to the Italian parliament, cardinal Ratzinger said: "With regard to the relationship between Church and politics, [American catholics] have been handed down the traditions of free churches, in the sense that only a Church that is not confused with the State is able to better guarantee the moral foundations of the whole. In this way, the promotion of the democratic ideal appears as a moral duty that is deeply consistent with faith. Similar positions can be rightly seen as a continuation of Pope Gelasius' model adequate to our times."

Barbarians

In the 2nd century there were some light incursions. In the third they became heavy. In the fourth there were migrations of entire peoples. Up until the 10th century, countless barbarian invasions poured out over the very rich lands of the Western Roman Empire. From northeast and from the north: Picts, Caledones, Saxons, Frisians, Franks, Alemanni, Burgundians, Marcomanni, Quadi, Lugs, Vandals, Iutungi, Gepids, Goths, Iazigi, Roxolani, Alans, Bastarnae, Scythians, Borani, Heruli, Huns, Longobards, Normans, Hungarians. All barbarians.

The rich and civilized roman world attracted nomad peoples in search for new raiding grounds and a better future like bees to honey. Roman portrayals of these peoples were gruesome because they spread terror everywhere, they went by their violence, robberies, and plundering. Ammianus Marcellinus (330-400) in his *History* describes the customs of the Huns: "They have the custom of using a knife to cut deep into newborns' cheeks" so that when their beard grew it would be more than just peach fuzz "because of the wrinkles from the scars"; "their tenor of life is so rough that they need neither fire nor seasoned food; they rather eat wild roots and the half cooked meat of any animal, which they heat up for a short time in between their thighs and the back of their horses"; no law, no religion, no home, "animals bereft of reason."

Jerome, the great and learned father of the Church, raised in Rome, then monk in Bethlehem, friend to many roman nobles, rich and fervent Christians, was baffled and speechless. In one letter he wrote: "Rome sees her own womb transformed into a battlefield, and not to come out glorious, but to come out alive! Even worse: her's is not a battle, she is buying her own life at the price of gold and of every valuable she possesses!"; "Countless and dreadfully ferocious peoples have occupied all the Gauls. All that stands between the Alps and the Pyrenees, between the Ocean and the Rhyne, the Quadi, the Vandals, the Sarmatians, the Alans, the Gepids, the Heruli, the Saxons, the Burgundians, the Alemanni and – oh wretched State! – the Pannonians, our enemies, they have plundered everything"; "I will not speak of the rest to not give the impression I am despairing of God's mercy"; "These very things I said are a risk to those who hear them and to those who repeat them. We are not even allowed to let out a sigh; we! who do not want, or better yet, who have not the courage to cry over our sufferings."

There is a pain, the breadth of which makes it impossible to utter. The event was dramatic, unimaginable and yet, it happened: in 410 Rome (Rome!) fell into the hands of the Visigoths: "The city that conquered the whole universe is conquered"; "Who would have ever believed that Rome, built on the victories won over the entire world would have fallen down to the point of becoming the tomb of those people, whose mother she was." And behold the desolate conclusion: "He who held back the antichrist has been removed, and we would like to not understand that he is nearing." Pagan Romans adored Rome as a deity and believed her as eternal. But even Christians thought that Rome, especially after the empire became Christian, would have been protected by God until the end of time. And all things considered, they are not to blame for thinking so because Rome, the universal city, the city-world, endured within the Christian Rome. It endured because the Popes were here.

If the Catholic Church did not exist, the Roman church, nothing would have survived the catastrophe which over centuries fell unremittingly on the Western Roman Empire. Nothing civilized. No memory of over a thousand years of history which constitute the foundation of our civilization. Nothing of the Greek-Roman world would have survived the barbarian onslaught had not the monasteries, the Church, the Popes, the philosophers and Christian scholars offered protection and refuge to the masterpieces of classical antiquity. No codices, nor historical texts, nor philosophical works, nor tragedies, nor comedies, nor epic poems. Nothing would have survived.

The *Katéchon*

"Do you not remember that I told you these things when I was still with you? And you know what is now restraining [*quid detineat*; τὸ κατεχον] him, so that he maybe revealed when his time comes. For the mystery of iniquity is already at work, but only until the one who now restrains [qui tenet; Ὁ κατεχων] it is removed." Thus wrote Paul in the *Second Letter to the Thessalonians*. Paul addressed people who heard his preaching, people for whom his writing was crystal clear. Unlike those who had not heard that preaching and for whom this text was obscure: what exactly is Paul speaking about? Who is holding back the antichrist from revealing himself in all his destructive power (the *katéchon* precisely)? In the letter we quoted, Jerome took for granted that this power had a name: the Roman Empire. This firm belief was shared by many Christian fathers and scholars. Tertullian wrote: "The Roman Empire delays the maximum violence incumbent on the universe as well as the same end of the world with its terrible scourges"; "While we pray to delay the end, let us favor the perpetual enduring of Rome." In a passage taken from the *City of God*, Augustine (354-430) reviewed all possible interpretations of the nature of the katéchon and wrote: "I frankly confess I do not know what he means. I will nevertheless mention such conjectures as I have heard or read. Some think that the Apostle Paul referred to the Roman Empire, and that he was unwilling to use more explicit language lest he should incur the slanderous charge that he wished ill on the empire all hoped would be eternal [...] But others think that the words, 'you know what is now restraining,' and 'the mystery of iniquity is already at work,' refer only to the wicked and the hypocrites who are in the Church until they reach that number which forms the great people of the Antichrist, and that this is the mystery of iniquity, because it seems hidden."

The fall of Rome made such an impact on Augustine that he wrote *City of God*, a book which kept him occupied for almost the last twenty years of his life. Pagans took occasion of the sack of Rome to blame Christians and their God: the gods who made Rome great, once betrayed, have taken their vengeance by bringing about the end of a city which was destined to endure as long as the world itself. The pagans' accusation was truly grave, and it could not go unanswered: Augustine rose to the challenge and answered. Starting from the Bible, Augustine defined history as the battle stage between two cities animated by two different types of loves: the city of God places the love of God in the first place unto contempt of self and the city of man places love of self in the first place unto contempt of God. The war between these two cities – a war which takes place both amongst the peoples as well as within individuals – is destined to last until the end of times: "Certainly these two cities are muddled and united together in this world until they are not separated at the final judgment."

In *City of God*, Augustine reviewed the history of this battle between two cities inside Greek-Roman culture, preserved by Christian culture. This masterpiece turned the same accusation made against Christians, right back at the pagans. The cause of the sack of Rome is identified in the moral evils of the empire: the "collapse of morality has brought the state into such grave a ruin" that pagan authors themselves did not hesitate to foresee calamity. Even worse: despite calamity, the pagan people did not convert; "while spoiled in prosperity, adversity cannot heal you. Scipio wanted that your fear of the enemy would deter you from sinking deep into your lust; but you, even at the enemy's feet did not know how to restrain it; once the opportunity offered to you by calamity was lost, you have become the most unfortunate and have remained the worst." Despite this ruthless analysis, Augustine was a Roman, he loved his country and recognized the greatness of Roman character (*indoles romana laudabilis*): "All great Roman achievements at first were born out of love for freedom, then also out of thirst for power, consideration, and glory"; "Romans neglected their private interests for the public" and managed to "restrain their greed for money and many other vices in favor of this one only vice, that is, love for glory." Yet, Romans failed to adhere to the true religion and renounce demonic deities: "It's time to choose what you must pursue."

Augustine of Hippo

"Late have I loved you, Beauty so ancient and so new, late I have loved you": Christian poet, profound theologian, great philosopher and sublime writer, Augustine came to the Christian faith late in life, only after having pursued for truth and happiness elsewhere. The road travelled on before reaching Christ gave strength and depth to Augustine's faith and to his philosophical, biblical and human considerations. Thanks to his pursuit's intellectual restlessness, Augustine was enabled to answer those who in their doubt searched for an answer to the challenges posed in their lives by history and philosophy: first and foremost, the problem of evil. Augustine came from Manicheism which took evil so seriously that it hypostatized it, transforming it into a substance: in the Manichean vision, good and evil face each other as two juxtaposed deities. After approaching the faith, Augustine denied that evil was a substance because to admit this would have meant to deny that God is all-powerful: "Good things can exist without the evil ones," on the contrary "bad things cannot exist without the good, because the natures in which they stand, in so far as they are natures, are certainly good." All that God created, including body and matter, is good. The origin of evil and ensuing death and suffering, are to be found in the moral evil which induced Adam and Eve to sin, to rebel against God, thus to make a choice of death for themselves and their descendants: "Death was not inflicted by some law of nature and therefore God did not submit man to death, but justly because of sin."

The perverted action carried out by those who reject the supreme good – the creator – to make an idol of a lesser good – the creature – is a fruit of free will: "It was not something inferior which produced an evil will, but it became evil on its own; in a disordered and abject fashion, it desired something inferior"; "it was not corruptible flesh that made the soul sinful, it was the sinful soul which made flesh corruptible." What is the cause of such a ruinous choice? "Let no one search for the efficient cause of an evil will; such a cause is not efficient but deficient"; "the evil will is not natural, but contrary to nature, because it is corruption." Augustine's philosophy is Christian and therefore it is radically anti-Gnostic: body and matter are good. Death is a just punishment, a dreadfully painful reality, "angst-filled," provoked by perverted love which privileges one's own pleasure, ones own judgment, ones own definition of good and evil in opposition to that pointed out by God.

Why does the human will, which is free, freely make a choice which degrades man to evil and therefore to suffering and death? It is a mystery. And why does God allow for sin by creating man free? "Because He who gives to each according to his providence and omnipotence knows well how to make good use not only of the good but also of the evil [...] deeming his own power and goodness to be greater by drawing good even out of evil, more so than simply impeding it." Once fallen, having rebelled against God and hence becoming mortal, is man's free will still intact? By responsing to this question, Augustine answers Pelagius. Augustine's contemporary, a monk of British origins, like Arius very erudite and an ascetic,

Pelagius claimed that man is saved by his good will. Thanks to his good works. In *De Natura et Gratia*, Augustine said a definite no. After the fall, in order to be saved, grace is indispensable; good will alone is not enough. If it was not so, then there would not have been any need for Christ's incarnation and his sacrifice on the cross: after original sin, human nature is "wounded, plagued, damaged, ruined: it needs a sincere confession and not a false protection," as that envisioned by Pelagius.

The heresies which rose in successive waves throughout the centuries have often taken their cue from Augustine. Not because his thought had something contrary to the catholic faith; rather, because the depth of his reasoning, the penetration of his philosophy's analysis, the solutions found by him to the problem of evil and the human will are so deep and so vast, described in an erudite language and shooting forth from such wisdom of the heart, that some, to make them simpler, had took them in bits and pieces and distorted their meaning.

Compelle intrare

Are the sacraments administered by those who are or were apostates valid? This question was at the origin of a schism which lasted for a very long time, It survived Constantine's attempt to eradicate it and once it festered, led to armed combat: Donatism.

Diocletian's persecution produced *traditores*: people who fearing torture and death apostatized and handed over (hence the term *traditores*: those who carry, who hand over) sacred books to the pagans. In the year 311, in Carthage, a conflict ignited between bishop Cecilian and a party of Christians from Numidia who challenged the legitimacy of his election and appointed Donatus in his place. The Numidian bishops believed that baptism administered by *traditores* was not valid and hence it had to be repeated. Donatism gained ground under Julian the Apostate, the pagan emperor who did everything he could to damage the Church. The Donatists, who thought themselves so holy, pure and perfect, abandoned themselves to anti-Catholic violence: they looted churches, destroyed religious objects, desecrated the Eucharist, killed. With time, the conflict, which at first was religious, became political. It transformed into a nationalist movement which demanded independence from the yoke of Rome for the provinces of North Africa.

Augustine placed his faith and culture at the service of healing the schism: the sacrament's efficacy does not depend from the "purity" of the minister but from Christ. Otherwise, hope would be placed in a man and not in God. Through the minister, it is Christ himself who baptizes, and the sacrament is efficacious only through His merits. Augustine confronted the supposed purity of the schismatic church ("the church of the Numidians is great; we are the Christians, and only we") with biblical and philosophical arguments: the darnel cannot be separated from the wheat before the end of times; the city of God and the city of man coexist and no man is given the right to presume a nonexisting, total purity for himself and his own.

At first, the bishop of Hippo was kind in how he addressed the Donatist. He invited them to take part of a synod where they could confront eachother in a brotherly fashion. But after having received a harsh refusal in response, having witnessed the escalation of the violence and even having escaped by chance from an ambush, he requested that the magistrates intervene to punish the guilty and give back to catholics, still the majority party, the possibility to freely profess their faith. In 410, Emperor Honorius ordered that a public debate be hend in the presence of senator Marcellinus who was to act as arbiter betweent the two opposed fronts: the catholics came out victorious and the violence came to a halt. The Donatists came back en masse to the Church, while a segment of Circumcellions (the armed faction of the Donatist movement) resisted until the invasion of the Vandals.

"Go out to the highways and hedges, and compel people to come in, that my house may be filled"; *compelle intrare*. That is what the Gospel of Luke says, chapter 14, verse 23. Force them to enter: here is the supremely delicate issue surrounding the use of force in favor of religion. Augustine seemed to view the intervention by temporal authorities against heretical and sectarian violence as legitimate. In *City of God* he wrote: "Therefore, the commandment thou shalt not kill is not broken by those who have waged war on the authority of God, and seated in places of public authority have, in accordance with the law, that is according to the just dictates of reason, condemned the guilty to death."

The painful Donatist controversy, here recounted in the main, offers us the occasion to place some questions which are not always granted. When he was questioned by Pilate, Jesus answered: "If my kingdom were of this world, my servants would fight that I might not be handed over to the Jews." Is it right for the Church to behave differently from Christ by calling temporal authorities to its defense? More generally: can Christians serve in the military? Can a Christian state fight in wars? In response to these questions, let's keep in mind that the New Testament manifests no hostility whatsoever against the army. Some soldiers questioned John the Baptist on the matter: "And we, what shall we do?" And the precursor answered: "Do not extort money from anyone, nor use threats or false accusations, and be satisfied with your wages"; the first pagan to be baptized was Cornelius, a centurion; many Christians fought in the ranks of the imperial army throughout centuries of persecution.

"Wars waged on the authority of God," Augustine wrote. It is the age-old doctrine of the just war: a defensive war in favor of peoples threatened by injustice, violence, and invasion. The Church never imposed the heroism of love to the enemy on everyone, which at an individual level, Christians continued to practice anyhow.

Leo the Great

It is not a rule of thumb, but often God chooses his champions amongst society's cultured and wealthy, just like Mary normally chooses them among young girls, children, shepherds, that is, among very simple people. The missions assigned are very different. Leo, called the Great, an erudite Roman served as Pope (390-461, Pope starting from 440) in one of the darkest moments of the history of Italy and the Western Empire: invasions, looting, and brutality. At the end of a thousand-year history, every aspect of order, civilization, justice, administration, religion risked being swallowed up into the abyss. Leo held fast to Christian strength and roman dignity; he placed his hope in the salvation brought by Christ and was familiar with the strength, the composure, and the discipline of the tradition to which he belonged. In 476, at the threshold of the western emperor's demise, even if only symbolic, Leo not only carried out all functions of the papacy, but also those of government, administration and the people's supreme defense.

The west lacked a guide. The world was decomposing, and no temporal authority had the strength to endure or resist the collision with barbarians. Only the Church remained. Only the Pope. And it was the Pope precisely who, as imperial delegate, in 452 confronted Attila, chief of the devastating Huns and convinced him to leave Italy. Only three years later, it was Rome's turn against Genseric, king of the Vandals (the name itself vandal has remained deeply etched in collective memory), who for fifteen days laid Rome to waist. Once again, the only defense left, the only wall able to hold back barbarism was Leo who managed to convince Genseric to spare Roman lives and to exclude the three major basilicas from being looted: St. Peter, St. Paul, and St. John.

If on the temporal plain Leo was the only stronghold in defense of Rome and Italy, on the spiritual plain he was Peter's successor and with great resolve he vindicated the functions he carried out at a universal level. To Anastasius, bishop of Thessalonica, he wrote: "Preeminence over the others was entrusted to one only"; it was so established, that "through them [i.e. bishops with metropolitan responsibilities], the care for the universal Church should converge into the unique seat of Peter and nothing anywhere should ever dissent with its chief." In the Eastern Church, incessantly tormented by heresies, the latest fashion was Monophysism, which deprived Jesus of his human nature by asserting that only the divine nature existed in him. The council convoked in Ephesus in 449, which passed into history as the 'Latrocinium Ephesinum" (the 'Robber council' of Ephesus), led the Monophysite party to victory by illegal means. The Pope declared the conciliar decision null and induced the emeperor to convoke a new council. Gathered in Chalcedon in 451, the fourth ecumenical council[2] decreed the existence of two natures

---

[2] Gregory the Great honors the first four councils as the four books of the gospel. Respectively: in 325, the Council of Nicea condemned Arianism and approved the *symbolon* of faith (the Creed); in 381, the Council of Constantinople added certain details related to the incarnation of the *Logos* and the divinity of the Holy Spirit to the Nicene *symbolon*; in 431,h the

in Jesus: "One cannot believe that humanity may subsist without true divinity and divinity without true humanity," wrote Leo to Flavian, the patriarch of Constantinople.

The dissertation made by the humanist Lorenzo Valla (1405-1457) proving that the so-called Donation of Constantine was false (something which Silvester II at the turn of the 11th century was already well aware of), caused a great uproar and continues to do so even today. Through a complex and exhaustive philological and historical analysis, after seven centuries from its actual composition, which took place in the 8th century, Valla proved that the document was a fake: Constantine did not entrust the western part of the empire to the Pope. Valla's study is generally used to prove how those who occupy the highest ranks in the church have an insatiable thrist for power and to prove how shameless the pontifical attitude is because it is willing to use all means in order to justify its thirst for power and riches.

To pass a false document as true is reproachable; even more so if it is the Holy See doing it. However, in those times, false documents manufactured to prove ownership of buildings, churches and convents were not rare because many went lost in the gloomy vicissitudes of the times. Ownership of these properties, in any case, was certain. In fact, documents were created to deter the powerful or, better yet, the bullies of that day and age from taking possession of what was not theirs. Could something similar have happened with the Donation of Constantine? Could it be a forgery made in good faith, in the persuasion that Constantine really so decided? It's a fact that the stable transfer of the imperial capital to Constantinople-Bizantium, the uncertain fate of the Western Roman Empire and finally its disappearance, all contributed to leave an enormous power vacuum which only the Pope filled, and he filled it only partially. It's a fact, that the Pope stayed in Rome (Rome!) and that he inherited the universal authority which earlier was owed to the ancient capital

---

Council of Ephesus defined Mary the mother of God (*Théothokos*); in 451, the Council of Chalcedon asserted the double nature of Christ: Jesus is true God and true man. Two natures in one sole person: "The difference between the natures is never cancelled by their union, on the contrary each preserves its properties so that both converge to constitute one single person or hypostasis."

of the empire. It's a fact that, if no one questioned the Donation's authenticity for so many centuries, then it must not have been deemed unlikely.

The Last shall be First

Ireland was never part of the Roman Empire: Latin was never spoken there, it never developed an urban and civil life, it was always divided amongst many clans, and it was never converted. That was until Patrick (387-461), a sixteen-year-old boy, a catholic from a Roman family of British origin, was kidnapped by pirates and ended up as a slave in the service of an Irish clan chief. Patrick spent his six years in captivity shepherding a flock and praying incessantly. He learned Gaelic as well as the religious customs of the Druids to whom his master belonged. Then he escaped and returned home. At home, he decided to follow an invitation made to him in a dream by people who were begging him to return to Ireland. And something extraordinary occurred: Patrick returned to the place he had seen as a slave. He returned to the place of his suffering. But before going, he studied, he visited monasteries, he was ordained a priest and then bishop.

Not all traditions surrounding Patrick's life are in agreement. But it is a fact that each Irish town carries the memory of the miracles he worked there. It is a fact that his preaching converted the whole island, starting from the chiefs of the various clans, whom he first addressed. The same symbol of Ireland, the shamrock is the plant used by Patrick to exemplify the difficult concept of the Trinity. The technique used by the apostle of Ireland to evangelize the Celtic pagan peoples is the same Jesus used and, after him, the apostles. Jesus, the apostles and Patrick (as well as all the first evangelizers of a nation) capture their audience's attention through wonder, through miracles. And so, just to say one for example, after Patrick there were no more snakes in Ireland, just like after Paul there were no more vipers in Malta.

Patrick's life was a constant act of prayer and penance. It was a continual battle against the devil to obtain from God protection for a newly converted people. And God blessed his apostle's efforts: a great fervor spread everywhere, many vocations, and with these many monasteries. Since Ireland never came to know the civilized life of Rome and its customs, Irish bishops never dwelt in palaces nor did they run dioceses by retracing Roman administrative divisions; instead, they were often monks dwelling in monasteries and the boundaries of their diocese matched the areas of influence of the various clans. The peculiar feature of Christianity in Ireland is the presence of these monasteries which had spread everywhere. They became great cultural centers and missionary foundries. Nowadays, almost nothing is left of those monasteries except some ruins here and there. After the Vikings destroyed them, they were rebuilt. But after the English Puritans, the pure of Oliver Cromwell (1599-1658), destroyed them, they could not be rebuilt again.

Patrick had an extraordinary veneration for the cross: that is why many commanding stone crosses are found everywhere on Irish soil; crosses that are very original, with a circle at the intersection of the arms, sculpted, of imposing stature and rising on solid foundations. Generally, they were placed in front of monasteries, but now that the monasteries are gone, only the crosses remain, an extraordinary witness to a time of great strength and beauty.

The monks and missionaries of Ireland were the last to embrace the faith but became the first. They re-evangelized Britain, France, Switzerland, and Northern Italy. After the invasions, all had embraced paganism again or heresy. This was the typical charism of Irish monasticism: the *Peregrinatio pro Christo*, of Colombanus (543-615), its most renowned personality. He represents a very demanding version of monasticism and therefore is not always well thought of. The founding of the monastic centers of Luxeuil and Bobbio, notorious cultural centers, can be traced back to him. One of the twelve companions with whom he left Ireland founded the monastery of St. Gallus. In Benedict XVI's catechesis on him, Colombanus is defined as a "European saint" because "as monk, missionary, and writer he worked in various countries in western Europe. Together with the Irish of his time, he was well aware of Europe's cultural unity. In a letter written around the year 600 and addressed to Pope Gregory the Great, for the first time the expression '*totius Europae* – of all Europe,' is used in reference to the Church's presence throughout the continent." Just a curious fact: Colombanus "introduced the practice of private and repeated confession and penance into the continent; it was called 'tariff' penance because of the proportion established between the gravity of the sin and the type of penance that the confessor should give."

Ruins of Clonmacnoise monastery, County Offaly, Ireland

A First-born Daughter

During the 4th century, barbarians entered the Roman territory en masse and so came into contact with the empire during its Arian phase. These entire pagan peoples thus converted to Arian Christianity because they were evangelized by heretical apostles, like bishop Ulfilas for example, who translated the Bible into Gothic. Visigoths, Ostrogoths, Suebi, Vandals, Burgundians, Longobards, all became Arians. All converted en masse because when their chief converted, the rest followed suit. This gave birth to national churches. Moreover, in part also for religious reasons, they harshly oppressed the pre-existent Roman Catholic population.

There is only one exception, one barbarian tribe passed from paganism to Catholicism directly: the Franks. The story of Clovis'

(466-511) conversion, the first in the long Merovingian dynasty was recounted by bishop Gregory of Tours (538-594) in the *History of the Franks*. While in war with other barbarian tribes – Clovis' whole life was one continuous war – Clovis was about to suffer a terrible defeat. He turned to the Lord in anguish and offered Him the following proposition: my wife (the catholic Clotilda) says that you give victory to those who turn to you; if you save me and give me victory, I will convert. And so it happened. A saint led Clovis to baptism, Remi, bishop of Rheims, who baptized the king with great solemnity and anointed him with oil that – according to tradition – was brought directly from heaven by an angel. The king's anointing gave his power a sort of divine investiture, which made him quite similar to the Lord's anointed par excellence, namely, David. From that Christmas Eve of 496 in which Clovis was baptized, to the crowning in 1824 of the very last Bourbon king Charles X, all kings of France were solemnly crowned in the Rheims cathedral.

Clovis' conversion facilitated the process of making peace and mixing between the Frank invaders and the Roman people, especially its aristocracy, which gave this kingdom a much greater stability than the neighboring Arian kingdoms. When Visigoth Spain caved in under the Islamic invasion – the Visigoths converted to Catholicism all too late – Frankish Gaul stood its ground. Charles Martel halted the invasion at Poitiers in 732 and Charlemagne's counterattack sent the Muslims back beyond the Pyrennes and the Ebro. The Marca Hispanica was born. France was called "Firstborn daughter of the Church."

In Clovis' time, and for many centuries thereafter, the Church was the only hierarchically organized institution, governed by clear laws derived from Rome's legal heritage, with educated and hence also precious bishops. Clovis, newly converted to Catholicsim, did indeed support the Church. He gave it privileges and guaranteed ownership of its properties. At the same time though, he acted as if Church structures, hierarchies, and properties belonged to his sphere of competence. In fact, it was the king who convoked synods, named bishops, and approved canonical norms. Since the dawn of its life, the French church manifested the typical feature which accompanied it throughout the centuries: it lacked a true primate because, in practice, the king was its primate.

Because the king and his stewards appointed bishops and abbots chosen from among their own companions at arms, relatives or friends, very soon the discipline, morals and even cultural preparation of the clergy and religious were seriously deficient. So much so that when Charlemagne wanted to reform the Church and establish the Palace School, he will have no better alternative than to turn to Alcuin, a monk from York. The poor customs of the French church were later proudly vindicated as the distinctive traits of the "Gallican church", as if they were something to boast about; these Gallican customs were upheld not only by kings but also by the prelates, bishops and religious. Against the universal Roman Church, the French elite go about proud of the Gallican church's local features; only until the revolution.

Western monasticism: Benedict

On March 21, 547, two monks, simultaneously and in two different places, had the following vision which Gregory the Great, the outstanding biographer of Benedict of Nursia set down in writing: "They saw all the way from the holy man's cell, towards the east even up to heaven, hung and adorned with tapestry, and shining with an infinite number of lamps, at the top whereof a man, reverently attired and radiating light, stood and demanded if they knew who passed that way, to whom they answered saying, that they knew not. Then he spoke to them: 'This is the way,' said he, 'by which the beloved servant of God, Benedict, ascended up to heaven.'"

A Roman from a noble family, Benedict (480-547) lived completely alone for three years in a cave near Subiaco. Quite casually the holiness of his life was discovered and suddenly his fame spread everywhere. However, such renown was accompanied by the envy, jealousy and hate of some who did not manage to live in such a holy manner. So much so that it was only owing to his extraordinary prophetic gifts that he was able to escape those who wanted him dead for two times. These murder attempts were the occasions God used to make Benedict become Benedict: the founder of western monasticism. Leaving Subiaco behind, he moved to a mountain which towers over the Cassino valley. The first thing he did when he arrived, was to destroy the remains of Apollo's temple which local farmers still venerated: he "beat in pieces the idol, set fire to the woods, and in the temple of Apollo, he built the oratory of St. Martin, and where the altar of the same Apollo was, he made an oratory of St. John: and by his continual preaching, he brought the people dwelling in those parts to embrace the faith of Christ." Benedict's feats against paganism provoked a furious reaction by the "age-old enemy," the devil, who "did in open sight present himself to the eyes of that holy father horrendous and enraged."

In our eyes, the destruction of pagan idols and temples seems incomprehensible. Yet Benedict, who certainly was a man endowed by God with extraordinary gifts, did exactly that. Another Benedictine monk would later do the same: Boniface, the apostle of Germany, who eighty years old died a martyr because he tore down the great oak considered sacred by the Frisians, the primitive inhabitants of Holland. For a very long time, the Church believed that the battle against paganism, that is against the devil, his idols and his rites, needed to be waged with great resolve even by in some cases, destroying objects and temples. Today, this would certainly not be the case. And yet it was done for a long time. Were all our Catholic ancestors violent barbarians? Also the greatest among them? It's a worthwhile question to ask oneself because maybe, nowadays, something is eluding us.

Benedictine monasticism took a predominant seat over all others because of its Rule. Defined as "minimal and drafted only as a beginning," in reality "it offers useful guidelines not only to monks but also to all those who are searching for a guide on their way to God. Because of its size, humanity and sober discernment between what is essential and what is secondary in the spiritual life, it was able to maintain its enlightening force up until today," wrote Benedict XVI in the catechesis dedicated to the patron saint of his pontificate.

Some of the Rule's guidelines: "Let nothing come before the Work of God," that is prayer; let each "obey every command given him" but the abbot must take into consideration the opinion of all his brothers because "the Lord often reveals what is better to the younger"; that man shall become abbot whom "the whole community acting unanimously in the fear of God, or by some part of the community, no matter how small, which possesses sounder judgment." Benedict foresaw that in the future his followers would distance themselves even a long ways from his Rule – which in fact did happen – and therefore he prescribed: "May God forbid that a whole community should conspire to elect a man who goes along with its own vices." If so, after having informed the bishop, let "the abbots, or Christians [...] block the success of this wicked conspiracy and set a worthy steward in charge of God's house" because otherwise, "to neglect to do so would be to sin."

It will also happen, and it will be the worst of scenarios, that abbots are not elected freely by the monks but rather coerced on the monks by the powerful in the area who in this way wanted to reward their own friends to the detriment of religious life and the proper charism of the monastic community.

A New Civilization

In the *First Letter to the Corinthians*, Paul wrote: "Anyone unwilling to work should not eat." Benedict followed along the same line: "Idleness is the enemy of the soul. Therefore, the brothers should have specified periods for manual labor as well as for sacred reading." Nothing could be farther from the Roman ideal of life which exhalted idleness with its pleasures and despised manual labor which was intended only for slaves. Medieval life is cadenced by Benedictine industriousness which brought about innovation and improvements in every field of human activity. It also firmly stayed greedy profiteering because the Rule commands that "the evil of avarice must have no part in establishing prices; rather let them them be always a little lower than people outside the monastery are able to set, so that in all things God may be glorified." Starting with Luther and in subsequent waves, when hate for the Catholic Church led to the suppression of monastic and religious institutions, the inevitable result of robbing the Church of the goods it administered, was pauperism, that is, misery for the general population.

"The abbot should avoid all favoritism in the monastery," "A man born free is not to be given higher rank than a slave who becomes a monk, except for some other good reason"; let no one dare to "retain anything as his own, nothing at all – not a book, writing tablets or stylus – in short, absolutely not a single item"; "All things should be the common possession of all, as it is written, so that no one presumes to think or call anything as his own." Every day, monks coerced their will under the yoke of an iron discipline in order to practice charity. Clumsy imitators appeared over the centuries who were not even remotely near to that absolute tension towards heaven which alone, and it alone, is able to make this style of life possible: Communism's attempt to abolish private property, brought about disastrous consequences.

Benedict XVI wrote that the monastery at Montecassino, visible from far off, "carries a symbolic character: the hiddenness of monastic life has its raison d'etre, but a monastery has also its public purpose in the life of the Church and society. It must make faith visible as the strength of life." "St. Benedict of Nursia, with his life and work had a fundamental impact on the development of European culture and civilization" giving life, "after the fall of the political unity created by the Roman Empire, to a renewed spiritual and cultural unity given by the Christian faith which was shared by the people of the continent." The reality which we call "Europe" was born exactly like this. The Pope went on to say: "Today, Europe – which has just exited the last century deeply wounded by two world wars and after the fall of the great ideologies which reveled themselves as tragic utopias – is now in search of its own identity. To create a renewed unity that may be lasting, while political, economic and juridical instruments are certainly important, it is necessary also to foster an ethical and spiritual renewal that draws from the continent's Christian roots; otherwise Europe cannot be rebuilt. Without this vital sap, man remains exposed to the danger of succumbing under an age-old temptation: that of wanting to redeem himself – a utopia that in 19th century Europe, as Pope John Paull II laid bare, in so many different ways produced 'an unprecedented regression in humanity's tormented history.'"

Modelled on the first Montecassino, monasteries scattered in the thousands throughout all European regions and created a new civilization model. While they preserved classic culture from destruction, they gave life to a new culture. Benedict of Nursia persued the primacy in charity: the Rule established that there be a porter at the door of the convent who "as soon as anyone knocks, or a poor man calls out, should reply, 'Thanks be to God' or 'Your blessing, please'; then, with all the meekness that comes from the fear of God, he provides a prompt answer with the warmth of love." Charity is the distinctive icon of monasticism: charity practiced within the convent amongst the monks and without towards all.

Flavius Petrus Sabbatius Iustinianus

"In the time of King Totila, there was a certain Goth called Galla, a follower of the Arian heresy, who, did with such incredibly monstrous cruelty persecute religious faithful of the Catholic Church, that whomever fell into his hands, priest or monk soever, he shamelessly sent to the Creator." Gregory the Great, in *The Life of Saint Benedict*, described the situation at the time of the Goths. Justininan (527-565), having to confront the Persians, long-standing enemies of the Empire, in the east, as well as the Vandals and the Goths in the west, rose up to defend the Romans. The last emperor of Latin culture and language, Justinian reconquered southern Spain, Northern Africa, Italy, and Dalmatia. But he did so at the cost of devastating and depopulating entire regions. Rome was won and lost multiple times. The hard-won victory earned after two decades of battles against the Goths was short-lived. In fact, few years passed before new barbarian tribes occupied the freshly conquered territories: only three years after Justinian's death the Longobards took over Italy. Yes, it was an extremely high human cost that was spent in defense of the Roman peoples, but it was also defending the ideal of a universal empire, an institution which, at least on the western side, had already lost all its vital impulse.

A kingdom that wants to grow in strength must prove itself artistically and culturally vibrant. In art and architecture, Justinian accomplished true wonders. He rebuilt Saint Sophia (dedicated to Christ, Wisdom of the Father), which in those days was the largest church in the world, an unsurpassed example of architectural perfection, a shining display of gold and mosaic tile and an endless source of inspiration to religious architecture for centuries to come. He also built Ravenna, the imperial capital of Italy and the precious gem of byzantine architecture. On a cultural level, Justinian erected a monument which represents the most relevant and original feature of Roman culture: Roman law. He redacted the *Corpus Iuris Civilis*, a collection of all laws passed from the time of the Republic up until the most recent passed by Justinian with all their respective commentaries. It is a juridical creation of such unique value, that still today it is referred to by scholars and legal experts around the world.

A kingdom that wants to grow in strength also needs a great social and religious cohesion. Hence, Justinian often intervened in the religious and cultural arena: one single empire, one single faith, one single vision of life. In 529, mainly as a symbolic deed, Justinian shut down Athen's school of philosophy; he also dismantled Hellenistic culture, banned paganism, forbid Jews from using Hebrew as their liturgical language, destroyed the synagogues of Samaritans, and banned Manicheism.

Though Catholicism was already the empire's official religion at the time, the relationship with the Catholic Church regressed. As in the gloomy days of Constantine II, again, the emperor demanded that the Church's magisterium should adjust itself to his own religious beliefs. He imposed on the Church the imperial maxim: *Regis voluntas suprema lex*. The Monophysite heresy, which acknowledged only one single nature in Jesus, that is the divine, only seemed to have been defeated in Chalcedon. At the root of the Acacian schism that took place between 484 and 519, the first serious rupture between the Catholic Church and the Byzantine, was Monophysitism again. Though Emperor Justin, Justinian's uncle, had brought the empire back to orthodoxy, the reunification was superficial: many eastern bishops still adhered to Monophysitism. During Justinian reign, the fact that Empress Theodora was a Monophysite made a huge difference. After having coerced Pope Silverius to abdicate by accusing him of treason, he exiled him to Ponza, and in 547, Justinian deported the Pope's successor Vigilius, to Constantinople. However, Vigilius refused to underwrite a document which condemned the Three Chapters, that is, the three anti-Monophysite writings approved in Chalcedon. Regrettably, under pressure from the emperor and after various ordeals, the Pope gave in. In 553 he subscribed the condemnation of the Three Chapters, a repetition of the Liberius incident. This time, however, it was more serious: part of the Western Church, first and foremost Milan and Aquileia, joined the schismatic churches because they did not accept the Pope's surrender.

One last thought: in 554, after achieving victory in the Gothic War, Justinian promulgated the *Pragmatic Sanction*, an edict formally requested by Pope Vigilius (at the time held captive in Byzantium!) which repealed Gothic legislation and extended imperial law to Rome and Italy. Although this edict had a minor impact on daily life, it set down a precedent: in fact, all future attempts to bend the Holy See to the will of temporal authorities in power, drew from and referred to the *Pragmatic Sanction* as well as Justinian's Roman law. Within the wider perspective of Church history, Justinian's legacy is a heavily negative footprint: the phony procedure and deposition of Silverius, a holy Pope; the coerced election of Pope Vigilius, a weak and ambitious man; and finally, the constant theological, liturgical as well as administrative interference with Church affairs.

Gregory the Great

Gregory the Great (540-604, Pope from 590), was Pope at the end of the 6th century. Italy was in dire straits: after having just put behind a very harsh confrontation with the empire, it was now invaded again, this time, by the Longobards, an Arian, pagan, and very violent people who set siege to Rome, destroyed Montecassino and threatened to take over all of Italy. Gregory was a member of a powerful and rich family belonging to Roman senatorial aristocracy. Before becoming Pope, he had served as Praefectus Urbi (Urban prefect), then papal envoy to the byzantine imperial court, and finally he had transformed his father's house into a monastery (one of the many that were to be established on his lands) where he retreated to lead the life of a monk. Once he was elected Pope, he confronted the enemies of the Holy See with firmness, legal and biblical wisdom, with diplomacy, with faith. There were hardships everywhere: the situation of Rome and Italy was dire and one could not count on imperial support; the Patriarch of Constantinople made constant demands; Pope Vigilius had left a schism behind; the quality of the clergy's formation needed careful consideration; the Longobards created deserts everywhere and their expansion needed to be stemmed; many private and imperial donations (partially dispersed as a result of the invasions) which required careful administration. Gregory faced a mountain of issues.

He set himself immediately to work. He assured that Rome had rations supplied during times of plague and war; he established schools to form a select clergy adequately prepared and morally irreprehensible for any place that required its presence: biblical schools, schools – famous to this day – for cantors, liturgical schools, schools for administrative officials. He reorganized the papal estate's administration everywhere (Africa, Gaul, Sicily, Sardinia, Corsica, Campania, Lucania, Picenum and in the Balkan Peninsula) by centralizing and appointing a person responsible for each area who gave account to the Pope directly. He also wrote letters (847 were conserved to our day) to give counsel, correct, command, instruct, and maintain relations with the byzantine court (he always claimed to be a loyal subject of the emperor without this being a reason for him to not be frank when problems emerged). He instituted a register so as to be able to preserve all acts of the apostolic see. Finally, as bishop of Rome and therefore of the universal Church, Gregory personally oversaw the evangelization of Roman territories which had been invaded by barbarians and regressed to paganism and sent 40 monks led by Augustine to Britannia.

Gregory was called the Great.

Let us examine two significant issues faced by Gregory over the years:

- The council of Constantinople in 381 gave the imperial city's patriarch the second primacy of honor after Rome. This title has nothing to do with the evangelization (which is at the original purpose of the patriarch's institution) but only with the fact that Constantinople was the empire's capital. In Gregory's time, the Patriarch of Constantinople, John, had himself called "universal" bishop. This was the first of many attempts to strip Rome of its uniqueness and universality by transferring it elsewhere, some other city, kingdom or institution. Gregory confronted the thorny issue in several letters: "All those who know the Gospel, clearly know that it is by the word of the Lord that the care of the universal Church was entrusted to the holy apostle Peter, prince of the apostles"; nonetheless, no bishop of Rome ever flaunted this title ("if one has himself called universal patriarch, the name patriarch will become diminished for the others"); yet "John, most holy brother with me in the priesthood, does all he can to be called universal bishop"; John caused a scandal with this claim: "Let him turn back, therefore, onto the right way, he who is the author of the scandal and all grievances will come to a halt. I am, in fact, servant to all priests." *Servus servorum Dei*: since then, all Popes have made use of Gregory's definition;

- In November of the year 602, Gregory wrote to Paschasius, bishop of Naples, with regard to protests made by certain Jews who lamented not being able to celebrate their own religious festivities according to custom. Gregory's letter, in continuity with Saint Paul's teachings, laid down the conduct which the Catholic Church had to follow towards Jews: those who want to hinder Jews from freely professing their faith, prove that it is not from a desire to convert them that they do so, but rather out of cunning, out of concern only for their own self-interest. Jews are not conquered for Christ with harshness but with affection (*blandimentis, non asperitatibus*): "Whoever, with a sincere intention, desires to bring to the right faith those who are far away from the Christian religion must do so with affection and not harshness"; "whoever should act otherwise and would like under this pretext to distance them from the customary worship of their rite, demonstrates to be more concerned with their own interests rather than with those of God (*suas illi magis quam Dei probantur causas attendere*)."

The blind gods roar for Rome fallen

In the poem *The Ballad of the White Horse* Chesterton wrote: "The blind gods roar for Rome fallen." Chesterton's meaning is clarified by reading the *Ecclesiastical History of the English People* written by the Venerable Bede (672/3-735). Though it is a most enjoyable and also quite poetic read, it becomes rather hard to keep track of the evangelization's dynamics when, at the turn of the 5th century, Roman presence on the island came to an end. Under Roman rule, time flowed regularly, the same for everyone everywhere, cadenced on the years since the foundation of Rome, since the foundation of the empire and since the birth of Jesus; during barbarian times – with the Angles, the Saxons, the Jutes – time splits and even triplicates to keep up with the history of various tribes and kingdoms without a main thread: "In the year 693 of Rome, sixty years before the incarnation of the Lord" Julius Caesar arrived in Britannia; "In the year 798, Emperor Claudius, fourth after Augustus…"; "In year 156 of our Lord, Marcus Antoninus, fourteenth after Augustus…," and so on and so forth with distinct precision up to the arrival of the tragic end: "In year 1164 since its foundation, Rome was taken and looted by the Goths. Since that moment, Romans ceased to govern Britannia, after about four hundred and seventy years since Julius Caesar had set foot on the island." Deprived of its defenses, Britannia "had no other choice but to become itself a prey": Gaels in the west, Picts in the north, "it became immersed in terror and pain for many years." "As lambs with ferocious beasts, so are the wretched citizens ravaged by enemies." After the Gaels and the Picts came the Saxons – eastern, southern, and western – and the Angles – eastern and central – and the Mercian and then the Northumbrians. It was total chaos.

Yet the Lord never abandoned the Island and a new evangelization began: "In the year 582 of our Lord, Mauritius, fifty-fourth after Augustus, rose to the throne and held the reign for twenty-one years. On the tenth year of his reign, Gregory, eminent man for knowledge and works became Pope in the Apostolic See of Rome and was Pope for thirteen years, six months and ten days." Gregory, "by divine inspiration," sent Augustine with 40 monks to preach the Gospel to the Angles. The missionaries, at first, "overwhelmed by paralyzing terror, thought of returning home rather than head to the barbarian, ferocious, unbelieving peoples, whose language they did not even know," but Gregory did not give in and spurred them forth, exhorted them, admonished them: "It would have been better to not even start on a good work than to think of turning back." Having found their courage again, the monks took off on mission, and the mission is such a success, the preching of Augustine is accompanied by so many miracles, that Gregory, greatly consoled, wrote: "For love of Him [Jesus] we searched Britannia for brothers we did not know, and for his gift we found those we searched for without knowing."

Bede recounts an episode, really one of a kind, which took place during Paulinus' mission – one of the monks who took off with Augustine – in the court of the Northumberland King Edwin. Before authorizing them to preach, the king first asked the men in his company for their opinion. One of them expressed himself thus: "Your Majesty, when we compare the life of men on earth, with that time of which we have no knowledge, it seems to me as when, while you are having dinner with your dignitaries, in winter, while the fire is lit and the halls are heated, while outside a storm of rain and snow is raging, suddenly a sparrow speedily flies in. He makes his flight swiftly in through one door and out through the other. For this very short time that he is inside he is safe from the winter storm and thus spends but a moment of tranquility; immediately after, he vanishes from sight into the storm from whence he came. Such is the life of man, it remains in sight but for a moment, and we know nothing of what it will be after nor what it was before. Therefore, if this new teaching has brought any more certain knowledge, it certainly deserves that we should follow it."

The Anglo-Saxons converted with such fervor that, following the Irish example, they became protagonists – *peregrine pro amore Dei* – of the evangelization effort among the continent's Germanic tribes. Bede, a cultured and erudite monk of Anglo-Saxon origins but an heir of classic culture, is the father of English historiography. This is a positive instance of how, thanks to Christianity and Christian monks, barbarian invaders mixed with the preexistent Roman population and inserted themselves as the protagonists of the Catholic Roman World.

Mohammed

During its one thousand and five-hundred-year history, Islam was always an unshakable enemy of Christianity: to understand why, we must keep in mind a few features which distinguish its doctrine. Let's briefly examine them.

Mohammed (579-632) possessed an oral knowledge of both Judaism and Christianity and was also a genius of social and religious organization. "There is no God if not Allah and Mohammed is its prophet": this is the maxim that summarizes Islam's faith. Islam means "submission." It includes a firm denial of the Trinity and of Jesus' divinity, and holds faith in Jesus as a prophet and in Mary the Virgin mother of the prophet. Islam is God's final revelation to man. Previous revelations, made to Jews and Christians, who are also "people of the book," are also partially integrated in the revelation entrusted to Mohammed, but they are rejected in their specific natures: there are no elected people and there is no incarnation. God is one. All men fall under two categories: the house of peace and the house of war. The house of peace, or Islam, must fight the house of war unto victory. In the end, Islam fights on behalf of God and so shall win. All people shall profess the true religion by adoring the only God, Allah.

Mohammed's life is defined by two events: the start of the revelations made to him by the archangel Gabriel in 610; and the flight from Mecca to Medina in 622, year which marks the first Muslim calendar year. As a man blessed by God, Allah granted Mohammed many privileges: one fifth of all loot obtained in any one conquest (Quran 8, 41) and one "special privilege reserved for you only, and not for the rest of believers," "it will not be sin for you," "it is lawful for you" (Quran 33, 50-51), to have more than four wives (the number of wives that the Quran allows males to have, without counting concubines)[3]. According to the greatest historian of Islam's

---

[3] This is the full text of verses 50-51 from Sura 33: "50. Oh Prophet! Behold! We have made lawful to you those wives to whom you have paid their dowries, the slaves who you possess and who Allah has given to you as spoils of war. The daughters of your paternal uncle and the daughters of your paternal aunts, the daughters of your maternal uncle and the daughters of your maternal aunts who have emigrated with you and every believing woman who may offer herself to the Prophet, if the Prophet wants to marry her. This is a special privilege reserved for you only, and not for the rest of believers. We are well aware of that which we have enjoined on them concerning their wives and the slaves whom they possess, so, let there be no shame for you whatsoever. Allah is ever forgiving, merciful. 51. If you will have those whom you wish to wait, and will call to yourself those you desire, and if you will go back to take again one whom you had made to wait, there will be no sin for you, so that let them be comforted and let their affliction cease and let them be content with what you shall have granted them. Allah knows what is in your hearts. Allah is wise and magnanimous."

first three centuries, the Persian Tabari, Mohammed had 15 wives, without counting concubines. After the death of his first wife Khadija, a rich widow, his favorite wife became Aisha, the daughter of Abu Bakr, a great friend and future first Caliph. He married her when she was 6 years old, and their marriage was consummated when she was 9.

That which the Quran calls the house of peace knew war since the very beginning. And it was not only against external enemies but also amongst the same members of the Muslim family. In fact, upon Mohammed's death, four elected Caliphs succeeded him (two of his fathers-in-law and two of his sons-in-law). All were murdered but one, the first, Abu Bakr who died of natural death after two years. Ali's murder (Mohammed's cousin and son-in-law by way of marriage to Fatima, the only daughter who survived the prophet's death) is at the origin of the division between Sunnis and Shiites. The hereditary Omayyadi Caliphate (660-750) came to an end because the Omayyadi family was exterminated (only one survivor managed to escape, and he established the Cordoba emirate in Spain).

"God created man in his image; in the image of God he created man; male and female he created them" (*Genesis* 1, 27). This is an expression that in Islam is absolutely meaningless: man and woman are radically different; man is unmistakably superior to woman and in paradise, an uninterrupted series of virgins shall delight the stay males. Furthermore, not even man is created in the image of God: man must only be submitted to him. God is neither father nor spouse (as the Song of Songs and the prophet Hosea, amongst others, revealed) God is completely different from man. The Jewish concept of covenant and that of analogy, developed by Christian philosophy from the scriptural verses of Genesis, are unthinkable for a Muslim. The Christian conception of Jesus' divinity and the consequent possibility that man may become son of God in Christ is unimaginable.

What must one do to be a good Muslim? One must obey God and his prophet. In the Quran, however, not all teachings are homogeneous: in fact, opposite behaviors are viewed positively with regard to the same issue. This makes it quite hard, in principle, to deny that the practical consequences of observing Quranic teachings do not match divine revelation. For example, when it says: "In truth, the only reward of those who make war upon Allah and His messenger and strive after corruption in the land will be that they will be killed or crucified, or have their hands and feet on alternate sides cut off, or banished from the land" (Quran 5, 33); or when it says: "I will throw terror into the hearts of the non-believers: smite them between head and neck, strike them on each finger [...] It certainly was not you who killed them, it is Allah who has killed them" (Quran 8, 12-17). Therefore, it is very hard to deny that those who put these commands literally into practice – something which happened repeatedly throughout the centuries starting from the same Mohammed – is disobeying Allah. Holy is that war which submits the infidels (*Jihad*).

I am who I am

Though the Quran speaks about "peoples of the book," thus taking for granted that God's revelation reached its climax with Mohammed, the Quran's and the Judeo-Christian vision of the world are radically different. To Moses, after insisting, God revealed his name: "God said to Moses: 'I am who I am'" (*Exodus* 3, 14). In the Gospel of John, chapter eight, Jesus attributed that same name to himself three times: "You will die in your sins unless you believe that I Am" (8, 24); "When you have lifted up the Son of Man, then you will know that I Am" (8,28); "Before Abraham was, I Am" (8,58).

"I Am" created man in his image (better yet, "In our image," *Genesis* 1,26): therefore, even man is. Man's being derives from God's being. The Quran attributes 99 names to God but being is nowhere among these. Because God is completely different from creation. Not even creation has a nature or a being because it results from God's continued stance. Fr. Gianni Baget Bozzo (1925-2009) writing about Islam used words of rare depth: "Creation is a fundamental concept of Christianity precisely as a reality which is other from God, although its origin and foundation is in God. For Islam, creation exists only as a constant production of the divine will: God is the sole cause of all events. The concept of nature therefore has no place in Islamic thought, and contrary to Christianity, it acknowledges no autonomy in created causalities."

In Islam, both the problem of evil and the problem of free will are strictly not posed as a question: evil is the infidel, "A nothingness which rebels against the sole cause of its existence." A nothingness which must be annihilated: "This is the subtle form of nihilism which pervades Islamic thought and which, not by chance, has found annihilating actions, that is acts of war, to be its proper form of civil and social action. At the same time, annihilation, death in battle is the manner by which the Muslim may enter a second space of creation: not life in God, as in Christianity, but a rewarded existence."[4]

"Islamic religion introduces a gnostic dimension, the theme of an evil existence," an evil existence which is not tied to matter per se, as in ancient Gnosticism, but to the presence of non-Muslims: "The God of the Quran posits those realities which oppose the Quran as existential evil"; evil is something outside of the Islamic universe and it exists "as a historical entity in the infidel universe."

Contrary to the God of the Bible and of the prophets, who are people and as such are capable of establishing relations and are endowed with free will – namely, the possibility to say yes or no to God – for the God of the Quran, man is not even a person "because before God it is not substance," and lacks ontological consistency. Mohammed is a passive instrument: Quran means recitation and Mohammed is a man who recites on God's behalf. God is an absolute subject which annuls any human individuality: hence, the Quran is "an intrinsically non-historical fact," solely a divine act, unchanging and perfect. "Not only did Islam reject the Quran's historic dimension, but it has also rejected all thought on God. That is to say, it rejected the application of Greek metaphysical categories to God." Thus wrote Baget Bozzo in *Di fronte all'Islam (Standing before Islam)*

In his *Lectio magistralis*, held in Regensburg in 2006, Benedict XVI also questioned himself about the relationship between faith and reason within Islam. In this respect, the Pope quoted a dialogue held in Ankara in 1391 between Emperor Michael II Palaeologus and a wise Persian. Michael II asked him: "Show me just what it is that Mohammed brought that was new, and there you will find things only evil and inhuman, such as his command to spread the faith he

---

[4] See Baget Bozzo, *Maometto, Cristo e l'Occidente (Mohammed, Christ and the West)*, "Il Foglio", August 5, 2005.

preached by the sword." The emperor, "after having expressed himself so forcefully, then goes on to explain in detail the reasons why spreading the faith through violence is unreasonable. Violence is in contrast with the nature of God and the nature of the soul. "God", he says, "is not pleased by blood – and not acting according to reason, 'σὺν λόγῳ,' is contrary to God's nature. Faith is born of the soul, not the body. Whoever would lead someone to faith needs the ability to speak well and to reason properly, without violence and threats... To convince a reasonable soul, one does not need a strong arm, or weapons of any kind, or any other means of threatening a person with death." Starting from this dialogue, Benedict XVI asked himself: "Is the conviction that acting unreasonably contradicts God's nature merely a Greek idea, or is it always and intrinsically true?"

Having said this, it must be said that the Quran, written in a perfect and even melodious classical Arab, contains very nice passages about Allah the merciful, the all-powerful and benevolent protector of those who honor him: "In the name of God the all-powerful and merciful" (*Bismillah ir-Rahman ir-Rahim*). This is the invocation by which every pious Muslim begins each day and with which he faces each important stage of his life.

An agreement conceded

After Mohammed's death, Arabs began spreading throughout Persian and Byzantine regions. In Constantinople, since Arius' time, that is three centuries earlier, the faith was threatened and corroded by heresies: Arianism, Nestorianism, Monophysism, Monotelism, and an infinite series of their ramifications leading to an unending stream of sectarian controversies. The empire's Patriarchates, the mother cities evangelized by the apostles, were pitted one against the other: Alexandria against Antioch; Constantinople against both. The unity Jesus had enjoined on his friends was dissolved. Moreover, there were wars which for centuries pit Persians against Rome, a conflict wherein neither of the two ever managed to achieve ultimate victory. The cost of war raised taxation in the Byzantine Empire to unbearable levels. This is the stage at which the Arab tribes emerged, and when two strive for a bone, a third runs away with it.

Mohammed died in 632: within ten years of his death, from 633 to 643, Persia suddenly tragically succumbed. In 637, Ctesiphon, the capital was stormed after a three-month siege and after plundering for a thousand and one nights. In 636 it was Byzantium's turn. In 637 the Caliph Omar (634-644) entered Jerusalem, Israel's holy city which, after being destroyed at the hands of the Romans, had become a Catholic city full of churches and monasteries. Syria and Egypt followed the fall of Palestine. Under Uthman (644-656) Armenia and Cyprus were occupied. The Umayyad (661-750) completed the conquest of North Africa and in 711, pushed towards Spain. In the east, Islam arrived all the way to India and Turkistan. In 697, Constantinople was put under siege for the first time and the empire survived, although in Asia it was deprived of Syria and Egypt, its richest provinces, and reduced to the current area of Turkey.

In 637 a pact was made between Caliph Omar and the people of Jerusalem. Omar granted Christians "safe-haven for themselves, their money, their churches, their crosses, their sick and healthy, for the whole community; none of their churches are to be occupied or destroyed and no part or whole part of their property should go missing, and none should be illtreated." In exchange for the Caliph's benevolence, Christians must pay a tax (*jizya*, or protection tax) and must expel "Romans and bandits"; but whomever "wishes to take his money and leave with the Romans, he shall be guaranteed safety until he reaches them."

On their part, Christians promise: "We shall not build new monasteries, churches, or hermitages inside or outside your cities; we shall not repair religious edifices fallen in disrepair nor shall we restore those which are in the Muslim quarters of the city; neither by night or day shall we refuse entrance to Muslims in our churches; we shall open the doors to travelers and pilgrims; we shall give hospitality to every Muslim traveler in our home, and offer him room and board for three nights; we shall not hide spies in our churches or our houses, nor shall we offer asylum to any enemy of the Muslims. We shall not teach the Quran to our children nor shall we make public showing of the Christian religion, nor shall we invite anyone to adhere to it; we shall not impede, however, any of our relatives from embracing Islam, if they should desire to do so. We shall honor Muslims and will grant them our place in our assemblies when they should desire to attend them; we shall not imitate them in dress, nor in headwear, nor turbans, nor footwear, nor hairstyle; we shall not use their manner of speech, nor adopt their nicknames, nor ride horses, nor carry swords, nor carry weapons, nor shall we make Arab inscriptions on our rings; we shall not sell wine and will shave off our beards; we shall continue to wear the same kind of dress wherever we shall be; we shall gird our waists with belts. We shall not set the cross over our churches nor shall we place the cross or our sacred books in the Muslims' streets or markets; in our churches we shall clap lightly; we shall not recite our prayers in a high voice when a Muslim is present; we shall not carry palm branches nor our votive images in procession along the streets; during funerals we shall not sing loudly, nor carry candles along the Muslims' streets or markets; we shall not take anyone slave who had been in the past property of a Muslim, nor shall we act as spies in their homes; we shall not strike any Muslim. We promise to observe these rules so as to benefit ourselves and all those who believe in a religion similar to ours; in exchange we shall receive from you protection. If we should violate any condition contained in this agreement, then we shall lose any right to your protection and you shall have the right to treat us as enemies and rebels."

Christians, by entering into this agreement with Omar signed their death: a slow but certain death. Moreover, when any Muslim wanted to become Christian, he was inevitably killed, as guilty of committing the worst kind of sins, dishonoring Allah; for this same reason, every territory conquered by the true faith could not pass under any authority different from the Muslim. Nonetheless, Omar's agreement granted the best conditions Christians could ever hope for under any Muslim rule. In fact, Mohammed's followers repeatedly resorted to the sword and to terror.

From Britain to Germany

The British evangelized the tribes dwelling in the areas of Germany and Holland: monks, nuns, benefactors, princes and kings. The whole Christian community made a great and intense missionary effort to convert the remaining pagan and barbarian brothers on the continent. Born from one Pope's resolve, the work of evangelization done by the English church was in very close communion with Rome. In all ages, missionaries always viewed keeping communion with Rome as of utmost importance to avoid the danger Paul speaks about in his *Letter to the Galatians*, of "running or having run in vain."

English missionaries, communion with Rome, protection offered by Frankish stewards: these were the main features of the mission in the German lands lying east of the Rhine. The Franks, who had been Catholics for some time already, wanted also to take part in the evangelization of the Germans. But their interest was not only religious. It was also political because if the Saxons converted, it would have become easier to place them under Frankish sphere of influence.

The mission began at the end of the 7th century when the monk Willibrord, together with 11 companions (12 are the tribes of Israel, 12 the apostles, 12 is a number which often repeats itself in the history of the Church) left Britain for Frisia (Netherlands). Communion between Rome and the English church was total, even in the slightest details: Willibrord went to see the Pope twice and the Pope nominated him missionary archbishop. Despite the protection offered by Pepin of Herstal, a considerable number of monks were slaughtered. Nonetheless, the evangelization carried on with a new generation lead by Boniface (675?-754), the apostle and patron saint of Germany. His story is truly beautiful.

Having entered as a child in a monastery and become famous for his wealth of knowledge and faith, at 40 years old, he abandoned his studies and his teaching post to join the evangelization effort to the Saxons on the mainland. Boniface took off on mission late in life. He left behind a peaceful and secure life at a very advanced age especially in those times. Moreover, it was not a dangerless endeavor nor was it easy, nor physically comfortable. The peoples he was going to meet were "ferocious and ignorant." Boniface was in constant movement. From 716, the year he left London, until his death in 754, his existence was a constant going and coming back out of love for the mission in Germany, for the reorganization of the Church in France, for the constant contact with Rome where he went three times. Pope Gregory II considered him his "right hand man" and ordained him "regional bishop" of Germany. Boniface's activity was tireless: he established new dioceses, celebrated synods, and reformed the

Frankish and Bavarian churches. Thanks to the English church's constant help – which beyond praying, also sent men, women, paraments, books, sacred ornaments – he established male and female monasteries with a dual purpose: spread the Gospel and improve the quality of civil life. Boniface, in fact, was convinced that the Christian faith itself brought about an improvement on all levels of existence, starting from everything having to do with art and culture. Germany's center for the mission was the Fulda monastery, founded in 743 and then made primatial see of the German church. Boniface managed to guarantee Fulda's exemption from local jurisdiction. This is a recurring trend: each time a religious institution needed protection for its original charism, it turned to Rome as the only one capable of guaranteeing its freedom from the pressures posed by local temporal and spiritual authorities.

You will be my witnesses "to end of the world," said the risen Christ to his disciples. Boniface never stopped. Even at the end of his life, he moves forward, he continued. In fact, he went to Frisia. At 40 years old, he left Britain. When he turned 80 he started over again and went to Holland. He was truly a courageous and tireless apostle. Before leaving he wrote to his friend Lullo, his successor as bishop of Magonza: "I desire to complete the purpose of this trip; I cannot in any way renounce the desire to take off. My end is near and the day of my death approaches; having laid down the mortal remains, I shall rise to the eternal reward. But you, my dearest son, call the people back unceasingly from the quagmire of error, complete the construction of the Fulda Basilica and there you shall lie my body, finally aged by many years of life, to rest."

In 754, assailed by the Frisian pagans who want him dead, Boniface neither retreated nor allowed his own to defend themselves: "My children, cease from fighting, put war aside, because the witness of Scripture admonishes us to never return evil for evil, but rather good for evil. Behold the long-desired day, behold our end has arrived; courage in the Lord!" The patron saint of Germany entrusted a precious heritage to the Germans: communion with Rome as the guarantee of true faith and of the same quality of life. He wrote to Pope Zachary: "I never cease to invite and submit to obedience to the Apostolic See, those who wish to remain within the Catholic faith and within the unity of the Roman Church as well as all those whom

God grants me as auditors and disciples." Seven hundred and fifty years later, Germany forgot its patron's warning and, wanting to go alone without and against Rome, opened an era of wars, and ultimately of barbarism.

Heretical Byzantium

Prepared by centuries of abuse by the temporal over the spiritual power, a generalized anti-Catholic persecution arrived also in Byzantium.

In Heraclius' (614-641) time, the empire is under attack by the Avars, Slavs and Persians. The Persians arrived all the way to Jerusalem, looted it and took the relic of the Holy Cross back to Persia. In such distressing times, Heraclius tried to find renewed strength for his kingdom by unifying the religious creed. This unity had been compromised by the Monophysite beliefs spread mainly throughout Syria, Egypt and Armenia. Instead of returning with firm resolve to Catholic orthodoxy, to accomplish his goal he became the promoter of a new heresy, Monothelitism: yes, there are in fact two natures in Christ, however there is one will only; the divine will. Under Constans II (641-668), the situation spiraled out of hand. Pope Martin I, after condemning Monothelitism, was deported by the emperor to Byzantium where he was put under trial, ill-treated, condemned for high treason and then exiled to Crimea.

Peace between Rome and Byzantium was reached in 680, two years after the imperial capital's victorious resistance against Islam's first assault. It was reached in the sixth ecumenical council which condemned Monothelitism and clarified that in Christ there are "two natural volitions or wills" which are not "in opposition, far from it, but the human will is subordinate; it neither resists, nor does it oppose itself, but rather submits itself to the divine and all-powerful will."

Monothelitism is not the only heresy which obtained sponsorship in the court. In 725, the empire had a very violent heretical disturbance which implicitly attacked the incarnation, that is to say, the same foundation of the Catholic faith. Form 726 to 787 and again from 815 to 842, the empire became heretical. Since the Edict of Thessalonica in 380, the empire had been obliged to defend the

Church it claimed for its State religion. Now, for over one hundred years, a very long time, it had become the maximum center of heresy and therefore the Pope's and the Church's worst enemy. This internal contradiction could not be sustained for long.

By the time Leo III the Isaurian had unleashed the iconoclast war, the empire was unable to strike directly against the Popes and deport them to Byzantium anymore. The last attempt at using violence against the Pope to bend him under the heretical imperial will, was carried out by Justinian II who ordered Pope Sergius I (687-701) deported. But the people and the same troops which were stationed in Italy turned against him and defended the Pope.

The persecution that emperors could not extend to the west recoiled with unheard of ferocity against the Eastern Church and against those people who incarnated its prestige and authority: the monks. The patriarchs of Constantinople, with few exceptions, generally submit to the emperor's will, including his theological views. The monks don't. Moreover, the monks administered great riches and guarded Christianity's historical memory: icons. So, the imperial persecution was unleashed against icons and whoever protected them. The empire systematically began to destroy icons. In the process, it tortured, mutilated and killed monks. This first appalling devastation of an immense artistic, cultural and religious wealth to the detriment of the Church was carried out by authorities who called themselves Christian.

Leo III and his descendants, by means of this iconoclastic battle, chose to imitate a Jewish and especially Muslim practice: for them it was forbidden to represent God through images. This prohibition is perfectly comprehensible when between God and man there exists an abyss, as in Islam. Instead, it is absolutely meaningless, or rather it is even blasphemous when faith is placed in a trinitarian God which supposes the Word – second person of the Trinity – assumed a body so as to redeem from death the children he had created for life. It is obvious that the body of Christ, true God and true man, can be represented. Not only: it is Christ himself who left a memory of his body in the acheiropoieta (not painted by human hand), the image par excellence which is the Holy Shroud[5].

To deny the legitimacy of painting and venerating icons is the same as denying the incarnation: thus wrote John Damascene (676-749), perhaps the greatest theologian of those times. Leo III's claim to be "emperor and priest," as he wrote himself to Gregory II, drove the empire into a heresy which denied the very foundation of Christian faith. Yet another violent injustice of the gravest proportions perpetrated by temporal authorities who arrogantly presumed to be competent in spiritual matters. This act had consequences of historical proportions: while until the 8th century Popes de facto were and called themselves the emperor's subjects, though they indeed were very autonomous in the administration of Saint Peter's lands (Lazio and parts of Umbria up to Perugia), from the third decade of the 8th century onwards, Popes began to look around them to see if someone in the west could offer protection against heretics and barbarians. They started trying to guarantee a minimum of defense for Peter's ship against the periodical storms which knocked it about.

While the empire, in 843, officially repudiated iconoclasty and with great solemnity instituted the Feast of Orthodoxy celebrated from that day onwards every first Sunday of Lent, in the west, the situation radically changed because the Pope had become a king and a new Roman Empire was born.

The Pope King

The "first-born daughter of the Church" offered the Pope the support he sought in the west. At the head of all Frankish kingdom, the most stable of all Barbarian Kingdoms, were the Merovingians who passed into history as the "do-nothing (lazy) kings." They held

---

[5] In the Gospel of Matthew, Jesus foretold that he would leave a sign: "The some of the scribes and Pharisees said to him: 'Teacher, we wish to see a sign from you.' But he answered them: 'A perverse and adulterous generation demands a sign! But no sign shall be given to it except the sign of the prophet Jonah'" (Mt 12,38-39). Jonah stayed for three days in the belly of the fish just like Christ's body stayed three days in the sepulcher: it is very probable that the sign left by Jesus is the Holy Shroud.

power by right but not in practice. The ones who really governed were the palace stewards, amongst whom the most famous was Charles Martel, who in 732 defeated the Muslims at Poitiers. His son, Pepin the Short (714-768) requested Pope Zachary for authorization to put an end to this anomaly of a king who does not govern and a steward who does: why not change the steward, who practically is already governing, into the rightful king?

Pepin ask the Pope as if it were his own right to dispose of the regal crown. He ask the Pope and not the emperor, who being in charge of governing the roman world could rightfully award or deny regal titles. The request itself shows how in the West there existed no authority above that of the Pope. Moreover it shows that this authority was acknowledged by all (this is the period in which "Constantine's Donation" was drafted). We must also keep in mind that, when mid-way through the 8th century, Pepin made his request to the Pope, the empire was governed by Constantine V, son of Leo III, a violent iconoclast: as an enemy of the Church, the empire rejected the responsibility assumed under the Edict of Thessalonica in 380 to defend the Church. So the Popes could rightfully do without the empire's consent. In embryonic form, here is origin of the practice of excommunication cast by Popes against apostate or heretical emperors or kings: people who oppress and bully the Christian people as tyrants and not as faithful stewards of the Gospel.

In 751, Zachary granted Pepin the right to become king and Childeric III, the last of the Merovingian dynasty, took the road towards the convent. Three years later, Stephen II, the new Pope, moved to Rome so as to personally crown Pepin as king of the Franks. This unique deed (which the Pope will become obliged to repeat against his own will in 1804 by the French emperor, Napoleon Bonaparte) can be understood only by keeping in mind the extraordinary hardships of the times: the Longobard conquest of the Byzantine lands in Italy including the capital Ravenna, the devastation of the Roman Dukedom and Rome itself under imminent threat. Not only did Stefan II crown and anoint Pepin king of the Franks, but he also conferred the prestigious title which gave him authority even over Rome itself and therefore, over the entire west: the Pope named Pepin and his sons *Patricii Romanorum*. This marked the beginning of the passage from Byzantium, the second Rome, to the future Aachen.

Pepin, on his part, rushed to Italy in order to fight the Longobards and hand over the lands stolen from Byzantium to the Pope: Ravenna's Exarchate and the Duchy of the Pentapolis. These lands were never returned to their legitimate owner, Byzantium, but were donated to the Pope on the basis that the empire was heretical.

By this move, which is both political and religious, the Pope became king. The Pope ceased to be anyone's subject. He did not need anymore to obey the whims of authorities to whom he was subject. To summarize, the crown guaranteed the Pope's religious liberty, the magisterium's liberty: the *libertas ecclesiae*. The pontifical state born in 754 is one of a kind in the whole world. Its uniqueness comes from the fact that it did not grow into existence from someone's or some kingdom's will to conquer. Rather, it came from the gratitude shown to Peter and his missionaries by peoples who were once pagan and barbarian and who were Christianized and Romanized.

When about one thousand one hundred years later, the Papal States were conquered by the House of Savoy, Pius IX, the Pope saint who reigned at the time (1846-1878), repeatedly reminded the faithful of the reasons why it was important for the Church to have its own state: we shall mention a few here because we are convinced that these are useful to understand the nature of the problem; today, in fact, this aspect of the Pope's temporal authority is very far from most Christians' sensibility. In the papal address *Quibus quantisque*, written in 1849 on Gaeta while the Republic was violently taking over Rome, the Pope wrote: "The faithful, the peoples, the nations and kingdoms would never give the Roman Pontiff full trust and respect if they saw him not completely free but rather subjected to the dominion of some Prince or Government. In fact, the faithful, the peoples and the kingdoms, would never cease to have doubts and apprehensions about the Pontiff, whether he did not conform his actions to the will of that Prince or that Government of the State in which dwelled. Therefore, with this convenient pretext, they would often have no scruples in opposing those same acts." In 1859, just when his kingdom was about to be invaded and dismembered, Pius IX remembers: "Certainly, all are aware of how by the singular wisdom of divine Providence, amongst the multitude and variety of secular Princes, also the Roman Church was given a temporal dominion free from subjection to any other power. In this way, the Roman Pontiff, Highest Pastor over the whole Church, without being submitted to any Prince, throughout the world and with absolute freedom, can exercise the supreme power and supreme authority, given to him by God, to pasture and lead the whole of the Lord's flock" (encyclical *Ad gravissimum*). In 1872, when everything had been already arranged, Pope Pius IX, imprisoned inside the Vatican, wrote the letter *Costretti nelle attuali tristissime circostanze* (*Coerced under the present very sad circumstances*) to the Secretary of State Antonelli: "While his supreme power is subject to the abuses and whims of a contrary authority, while his high ministry is marked by the influence and rule of political passions, while his laws and decrees are not exempt from any suspicion of partiality or offence to the each nation, the Pope is not and will never be free and independent"; "History itself abundantly proves that each and every time Roman Pontiffs were placed even for a short time under the authority of an alien power, what ensued were conflicts between the two authorities and instances of distress for the Christian family"; "Since the religious liberty of Catholics demands as premise the unalterable liberty of the Pope, it follows that if the Pope, supreme judge and living organ of Catholics' faith and law, is not free, they will never be assured about the liberty and independence of his act."

It's worthwhile mentioning that, still today, the Pope possesses a state: the minuscule yet important State of the Vatican.

Charlemagne

Charles (742-814) became king upon the death of his father Pepin in 768. From that moment onwards, his life was a constant battle on all fronts: south, east, and west. He successively confronted the Longobards, the Saxons, the Frisians, the Arabs, the Bavarians, and the Avars and defeated them all.

Gifted with great intelligence, although semiliterate, he understood how important culture was to govern the kingdom well. So from among the peoples in his dominion, he chose the best minds of the time and gathered them to his court. He had a stroke of genius because he took advice from people who had the adequate religious and cultural tools. In this quite scholarly environment he became immersed in, everyone was assigned a name expressing his true nature and his mission in life: Charles had himself called David, the new David, just like the Franks were the new Israel.

Culture is not enough to keep a kingdom united; religion is indispensable. On this front, Charles was resolved to have all become Catholic. Were the Saxons putting up a fight and causing problems? They must be converted. They don't want to? Let them be killed. And so, while baptisms en masse took place, on the other hand thousands of people who refused to convert to Christianity were killed. In chapter nine of the Gospel of Luke, Jesus reproached James and John harshly when they wanted a fire to descend from heaven and punish the Samaritans who did not welcome the Messiah. Faith cannot be imposed. It may be coincidence but, in the 16th century, the furious rebellion against Rome began in Saxony, precisely.

Charles had himself anointed with consecrated oil. This sacramental seemed to raise him out and above the lay man's condition. It endowed him with a priestly function, almost like that of a bishop. In fact, Charles deemed it his duty to care for the Church and felt that he was to be her defender and protector even in the most trifling matters. He reformed the Frankish Church, appointed bishops and abbots, summoned synods, gave capitularies – the decisions reached by synods – legal value, unified the liturgical tradition by taking as a model Roman praxis, introduced Gregorian chant, promoted compiling Canon law, established wonderful libraries which he filled with precious codices, oversaw discipline in convents, ordered all monasteries to observe only the Rule of St. Benedict, promoted the evangelization to the east of the regions in his power – just as his grandfather and father before him – founded new dioceses in newly conquered lands, and used bishops as his most trusted men.

Nothing escaped his control, not even dogma.

Two examples:

- He rejected the decision reached by the second Nicene council in 787 decreeing the veneration of images as lawful (veneration is due to images, adoration is due to God); though this was

accepted in Rome, in 794 he convened a general Frankish council in Frankfurt and condemned the practice;
- He coerced the addition of *Filioque* when reciting the Creed. The Nicene-Constantinopolitan text reads: "The Holy Spirit who proceeds from the Father, and with the Father and Son he is worshipped and glorified." To stress the Son's equality to the Father, in Spain the following amendment was promoted: "The Holy Spirit who proceeds from the Father and the Son." Here is the *Filioque*. Leo III rejected the Spanish custom and its extension. However, Charles chose to enforce it and since then it became customary throughout the whole Church. Still today, the *Filioque* issue may just be the most serious point of controversy between the Catholic and Orthodox Church.

Stemming from his desire to make a civilized kingdom, Charles called Alcuin from York and charged him with organizing a school able to form lay and ecclesiastical functionaries. Charles was well aware that his arrival opened a new stage in history distinguished by a rebirth of civil, cultural, administrative and religious life. Historians speak about the "Carolingian Renaissance." Charlemagne's Palace School was so innovative that the so-called "Carolingian minuscule" (lower-case), which makes use of simple and elegant characters which are easy to draw and recognize, is still today the most widely used writing style in the whole world.

In 2004, when he was being awarded the Charlemagne prize in the Vatican, Pope Wojtyla outlined Charles' character: "The king of the Franks, who made Aachen the capital of his kingdom, made an essential contribution to the political and cultural foundations of Europe. That is why, already among his contemporaries, he merited the title of *Pater Europae*. What took shape in Charles' empire was the successful union between Classical culture and Christian faith together with a variety of peoples' traditions. The multiform development of this union over the centuries has become part of Europe's spiritual and cultural heritage."

Charles, also known as the Great (Magne).

Translatio Imperii

It is Christmas Eve of the year 800. In Saint Peter's, Charlemagne was crowned Roman Emperor by Leo III who placed a "most precious" crown on his head. How long had Leo pondered this gesture? Was Charles aware of the Pope's intention? Sources on this matter are not in agreement. However the fact remains and it is unique: a Pope transferred the seat of the Roman Empire from one part of the world to the other and it was he himself who chose on whom to place the imperial crown (just like another Pope had done with the Frankish royal crown, albeit the magnitude of that event was infinitely smaller). How is it possible that the most important and prestigious office in the world, an office which preceded the birth of Jesus and therefore even the existence of the Church, be at the behest of a Pope? In the following centuries, to contrast the Pope, emperors repeatedly vindicated the fact that the empire existed earlier than the papacy. However, at the time, no one questioned Leo's decision because no one held a remotely comparable universal authority.

Why did the Eastern Roman Empire or Constantinople tolerate what appeared to be such a blatant abuse of power? It did so because Constantinople was weak. Since the year 787, it had rejected Iconoclasm (at least temporarily) and so distanced itself from heresy. However, the year 797 marked the beginning of a very delicate phase. Irene, a woman, held the imperial throne. She blinded her son Constantine VI and assumed the title used for the emperor: basileus. In the West, that the empire should be held by a woman was inadmissible. So the seat was deemed vacant. Leo III took advantage of this void and by moving the empire to the west, brought the papacy's relationship with Byzantine imperial authority to a definite close.

Seemingly, by so doing, the papacy acquired boundless power. However, upon closer inspection, this was not the case, neither for Leo III nor for any other Pope. The point is that, when the Pope became king, or in any case since that moment, it became remarkably more pronounced, Roman noble families ignited a succession of battles without quarter to ensure that Peter's throne would be occupied by one of their family members. This is the context in which Leo III was accused of adultery and perjury, and under this pretext was assaulted, beat up and imprisoned. Once he escaped, Leo went to Paderborn to place himself under Charles' protection. But also the enemies of the Pope requested the king to become involved. As a Roman Patrician, Charles became the third-party authority who could act as judge between the Pope and his accusers. However, by so doing, Charles disregarded the fact that ultimately the Pope is the *prima sedes* on earth, that is, the highest level of judgment. Instead, he acted as if he were the *prima sedes* himself. The episode is interesting because it proves how despite the throne, the Pope's indisputable authority coexisted with his weakness: weakness with respect to the Roman nobility and its factions, and in future centuries with respect to Europe's ruling dynasties.

Charles had the Pope escorted to Rome and summoned a synod to resolve the issue. However, no one can sit in judgment over the Pope because *prima sedes a nemine iudicatur* (let no one dare judge the first seat). So, a compromise was reached by which Leo "spontaneously" made a sworn deposition attesting his innocence. Charles' crowning as Roman Emperor took place two days after the trial against the Pope came to a close.

Mutatis mutandis, various features of Charles life are similar to that of Constantine. Both inaugurated a new age, with new features and problems. The novelty which they introduced and which both considered of utmost importance is their view about the scope of the prince's authority in the religious sphere. Note that Constantine was a Roman Emperor who governed over an immense state with its own juridical, cultural, administrative and military traditions. These were efficient, part of a well-oiled machine and tested through centuries of use. Charles was a man who could barely read and write and who had to build everything up from scratch, or almost so. After centuries of invasions and an endless fragmentation of power, Charles is owed the merit of unifying a great expanse of land in the center of Europe, a state with Aachen as capital which called itself Roman; though its being Roman rested mainly in the mere fact that it was created by the Pope, true heir of Rome's universality. Nevertheless, an empire it was, and as such nurtured universal ambitions.

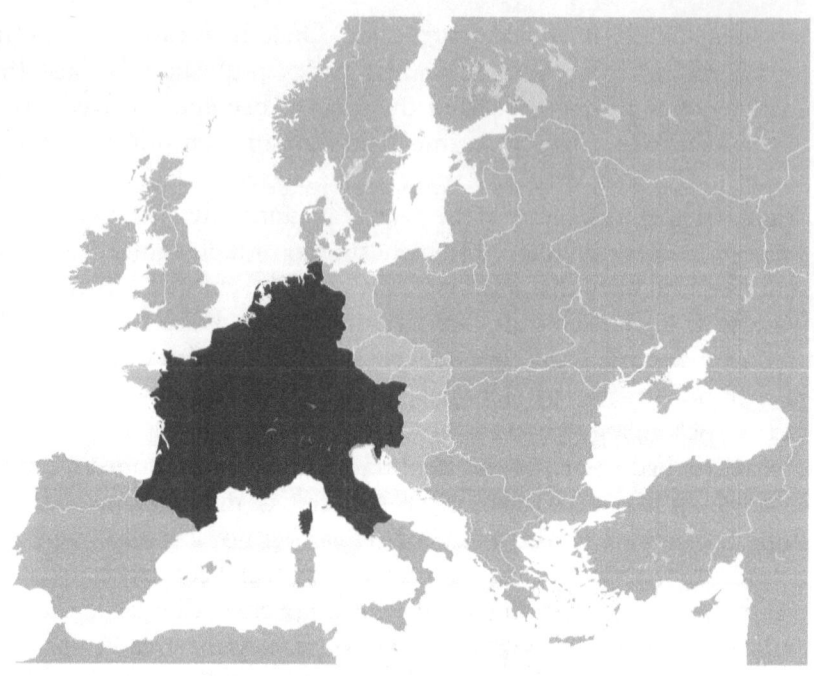

Map of the Carolingian Empire in 814

As with Constantine and the Roman Empire, all the pieces were set for recurring and inevitable tensions to arise between the papacy and the 'Holy' Roman Empire. In fact, while it is undeniable that the empire existed well before the papacy, it is also true that it was the Pope who solemnly crowned the emperor in Saint Peter's. So, if one cannot be emperor without the Pope awarding the crown, the Pope cannot govern without consent from the imperial force. From now on, the relationships formed between the two highest authorities in the west depended mainly on the moral and personal strength of those men who wore the two highest crowns. Excommunication was the Pope's weapon of choice while brute strength was that of the emperor. The duel went on for centuries with very few exceptions until the Holy Roman Empire disappeared and a new empire was born. The new empire was neither Christian, nor holy, nor Roman: it was the French Empire founded on a Freemasonic creed and invented by Napoleon Bonaparte in 1804 Paris.

Cyril and Methodius

Cyril (826-869) and Methodius (815-885), born in a rich family of imperial magistrates in Thessaloniki, became the evangelizers of the Slav peoples who dwelled in Central, Southern and Eastern Europe. These two brothers were sent as missionaries to Moravia by Emperor Michael III upon Prince Ratislav's request: "Since our peoples rejected paganism, we observe the Christian law; however, we have no teacher who is able to explain the true faith in our own language." Cyril and Methodius immediately began translating the Bible so as to allow the Slavs to hear the Word of God in their mother tongue. To do so, they invented a new alphabet (the Glagolitic alphabet which in time will be called Cyrillic from its initiator's name), perfectly apt to express the sounds of Slav languages.

The use of Slav in Catholic liturgy caused French missionaries, who had been working in Moravia since Charlemagne was enthroned, to cry out in scandal. In their view, the only permissible liturgical languages were the canonical: Hebrew, Greek and Latin. It was the beginning of the so-called "trilingual heresy." To resolve the matter, Cyril and Methodius went to Rome[6] carrying the relics of Clement I which Cyril had uncovered in Crimea, the land where the Pope had been exiled. Pope Adrian II endorsed the two brothers' work so emphatically that he had solemn liturgical services performed using the Slav language in the churches of Saint Peter, Saint Andrew and Saint Paul.

In Rome Cyril fell ill and died but Methodius, who was made bishop by the Pope, returned among the Slavs to complete their work of evangelization. Here the Frankish missionary zeal caught up with him, he was placed in prison for two years accused of having invaded another's episcopal jurisdiction. Once freed, Methodius took up his work again. But, upon his death, another persecution assaulted his disciples. They were imprisoned and sold as slaves. Sent to Venice as goods to be traded, they were recognized and freed by Byzantine

---

[6] On his way to Rome, Cyril stopped in Venice and there argued against the bogus nature of the heretical objections by recalling how the liturgy in vernacular was already used amongst the "Armenians, Persians, Abkhazians, Georgians, Sogdians, Goths, Avars, Turks, Khazars, Arabs, Egyptians, Syrians and many others."

officials who allowed them to take up the work of announcing the Gospel again, this time in Bulgaria.

John Paul II, one of the wonderful fruits of Cyril and Methodius' apostolate, being also a poet, took occasion of the eleven-hundredth anniversary since Methodius' death to write: "Incomprehension, blatant bad faith and even, for Saint Methodius, chains, accepted out of love for Christ, did not deflect either one or the other from the tenacious resolve to benefit and serve the good of the Slav peoples and the unity of the universal Church. This was the price they paid to spread the Gospel, for their missionary enterprise, for the courageous quest to find new life styles and effective ways to allow the Good News to reach the Slav Nations which were just taking shape"; "To translate the Gospel truths into a new language, they needed to carefully come to know in depth the interior universe of those to whom they meant to announce the Word of God, using images and concepts that would sound familiar to them"; "The effort of learning the language and mentality of these new peoples that were to be brought to faith was truly worthy of a missionary spirit, and the determination to assimilate and assume all the needs and expectations of the Slav peoples as one's own was exemplary. The generous choice to identify with their same life and tradition after having purified and enlightened them with the light of revelation, makes Cyril and Methodius true models for all missionaries who in different ages have welcomed Saint Paul's invitation to become all things to all, so as to save all."

Pope Wojtyla addressed the whole Church with an exhortation to celebrate "with solemnity and joy these past eleven centuries since the close of the apostolic work of Methodius, the first archbishop ordained in Rome for the Slav people, and of his brother Cyril, by recalling the entrance of these people on the stage of the history of salvation and their counting among the European nations who, in preceding centuries had already welcomed the Gospel message. All can appreciate with what deep exultation this first son of Slav stock, called after almost two millennia to sit in the episcopal see which belonged to Saint Peter in this same city of Rome, intends to participate to this celebration.

It was John Paul II's wish that, Cyril and Methodius, "children of the East, their fatherland Byzantium, by origin Greek, by mission

Roman, by their apostolic fruits Slavs," as Pius XI wrote, should become Patron Saints of Europe together with Benedict, Brigid of Sweden, Catherine of Siena and Teresa Benedicta of the Cross, born Edith Stein. Three men and three women.

Constitutio Romana and *Privilegium Othonis*

In 494, Pope Gelasius made an attempt to clarify what the rightful relationship between the Pope and the emperor should be; in 824, Emperor Lothair I, nephew to Charlemagne and son of Louis the Pious, laid out the rightful footing on which to build the relationship between emperor and Pope by means of a document which passed to history as the *Constitutio Lotharii* or *Constitutio Romana*. The document draws the natural conclusions from one single fact: from the temporal point of view, the emperor is endowed with universal authority and as such is superior to that of the Pope, who is only a king and moreover in constant need of protection by Roman nobles. The substance of the document confirmed the Pope's autonomy as king but insisted on the fact that, once elected as custom demands, the emperor should express his approval of the Pope and likewise the Pope should swear an oath of fidelity to the emperor.

The Carolingians, and later also the Saxon kings, took the title of Roman Emperor very seriously and they were firmly convinced that Roman universal authority survived through them. This is abundantly proven by the iconography of the time: Lothair II's (855-869) beautiful cross, which is studded with gems, at its center holds a Roman cameo displaying an image of Augustus' profile. It is really interesting and hard to imagine that the cross, the most sacred icon for Christians, and in this case the precious cross used for the entrance procession of emperors into the Palatine Chapel of Aachen, carried Augustus crowned with a laurel in its center. This is the empire's undying *virus*, the eternal attraction to power, sublimated and encrusted within a cross.

Lothair's cross

The Carolingian version of the Roman Empire had a short life. It came to an end in 887 when Charles the Fat, the last direct descendent of Charlemagne, was deposed. Internal dissension compounded with the resumption of barbarian invasions, with the Normans, Danes, Magyars in the north and northeast while the Muslims pressed hard in the south, brought the first attempt at unifying the Christian lands of Europe to a premature end. By the second half of the 9th century, the Empire was dissolving. Nonetheless, the papacy was in no better shape because some Popes had nothing Christian about them: lustful, greedy and in some cases real evildoers; homicides, imprisonments, mutilations, bindings, a Pope left to die of hunger in Castel Sant'Angelo. They stopped at nothing. Once, the new Pope exhumed the corpse of his enemy Pope Formosus in order to put him on trial in the so-called *synodus ad cadaver*, condemn him and scatter his ashes to the four winds. The dark century of the papacy: this is how the 10th century was defined, and quite understandably so.

The Normans were stopped in Normandy which was then granted to them in 911 as a fiefdom by Charles the Simple, king of France. The Magyars were overcome in 955 by Otto I (912-973) king of Saxony. Finally, after a seemingly endless period of time, the barbarian invasions were put to an end with the Magyars. With Otto, and his father Henry before him, Germany assumed a leading role for the whole Catholic West and fought against the fragmentation of feudal power by establishing bishops (and abbots) as counts. These were bishops who besides the spiritual authority held also temporal authority in virtue of the lands that the emperor granted them. These bishops owed everything to the emperor, were faithful to him, and avoided all problems associated to succession because officially they could not have any heirs. In most cases, in the lands subject to the Saxon emperor, these men exercised good government and guaranteed a stable economic and cultural recovery. Once again the empire chose its officials within the Church and once again linked the evangelization to a colonial-style foreign policy: Bohemia, Poland, Hungary, Denmark… these were all converted and absorbed under the imperial area of influence.

In 962, Otto was crowned emperor in Saint Peter's and that very same year he published the edict *Privilegium Othonis* which in essence took up the *Constitutio Romana* again. The following year he forcefully deposed John XII, the same Pope who had crowned him, accusing him of perjury, homicide, incest, simony and sacrilege. The practice by which an emperor deposed and then elected a Pope continued with Henry III of Franconia, who chose morally and culturally irreprehensible German Popes. These Popes began the reform of the Church which led to an inevitable clash with the empire.

Once Again 12

While in Rome the papacy sunk into the dark night of the struggle for power, in the center of France the Holy Spirit inspired a group of holy men, once again 12, who wanted to live their faith together by following the heroic footsteps of Benedict and by putting the rule in practice to the letter. Once again, the Church was stirred up by God's initiative. To do the will of God, the monks of Cluny made a most serious renunciation to worldly goods. And that is exactly why the world followed them. "When I am weak, then I am strong", wrote Paul in the *Second Letter to the Corinthians*. This word is so true that all the greatest innovations in Church history came from a small bunch of men, if not two or even one. God does not need the strength of men. At the turn of the 10th century, the Order of Cluny was supremely attractive because in an age of total disorder, it created order; in an age of total violence, it created peace; in an age of continuous destruction and licentiousness which undermined even the seat of Peter, it created hope.

The *Book of Judith* recounts how Abraham became "the friend of God" after "being proved by many tribulations." The lives of monks prove the truth of this statement and of how, by renouncing many of the even minimal pleasures of life, one may experience a communion with God which surpasses all intelligence. The same word "monk", which means alone, shows that God is enough. Moreover, it shows that this path can lead one to a life of perfection which is not available in social life. That is how the life of monks became attractive. Cluny was founded in 910 and at the start of the 12th century there were 1,200 monasteries of the Order of Cluny throughout Europe. From a human point of view, this was an awe-inspiring and surprising success for people who are not out to be successful.

The rule of Cluny is the same rule of St. Benedict with some adaptations. The order was increasingly centralized and so depended from the mother house in Cluny. Furthermore, this centralization and the order's direct dependence from Rome obtained by monks in order to guarantee their freedom from the local bishop's jurisdiction that was too often the object of pressures by local temporal authorities and whims (the same exemption Boniface had obtained for Fulda). In this way, the monks avoided abuses such as those suffered by the Benedictine abbeys, at this time reduced to a parking lot for old generals, children, friends and various relatives of the powerful. How the papacy, despite the unworthiness of those in power at the time, effectively guaranteed Cluny with the autonomy needed to freely live out its charism, is astounding.

The Order of Cluny served as a sword in the hands of holy bishops and Popes, and it pushed all Christians to emulate the good done by them as well as their saintly life in all fields. The authority of example healed society. The life of monks had a positive effect both on the diocesan clergy, who was lead to fight against Simony and Nicolaism, attachment to money and sex, the recurring sins of priests which during some centuries seemed unstoppable;, as well as on the laity, that was moved to respect the 'Peace and Truce of God' and spurred to hold back the violence through the respect inspired by certain liturgical times, solemnities as well as the inviolability of those spaces dedicated to God, churches and convents.

The heart of the Cluny reform was that praise which projects monks into the celestial liturgy's eternity. Liturgy and song. Liturgy, song and silence. Conditions needed to protect those gifts granted to monks daily by God. And a space suited to offer God the exultation of the spirit in blessing. Accordingly, the order developed its own architecture suited to foster spiritual recollection and prayer. It was a solemn architecture, both majestic and essential, projected toward heaven as were the monks' most heartfelt desires. The vertical push is a typical feature of the thirst for God expressed by Cluny's monks. This same vertical framework developed by Cluny soon became the main feature of gothic cathedrals.

The Cluny Order boasted of such universally acknowledged merits, that the enemies of the Church wanted to erase its very memory. In fact, the French revolutionaries furiously committed themselves to the titanic, extremely costly and most strenuous task of demolishing the order's daunting monumental complex stone by stone, thus transforming it into a quarry for publicly owned rock.

A New Millennium

At the dawn of the new millennium, the world started rapidly evolving on many fronts. After seven hundred years the invasions were finally over. A time of unending suffering, precariousness and death had passed. The population started growing again. People slowly flowed back to urban centers, new lands were tilled. Life started again. By the turn of the millennium, all the peoples who had invaded Europe had become Christian. Moved by the fervor of the new convert, by their gratitude towards the monks, and to Peter who had sent them, the new kings declared themselves vassals to the Pope: thus Poland; thus Saint Stephen's Hungary. In Kiev, thanks to Prince Vladimir, the immense Russian planes converted in 989. From the second half of the 11th century also the Normans in England and Sicily became the Pope's vassals while Rome blessed the initiatives begun by the Spanish to reconquer their lands overrun by Moors.

The Church of Rome, which was the heart of all this hustle and bustle, coming and going, however was still sick. But it was recovering. The papacy was still in the hands of the noble families of Rome which contended for its power while throughout the continent, Bishops, Archbishops, and Abbotts were appointed by emperors and kings: the Church had become completely subservient to the temporal power and acted as its vital organ. We can add also the typical evils of an all too worldly clergy summarizable in the two sins we just referred to: simony and Nicolaism. A plague for the Church, simony, was the sale of ecclesiastical positions. For example, in Milan, to become a subdeacon you needed 12 denarii, to become deacon you needed 18, to become a priest 24; the Nicolaitans, followers of the gnostic deacon Nicola, claimed to know more about sexual life than Christ and therefore permitted free sexual relations for all, including priests. St. John in the *Book of Revelation* says, "Yet this you have, you hate the works of the Nicolaitans, which I also hate."

Within the Church, the true novelty, or in any case truly relevant novelty, was that the Cluny reform had become so widespread that princes, emperors and Popes became convinced that religious life was in need of deep renewal. In this situation, Henry III of Franconia, a deeply religious and pious man as well as German king, so as to heal a degraded papacy now contended among three Popes, chose to descend upon Rome. Firmly convinced that the Church could be reformed only by managing to free the pontifical election process from the damaging influence of the Roman noble families, in 1046, Henry convoked a synod in Sutri, he deposed all three Popes and had a prelate elected from among the uppermost Saxon nobility. Suidger of Morsleben and Hornburg, a monk of the Order of Cluny and bishop of Bamberg, took up the name of Clement II. The name itself was his government program. In fact, Clement I (92-97) saint and martyr, was a Pope who distinguished himself by writing a dogmatic letter to the Corinthians. Clement II was the first of four Popes elected by Henry. He was enthroned on Christmas day and on the same day he likewise crowned Henry III Roman Emperor.

A very strong push for reform came from the third German Pope, Bruno of Egisheim-Dagsburg. He was a relative of the emperor and took up the name Leo IX (1049-1054). Though he accepted the imperial nomination, by riding on the back of a donkey into Rome, he in fact subordinated its validity to the approval of the roman clergy and people. He surrounded himself with collaborators of the most serious and decided kind from France and Germany. Furthermore, he exercised the universal primacy by personally visiting various Christian regions and there, by convoking numerous synods, fighting against the clergy's vices.

In Leo's time, the Normans had conquered the better part of southern Italy and in 1053, the Pope descended with an army into Puglia so as to defend the byzantine lands. His army however was defeated and he himself captured and held prisoner. Within a year, however, following the proclamation of the East-West schism, everything changed drastically. The schism had been preceded by centuries during which the byzantine patriarchs had been subjected to imperial rule and at the same time had repeatedly rebelled against Peter's authority. On July 16, 1054, the schism was consummated. The Pontifical legate, Umberto of Silvacandida, placed a bull of excommunication on the altar of Saint Sophia against the Patriarch of Constantinople, Michael I Cerularius and his collaborators. On the 24th day of the same month it was Cerulario's turn to excommunicate the pontifical legates and their supporters[7]. Although by this time Leo had already died, the motive which pushed the Popes to defend the Byzantine lands in Italy was now missing.

Henry III was a pious man. He acted in the best interest of the Church, and his choices undoubtedly had positive effects. However,

---

[7] On December 17, 1965, Paul VI and the Patriarch Athenagoras officially removed the mutual excommunication by means of a joint declaration.

the Church cannot allow that Pontifical elections are decided by the emperors.

In defense of the *Libertas Ecclesiae*

Is it right that the Pope is elected by the emperor? Is it right that local political authorities have the power to appoint the highest ecclesiastical offices? The battle in defense of the *libertas ecclesiae* was a real war. In fact, it subtracted a very consistent power from both emperors and kings. The war began midway through the 11th century and continued for various decades until a compromise was reached in 1122: the Concordat of Worms.

Nicholas II (1059-1061) was the first Pope who openly went against the Church's dependence on the empire which, for various reasons, had lasted already two centuries. In 1059, during a synod held in the Lateran, Nicholas set down the rules that were to govern all pontifical elections: only the cardinal[8] bishops chose the candidate and elected him together with the cardinal priests and deacons. They then passed him on to be acclaimed by the clergy and the people. At the same time, he approved a decree which forbade clergymen from accepting investiture to the government of any church from lay people and condemned the Nicolaitans. Moreover, the Pope called upon all lay people to become protagonists of the reform by refusing to receive communion from priests who lived in concubinage and by not participating to their services.

Nicholas II turned the Holy See's policy towards the Normans upside down by granting them the lands they conquered in vassalage. In exchange, the Normans tied themselves to the Holy See by an oath of vassalage, and so promised to respect pontifical domains and guaranteed that they would not interfere in any pontifical election. In continuity with Nicholas II, the new Pope Alexander II (1061-1073) granted the standard of St. Peter to the Norman Roger I of the House of Hauteville for the conquest of Sicily until then occupied by the moors and to the Norman William the Conqueror (who was favorable

---

[8] The name "cardinal" is applied to those bishops, priests and deacons who belong to the seven cardinal churches: the most ancient and important churches of Rome.

to the Church's reform) for the conquest of Anglo-Saxon England, which took place in 1066 in the battle of Hastings.

With Gregory VII (1073-1085), the struggle for the Church's independence became increasingly drastic. He is a key figure of the 11th century. "I have loved justice and hated iniquity, therefore, I die in exile": these were the words pronounced upon his death by Gregory, born Hildebrand of Sovana. The Pope who died as Jesus did while praying with the words of the psalms (Jesus recited psalm 21 "My God, my God, why have you forsaken me," while Gregory recited psalm 45) was proclaimed saint by the Church. He was a sign of contradiction: hated by most, loved and praised by many. Ultimately, he died exiled in Salerno where his ashes were laid to rest.

Gregory VII and Henry IV of Franconia faced each other in a grueling conflict which dragged on at the beat of excommunications and appointments of antipopes: the Pope demanded obedience and that the election of Church ministers be made without the interference by the royal authority. In 1075 he redacted one of the most important and interesting documents in the history of the Church: *Dictatus Papae*[9]. The *Dictatus*'s follows an iron logic: by God's

---

[9] So goes the decree:
1. That the Roman Church was established solely by God.
2. That only the Roman Pontiff can rightly be called universal.
3. That it is he alone who can depose or reestablish Bishops.
4. That his delegate, though he is inferior by order, in a council stands above all bishops and may pass sentence against and thereby depose them.
5. That the Pope may depose those absent.
6. That we must not have communion or stay in the same house with those who have been excommunicated by him.
7. That only he is permitted to enact new laws according to the needs of the time, make new congregations, turn an abbey into a rectory and vice versa, divide a rich episcopate and merge the poor ones.
8. That he alone may use the imperial insignia.
9. That all princes must kiss the feet only of the Pope.
10. That his name must be recited in church.
11. That his title is unique throughout the world.
12. That he is permitted to depose the emperor.
13. That if need be, he is permitted to move bishops from seat to seat.
14. That he has the power to ordain any member of the clergy from any church for any place he wishes.

will, Peter's magisterium is infallible; Peter must guide the battle between the city of God and the city of this world; kings have no priestly functions; if they are heretical they must be excommunicated because they are not apt to govern Christian peoples; the Pope has full jurisdiction over all ecclesiastical appointments.

It is a revolutionary framework which Henry rejected. An arm-wrestling match began wherein the emperor put Rome under siege and Gregory called the Normans to his aid. The Normans delivered him from the siege but placed Rome under the sword, fiercely looting and carrying away also a large number of slaves. Rome's people blamed Gregory for their disgrace, and so did not allow him to enter Rome. He also died in exile.

---

15. That whoever was ordained by him may be the head of another church, but not subject, and that no bishop can obtain a higher order.

16. That no synod may be called general if it not be lead by him.

17. That no article or book may be called canonical without his authorization.

18. That no one may revoke his word and that only he may do so.

19. That no one may sit in judgment over him.

20. That no one may dare condemn whoever appeals to the Holy See.

21. That the most important cases of any church must be remitted to his judgment.

22. That the Roman Church never erred nor will ever err, and this is so by the testimony of Holy Scripture.

23. That the Roman Pontiff, if ordained by canonical election, is undoubtedly sanctified by the merits of the blessed Peter; Saint Ennodius, bishop of Pavia, bears witness to this, with the consensus of many Holy Fathers, as it is written in the decrees of the Blessed Symmachus Pope.

24. That his subordinates, upon receiving his order and permission, are permitted to make accusations.

25. That he may depose and reestablish bishops even without a synodal gathering.

26. That no one is to be considered catholic if he be not in agreement with the Roman Church.

27. That the Pontiff may release subjects from loyalty toward evil doers.

The investiture controversy

Just like the reborn Roman Empire, Barbarian Kingdoms could not but appoint consecrated persons such as bishops and abbots to wield temporal power: basically, they were the only ones who had some understanding of law, had some education, appreciated art and literature and moreover were able administrators.

An investiture is the ceremony by which the king conferred governing powers to his prelates. During this solemn ceremony, the king (or emperor) handed both the symbols of temporal and ecclesiastical power over to the candidate: the pastoral staff for the office of bishop or abbot, and the ring which sealed the spousal union between a bishop and his diocese. After the investiture, the bishop swore an oath of loyalty to the kingdom by acknowledging himself as vassal and only then would he be consecrated. The very same dynamic of the ritual clearly shows how for the king (only for the king?) temporal power held a position of preeminence over the spiritual.

From the middle of the 11th century, the Church resolutely confronted its reform: it fought against simony and Nicolaism also by involving the common people and blessed the birth of new religious orders; however, the only way to obtain lasting results was to free itself from the tutelage of secular authorities. But to achieve this goal, it met with the comprehensible opposition of kings and emperors who were averse to giving up such ancient privileges and such a convenient government custom. In these circumstances the Popes entered into agreements with various kings and emperors; agreements which inevitably turned out to be compromises. The first were the concordats with England and France both signed in 1107. The terms contained in the concordat made with Philip I of France were more favorable because the king, who had been excommunicated for having divorced his wife and remarried an already married woman, found himself in a weak position with respect to the spiritual authority. In France, the king gave up the investiture of the ring and pastoral staff and the consecration took place immediately after the prelate's election while the bestowal of the fief and the oath of loyalty were moved to the end of the ceremony. The spiritual aspect took the center stage over the temporal. In England, the situation remained overall more favorable to the king: the bestowal of the fief and loyalty oath preceded the episcopal consecration.

In 1122, some years later, in Worms, after a never ending series of clashes, a concordat was signed with the empire which established differing modes of investiture for Germany and all other imperial lands: in German lands, the emperor presided over the election, bestowed the scepter on the bishop and received feudal homage while the consecration moved to the end; Italy and Burgundy instead kept the consecration immediately following the election. In the first part of his *Privilege*, Emperor Henry V wrote: "In the name of the holy and indivisible Trinity. I, Henry, by the grace of God august emperor of the Romans, out of love for God and of the Holy Roman Church and for our Pope Callistus and for our soul's recovery, hereby relinquish to God and his holy apostles Peter and Paul, and to the Holy Catholic Church every investiture made with ring and pastoral staff, and concede that all churches in my kingdom and empire should have canonical elections and free consecrations."

Below are also some excerpts from Callistus II's *Privilege*: "I, Callistus bishop, servant of the servants of God, grant you, my beloved son Henry, established by the grace of God as august emperor of the Romans, that the elections needed for the kingdom of bishops and abbots in Germany, take place in your presence, without simony or violence [...] By means of the scepter, let the candidate receive all royalties from you and accordingly execute in all justice his duties towards you. He who is to be consecrated in other regions of the Empire, let him instead receive the royalties from you by means of the scepter within six months, and accordingly execute in all justice his duties towards you, safeguarding the recognition of all the Roman Church's prerogatives."

"Give back to Caesar that which is Caesar, and to God that which is God's": what belongs to Caesar and what to God? At the turn of the second millennium, the spheres of competence were not so clear. In a context where all professed to be Christian, the marriage between temporal and spiritual power was very tight. Both powers – at least in theory – worked towards the establishment of a well-ordered society, as fair as possible, which allows for a peaceful life on earth and a happy and eternal life in heaven. In practice, however, the risk that secular authorities lorded over the spiritual was very high.

Consequently, once again, the Church attempted to put certain boundaries in place and demanded that they be respected so as to safeguard its independence. By so doing, with the best of intentions, the Church ran the risk of moving on an ideal plane following abstract principles of justice which did not take into account the real situations and the real balance of power. It also ran the risk of demanding that secular powers accept and abide by logical schemes and ideological models which were miles away from the concrete, limited, sinful existence of all but perfect men and women. By supporting its excellent argument, the Church risked losing contact with reality. This was the case of Boniface VIII.

Hermits, Patarini and New Orders

An exuberant life, a quest to find God filled with challenges. This was the Church at the start of the second millennium. The Cluniac order, rich in merits, had attained great power, great riches and great pomp. There was need of something which went beyond the Order of Cluny, new orders were needed which would safeguard poverty through total renunciation, forsaking everything, including the use of speech. Carthusians earmarked speaking to only one hour a week on Saturday. With the new orders, holy hermits appeared in all regions of Europe and a great religious fervor spread among the people. They demanded that bishops be bishops and that they stop meddling in simony and concubinage. The case of Milan is emblematic.

Milan was a rich city and a center of communication. The simoniac and dissolute practices of almost the entire clergy, starting from the bishop, caused a social and religious uprising. Bishop Bonizone of Sutri described the situation of Milan's clergy in *Book for my friend*: Guido da Velate, the chaplain of Henry III appointed bishop of Milan against the people's wishes, "was an illiterate man, he lived in concubinage, and was engaged shamelessly in simony"; among the clergy, "only 5 out of 1000 were found unblemished by the heresy of simony." The rebels from Milan were called Patarini, which literally means tattered rag collectors. They wanted a holy Church with a holy leadership and therefore demanded their commune's independence. In 1057 Milan revolted. Unexpectedly, the Holy See made an alliance with the rebels and in 1063, Alexander II sent the Standard of St. Peter to the Patarini. Milan's example was contagious. The uprising spread to other cities in Lombardy. The Pope's alliance with the communes solidified over time thus aligning the Church in defense of Italian independence.

A heroic search for holiness spread everywhere. Religious orders with the most diverse charisms were born: the order of Fontevrault was unique and highly original in that it comprised both a male and a female branch under the guidance of a female abbot. Why? Because under the cross, Jesus entrusted John to Mary. The abbey was partially destroyed during the French Revolution and subsequently, Napoleon transformed it into a prison.

Besides those with such singular features, while Romuald founded the hermitage of Camaldoli, Gualberto the hermitage in Vallombroso and Pier Damiani became Fonte Avellana's most renown personality, three main orders emerged: Carthusians, Cistercians, Premonstratensians. All three orders were born from an extraordinary impulse for penance, manual labor, the most radical kind of poverty, solitary life pushed to the limits of hermitage, the rejection of all comfortable certainty. To describe the spirituality of these orders, especially of the Carthusians who were founded by Bruno of Cologne (1031-1101), we shall turn to Benedict XVI and the homily he pronounced in Serra san Bruno, Calabria, where this monk went to spend the last years of his life. Pope Ratzinger so described the specific nature of Carthusian spirituality: "Retreating into silence and solitude, man 'exposes' himself, as it were, to what is real in his nakedness, he exposes himself to that apparent 'void' precisely in order to experience its opposite, Fullness, the presence of God, of the most real reality that exists and which exists beyond any material reality"; by leaving everything, a monk risks everything: "He exposes himself to solitude and silence in order to live off of nothing more than the essential. Exactly when he is living only off of the essential, he discovers a profound communion with the brothers and with every man." In a nutshell, this was Bruno's experience. In his own words: "I dwell in the desert with some brothers, [...] in a persevering divine watchfulness to await the Lord's return and immediately open the door to him." Benedict XVI commented: "*Stat Crux dum volvitur orbis* – this is what your motto says. The only fixed point amidst a world in constant mutation and upheaval is the Cross of Christ. Life in a Carthusian monastery participates to the stability of the Cross, that is, God's stability, his faithful love."

Carthusians "are" like Mary at the foot of the cross, unmovable in their solitude and silence. They fight against anguish and the void. Nowadays, no one knows how to simply "be" anymore: "People live immersed in a virtual dimension because from dawn till dusk they are drowned in audiovisual messages. Born in this kind of environment, it seems that the younger generation wants to use music and images to fill each and every empty moment, as if it were afraid of feeling that void." Still today, Carthusians "are": the sisters of the "Monastic Family of Bethlehem, of the Assumption of the Virgin and of Saint Bruno," a monastic order born recently, is made up of women who spend their lives in silence. Even meals are consumed alone in their cells while during liturgical hours they sing praises to God. Such praise makes the words of the psalms heavy as stones. Living words. Words made flesh.

A Conspiracy against Truth

When the time of invasions was thru, after three centuries of constant Arab raids and a partial occupation of its territory (8th century Spain, and starting from the 9th century also Sicily and part of southern Italy and Provence) Europe finally found the strength to challenge and push back Islam. Under the encouragement of the Standard of Saint Peter, in the name of and under the protection of St. James the apostle, whose tomb had just been miraculously discovered, helped by French knights, the Spaniards took back a large portion of their lands conquered by Islam. Inch by inch, not only the knights but the whole people, even the farmers vigorously rose up in arms. In 1085 they occupied Toledo, the center of the peninsula; in 1092 they landed in Valencia and the following year in Lisbon. In Italy commerce came back to life and the maritime republics competed for control over the sea and the coasts which had been at the mercy of Arab pirates for centuries. The Normans and their Sicilian campaigns we already described.

In the east, the millennium started off with the destruction of the Holy Sepulcher in 1009 by the Fatimid Caliph Al-Hakim. The Turks of the Seljuq dynasty advanced west and in 1071 defeated the byzantine army in Manzikert: the Christian hunting season was now open. Anguished by the foul news coming out of Byzantium, Gregory VII wrote to Henry IV: "Christians who dwell in the lands beyond the sea – the greater part of which are now being butchered by pagans in unspeakable bloodbaths, slaughtered everyday like cattle to the point that Christian people are being annihilated – compelled by the exceeding burden of their misery, they, our brothers, have humbly written to me imploring my aid in any way possible so that the Christian religion, God forbid, should not completely disappear in our times."

Gregory did not manage to mobilize the courage and faith of the Latin Christians, but a few years later the situation changed radically.

The date is still not certain, but most probably in 1901, Emperor Alexios I Komnenos wrote to Robert I, Count of Flanders, to relate what was happening to Christians who dwelled under Turkish dominion or who went on pilgrimage to the Holy land: "They circumcise the children and the youth of Christians on Christian baptistries and as a sign of despising Christ they spill the blood of circumcision in the same baptisteries. Then they force them to urinate therein. Then they drag them into churches and force them to blaspheme against the name and faith of the Holy Trinity. Then they afflict those who refuse to do so with countless tortures. Finally, they kill them. They prey on noble matrons and their daughters and one after the other, in a consecutive onslaught, they dishonor them with adultery like animals. Others morbidly corrupt virgins and then force them to sing depraved and obscene songs in the face of their mothers until they have not satisfied their vice"; "men of every age and order, youth, adolescents, old men, nobles, servants and what is worst and more shameful yet, clergymen and monks. And what pain! What was unheard of and never seen before since the beginning of time, bishops have been violated with the sin of Sodom; one bishop even died in this obscene sin. In countless ways they contaminate and destroy the holy places while others, they threaten with even more terrifying fates. Who can hold back his tears before all this? Who shall not feel compassion? Who will not be filled with horror? Who will not pray?"

The Turks destroyed "almost the whole earth, from Jerusalem to Greece," the islands, and "now, almost nothing remains except Constantinople which they are threatening to take away from us very soon unless the help of God and of the Latin Christian faithful quickly reaches us"; "We shall omit the rest so that whoever might read this may not be troubled." The Emperor concluded: "Act while there is time, so as to not lose the kingdom of Christians and what is greatest, the Lord's Sepulcher, so that you may avoid eternal judgment and receive your just recompence in heaven. Amen."

In 1883, Leo XIII wrote an encyclical, *Saepenumero considerantes*, to denounce what was being done to history when every cultural space was occupied by enemies of the Church: "Historical science appears as a human conspiracy against truth"; the lie boldly unravels itself amidst the weighty volumes and light books, amidst the loose pages of newspaper and the seducing theatrical apparata." Anti-Christian forces aim to incite hatred against the Church so as to prepare the grounds for persecution. To do so they carry out a cultural maneuver that consists in the falsification of history, especially, the history of Church and of the Papal State: "Too many people want to make the very memory of past events an accomplice to their crimes."

We can appreciate how actual the words of Pope Pecci are, especially with respect to what has been taught about the crusades in the last few decades. The Church was labeled a violent, oppressive, and intolerant institution while Islam was described as tolerant. The legend was told that the crusaders were moved by the desire to conquer lands, by the desire for looting. The normal habits of Muslims were projected on Christians: the tables were turned by anti-Catholic propaganda disguised as historical science.

Deus vult

Pope Urban II (1088-1099), a French monk of the Cluniac order acted as the soul of western Christianity and mobilized the West to aid Constantinople and the Holy Land. The Pope, acting as a universal authority, led all into battle. And everyone went: even to places never heard before, even to places where they were nothing more than a drop of water in a sea of enemies, where supplies had to arrive by sea from very far away or by land over a never ending road. Emperors, kings, dukes, farmers, members of the middle-class: the whole of western society was on the move. And those who because of their age or because they were women could not go, helped as they could from home: with prayers and with donations. It was all to help pilgrims. The crusades were armed pilgrimages which began after doing a rite of penance, after having entrusted the care of one's goods to the Church and after having drawn up a will and testament. The return was more than unlikely. New religious orders were formed, military orders. Monks who added a fourth vow to the three canonical of poverty, chastity and obedience: the defense in arms of all pilgrims.

Shaken by what he heard about the suffering of Christians, the Pope did not stop simply at answering Alexios' call to help the empire survive Islam's assault, but he conceived a much wider plan which aimed to redeem and free the land of Jesus from the "pagans." On November 27, 1095, Pope Urban II, in the Council of Clermont, before a host of mainly French knights and bishops, called on all Christians to free Jerusalem. The Pope's words echoed in sheer enthusiasm. Shortly thereafter, many sowed a cross on their shoulder and took off: *Deus vult*. The first crusade had begun. After centuries of abuses and suffering, the West surge forth to free its brothers and to make pilgrimages to the Holy Land safe and possible once again. The land where Jesus lived, preached, suffered, died and rose again was made accessible once again. Formally, the expedition was led directly by the Pope. However, he delegated command to a representative who was to act as supreme commander instead of Emperor Henry IV and the King of France Phillip. Both had been excommunicated for some time already.

It was not one army, but four who took off for Jerusalem. The entire cavalry answered to the Pope's call. But before and in tandem with it, the people had already mobilized: men, women, children, farmers... all answered the call of Peter the hermit and shouted *Deus le volt*. It was the "Paupers' Crusade." They went towards Jerusalem completely unprepared in the military arts, and were diverted by Emperor Alexios I Komnenos to places where, after exterminating Jewish communities along their way, were massacred by the Turks.

The Crusades were a unique historical phenomenon, even from the military point of view. All crusaders went in the name of the Cross, to earn heaven, to expiate their sins and out of Christian charity. Though they went together, they spoke different dialects and had different leaders. The rivalries which accompany all human activities were especially tense. Moreover, upon their arrival in Constantinople, they clashed with an Empire who asked only for that kind of help which it, as master, could manage as it pleased. Yet, it was this eastward moving sea of people who arrived in Jerusalem and conquered it. On July 15, 1099, after four hundred and sixty-one years, finally, the crusaders once again set foot in the key city of all history, not as assailed, murdered, and abused pilgrims, but as people who could freely practice their faith. But human nature is wounded by sin, and upon their arrival in Jerusalem, crusaders massacred the Jewish and Muslim people who remained (resident Christians had been previously kicked out because Muslims feared they would ally themselves with the crusaders).

For a span of two hundred years, a truly long time, from the day on which the Holy City was taken in 1099 to the fall in 1291 of Saint John of Acre, the last Latin vanguard in the East, there were eight crusades. Knights came from all parts of Europe and formed various crusader states which were fundamentally very unstable. Moreover, surrounded as they were on all parts by Islamic states, they were in constant need of help to ensure survival. Over such a lengthy timespan, all kinds of things happened. Great heroism and sacrifice, suffering, imprisonments, the construction of a network of fortresses, crusader castles set a day's march apart to allow supplies of food, weapons and men to arrive unharmed, safe from the snared of the enemy. But also betrayals. Great saints preached in favor of the crusades. Among them was Bernard of Clairvaux (1090-1153)[10], a

---

[10] Bernard was a mystic who received great revelations and who in 1118 drafted the Templar Order's constitutions wherein he wrote: "Certainly, not even the infidels should be killed if there were some other way to stop the excessive troubles and the oppression of the faithful which they cause." Following the order of Pope Eugene III, this Cistercian abbot went throughout France and Germany to call men to arms for a third crusade in defense of Christian lands threatened by the Turks. To the bishop of Cologne, he wrote: "The fame of your courage has spread throughout the

Cistercian monk who was deeply in love with Our Lady, the "star of the sea" to whom he dedicated some of the greatest hymns of all time. Frederick Barbarossa, an emperor died on crusade in 1190; another emperor, Frederick II, in 1228, during the fifth crusade, which was organized through diplomatic channels though he was excommunicated, entered Jerusalem and went to the Holy Sepulcher as a slight to the Pope and to faith, and thenceforth was called antichrist by Gregory IX; the fourth crusade was diverted against Constantinople by the Venetians causing the formation from 1204 to 1261 of the Latin Empire of the East; the King of France, Louie IX, a saint, died in 1270 also on a crusade.

A Sun upon the World[11]

The *Book of Wisdom* reads that creation "exerts itself to punish the unrighteous, and in kindness relaxes on behalf of those who trust in thee [oh God]"; in the *Letter to the Romans*, Paul wrote: "The creation waits with eager longing for the revealing of the glorious liberty of the sons of God." What the *Book of Wisdom* and St. Paul mean can be easily understood by observing how animals behaved with Francis of Assisi (1182-1226).

In the town of Gubbio there was a ghastly wolf who frightened everyone. They were so afraid that the town's inhabitants never left the town's confines. Francis went into the woods to meet the wolf

---

world"; "I would offer you a profitable deal. Take the cross: its stuff is cheap, but it is of great value; its value is the kingdom of God." While preaching before the King of Germany, Conrad III, who was quite unwilling to go, Bernard quoted the prophet Micah and shouted: "Oh man, what should I have done to you that I did not do?" Even Conrad went on the crusade. Bernard preached for the crusades, but he staunchly opposed harming the Jews in any way: "Whoever strikes a Jew to take his life is like one who harms the same Christ." Often called upon by kings and Popes for advice, he retreated from the world to live a life of strict penance. However, in fact, he was the most significant and more active person in the first half of the 12th century. About him, Pius XII said: "In the multiple and too often turbulent affairs of his time, he was a commanding ruler in holiness, wisdom, supreme prudence and counsel for action."

[11] Dante, *Paradise*, Chant XI.

and made a deal with him: you stop doing evil, and in exchange, everyday the people of Gubbio will give you food. The wolf agreed to the pact by shaking paws, and from thenceforth, so it was: For two years he meekly visited the town, house by house, until in his old age he died and was mourned by all. It also happened that Francis preached to the birds. The birds stood still and quiet listening to him until when he finished instructing them they rose up in midair to draw the shape of the cross in flight. Sometimes creation obeys the children of God. As at one time also the lions, when they spared Daniel in the den.

In the history of the Church, Francis occupies a place of absolute preeminence. He was the son of a rich merchant, a youth of handsome looks and great hopes who was captured alongside those from Assisi in a skirmish with the citizens of Perugia, was thrown in prison where he converted and changed his life. A lover of beautiful things, full of love for all creatures, he held leprous people and the physical decay of their bodies in horror. Meeting one on the road, he understood that, for love of God, he had to overcome his revulsion: he dismounted from his horse, embraced him and kissed him. Shortly before dying, while composing his *Testament*, he recalled that episode: "What seemed bitter, was changed for me in sweetness of the soul and body."

From the cross in the church of Saint Damien, Jesus addressed Francis with these words: "Francis, go and repair my home which, as you will see, is all in ruin." To restore the church of St. Damian, Francis went to the town of Foligno, sold all his father's merchandise, sold also his own horse and went home on foot. Quite understandably, his father exploded in anger and imprisoned him at home in a space so tight, he could hardly fit and which is still visible today. Freed by his mother, Francis confronted his father in public, standing in the town square before the bishop. There, he took off his clothes, gave them back to his father and was welcomed by his new father: "Until now, I have called you, my father on earth; from now on I can say with all certainty: Our father, who art in heaven, because in him, I have placed all my treasure, all my trust and all my hope."

Francis lived in extreme poverty and penance, but as it always happens, old friends and new companions followed him. In the *Testament* he wrote: "After the Lord gave me some brothers, no one showed me what I should do, but rather the Most High himself revealed to me that I should live in the way set forth in the Holy Gospel. I had it set down in writing with few words and great simplicity, and the Pope confirmed it. And those who came to take up this life, distributed all they had to the poor and were glad to have only one tunic, patched up inside and out, one cincture and some drawers. And they desired to have nothing more. [...] I worked with my hands and wanted to work; and I want that all other friars have some work as honesty requires. And those who do not know a trade, let them learn not out of greed for what they may receive from work, but to give good example and to keep idleness at bay. If there should be no recompense from work, then let us turn to the Lord's Table by asking alms door to door."

The Pope Fancis referred to was Innocent III: the poor one of Assisi went to him with twelve companions filled with worry because Innocent III was amongst the most powerful Popes in history. However, the Lord preceded Francis by sending his vicar a dream: the basilica of St. John Lateran is prevented from collapsing by a tiny poor man supporting it. The next day Innocent recognized Francis as the man from the dream[12].

Not only men but also women were attracted to the life of those who loved Our Lady Poverty. The first to follow him was a young girl from a noble family, Clare, also from Assisi. Francis welcomed her, and Clare's holiness earned her order, known as the Clarisses, approval for a rule of life which absolutely excludes any kind of private property, including collective property.

Leaving behind the lepers they took care of, Francis and his friars took off two by two to preach the Gospel. They started in Umbria and then went everywhere. In his youth, Francis wanted to go on a crusade. As a friar, anxious to become martyr, he took off on a crusade and managed something prodigious: he managed to meet the sultan, who according to Thomas of Celano's version admired Francis' courage so much that he converted. Whatever actually

---

[12] Also the very first "Wheel of the Exposed" which is located in Rome, near the Holy Spirit hospital in Sassia, was built in response to one of Pope Innocent's many dreams, wherein he saw the bodies of newborns who had been thrown into the river Tiber appear to him.

happened, without a doubt, Francis arrived into the Sultan's presence, preached the Gospel and came back alive. Other friars who took off with the same objective never came back because they died martyrs. On Christmas night of 1223, in the town of Greccio, in memory of the poor birth of the King of kings, Francis made the first nativity scene; on the night of September 14, 1224, the feast of the Holy Cross, after 40 days fasting, Francis received the Stigmata. On October 3, 1226, the "sun" Dante wrote about died in the Porziuncola, naked upon the naked earth.

Altissimu, onnipotente, bon Signore – Most High, all powerful, good Lord

Francis is the patron of Italy and is also father of the Italian language. The first poetic composition in Italian was written by him: *The Canticle of the Creatures*. Here is the text:

> Most High, all powerful, good Lord,
> Yours are the praises, the glory, the honor,
> and all blessing.
> To You alone, Most High, do they belong,
> and no man is worthy to mention Your name.
> Be praised, my Lord, through all your creatures,
> especially through my lord Brother Sun,
> who brings the day; and you give light through him.
> And he is beautiful and radiant in all his splendor!
> Of you, Most High, he bears the likeness.
> Praise be You, my Lord, through Sister Moon
> and the stars, in heaven you formed them
> clear and precious and beautiful.
> Praised be You, my Lord, through Brother Wind,
> and through the air, cloudy and serene,
> and every kind of weather through which
> You give sustenance to Your creatures.
> Praised be You, my Lord, through Sister Water,
> which is very useful and humble and precious and chaste.
> Praised be You, my Lord, through Brother Fire,

through whom you light the night and he is beautiful
and playful and robust and strong.
Praised be You, my Lord, through Sister Mother Earth,
who sustains us and governs us and who produces
varied fruits with colored flowers and herbs.
Praised be You, my Lord,
through those who give pardon for Your love,
and bear infirmity and tribulation.
Blessed are those who endure in peace
for by You, Most High, they shall be crowned.
Praised be You, my Lord,
through our Sister Bodily Death,
from whom no living man can escape:
woe to those who die in mortal sin.
Blessed are those whom death will
find in Your most holy will,
for the second death shall do them no harm.
Praise and bless my Lord,
and give Him thanks
and serve Him with great humility.

The *Canticle of the Creatures* and the spirit which inspired it changed history. For instance, the history of art. Giotto frescoed the walls of the St. Francis' upper church in Assisi and took note of the revolutionary Franciscan spirit: to live in severe poverty and penance yet not abandoning the world as the monks did but rather living in it by preaching, working, speaking with everyone and going everywhere to bring the good news of the Gospel; all done in communion with creation. Suddenly, art changed. It came out of classic and austere fixedness and by depicting everyday life, including animals and birds, acquired something familiar and natural wherein even miracles were a part of normal everyday life.

The Mendicant Orders (the Friars Minor founded in 1209 by Francis and the Dominicans founded in 1216 by Dominic) and their absolute novelty were God's answer to the challenges the Church faced in the twelfth and thirteenth centuries. Society was changing at a fast pace: it was in constant growth, people were transferring in masse from the countryside to cities, and the world was filled with heresies. Monks lived set apart, far away from populated centers and there was need of someone credible that could, as a true witness of Christ, preach the Gospel everywhere and fight off heresy. So the mendicant convents set camp right in the center of town and there was no more talk of *stabilitas loci*. Friars had to move freely according to the needs of the evangelization. What Benedict wanted for each convent made no sense anymore. The context had completely changed. The whole order needed to be united tightly around the superior general who, having an eagle's view over the whole, could better distribute the available forces. The mission became the heart, the main objective of the Mendicant Orders.

The great renewal which the Franciscans brought about was joyfully welcomed by the people who developed a true devotion towards Francis and his poor brothers. By a strange twist of events, no saint was ever honored, loved, remembered, venerated, prayed to in such beautiful and luxurious churches filled with gold and works of art as was the other Christ par excellence, as was the poor of Assisi, friar Francesco di Pietro Bernardone. On the other hand, no saint was ever hated by the enemies of the Church as was the lover of Our Lady Poverty. Those who slander Christians, those who look in horror at the pomp surrounding Popes, cardinals and men of the church, those who do nothing but judge the Church because of its incoherencies, its crimes and its duplicity (we should take a look at what kind of pulpit these accusations come from!); they have no weapons against Francis and that is why they hate him. Because Francis and the mendicant family he founded embodied and substantiated the truth that there is not only money, power and business in the world; because many people took Francis as a model and live in the world without making an idol of the world.

With the passing of time, Franciscans divided into more families: minor, conventuals, capuchins. Each searched for a more perfect observance of the rule. Some, the so-called spirituals turned poverty into an idol and ended up in heresy. In this respect, the cardinal archbishop of Milan, Blessed Alfredo Ildefonso Schuster (1880-1954), a monk, wrote with great clarity and depth: "Saint Jerome observes that many philosophers of Greek antiquity have despised and abandoned earthly goods reducing themselves to not possessing nothing"; "But perfection is not to be found here; hence the Divine

Teacher added in praise to the apostles: 'and you have followed me.' Behold where Christian perfection is to be found." Francis followed and did what Jesus had asked him: he repaired the Church.

Cathars in Languedoc

Gnosticism views reality we live in as the result of the battle between two deities, two juxtaposed principles: good and evil. Good is spiritual, disincarnate, free; evil is creator of the matter which enslaves us. In the second millennium, Gnostic Manichean doctrines spread throughout the west along trade routes with the east and although there were many sects inspired to Manicheism, the one that spread the most was the sect of the Cathars.

The Cathars, a self-chosen label which means the "pure", wanted to have nothing to do with matter. This is the extent of their purity. They considered themselves pure and enlightened because they felt certain to know the truth. If creation is the fruit of evil, of an evil deity who imprisons spirit inside matter, then in order to overcome evil, one must fight and overcome matter. According to the Cathars, man is split in two: body and soul. The soul is good, the body is evil. The soul has its origin in the good deity while the body, in the evil one. The only way to become free of this curse, the only road to happiness is to fight against the body to the bitter end. One must contradict each and every expression of the flesh, including the most beautiful. To do so, life itself must be destroyed starting from the cell which reproduces it: the family. Any sexual relationship is better than the one that takes place between husband and wife. Marriage is nothing but "prostitution and bedlam." It forces man to live in a never-ending state of sin. When a woman becomes pregnant, abortion is the only way to free her from the evil growing within her and death is the solution to all problems because only death frees from the prison of matter.

Cathars are divided in two groups: the perfect and the simple believers. Perfect are those who after having abandoned their respective families lead an ascetic and poor life. They never eat meat, milk, cheese and eggs. The perfect, guide the simple believers on to *consolamentum* (the completed process of initiation), they live together, obey an internal hierarchy, vow to never swear any oath. Believers live immersed in social life, they spread Cathar ideals amongst the catholic population, periodically attend the preaching of the perfect, to whom they owe "the homage of adoration." Amongst the believers, many are merchants and craftsman and they are not held to live honestly. Since they do not confess, they never receive any penance: they need not remedy any fraud they may have committed and can comfortably practice usury, which the Church sternly condemned. Believers need only that, before dying, one of the perfect imposes his hands on them to confer the *consolamentum*, a kind of viaticum to obtain forgiveness for all faults. The greatest feat believers can aspire to achieve is to commit suicide by practicing *endure*, or death by starvation. The perfect are the only ones who, because they are apostles and must spread true doctrine, may put aside any aspiration to commit suicide. Generalized fornication and shameless moneymaking for the believers; strict asceticism and poverty for the perfect: the Cathar morality relied on a double standard.

Cathars vehemently and totally condemned the Church: the hierarchy, the sacraments and all ecclesial institutions which they deemed demonic institutions. Many nobles subscribed to the Gnostic movement and took advantage of its battle against the Church to seize ownership of its goods. As soon as possible, that is, as soon as the balance of power allows for it, just like any common revolutionary, Cathars pass from theory to action: they organize armed gangs to destroy churches and convents, they attack defenseless people, desecrate hosts, threaten and kill both priests and religious, destroy tombs. Besides their pretentious spirituality, Cathar truth spread terror. The founder of the Dominican order, Dominic Guzman (1179-1221), used the following words to describe the situation of southern France: "They persuade the simple by their deceiving appearance of poverty and exterior signs of austerity."

Catharism arrived in Europe at the end of the first millennium and quickly spread to all regions. In England, in France and in Germany, by the second half of the 12th century Cathars were annihilated by the secular authorities, quite understandably, fully supported by the local population enraged against the heretics. The king of England, Henry II Plantagenet (1133-1189), as well as the king of France Louie VII (1120-1180), after having fought against them in their respective countries, in 1178 struck an agreement to conduct a military campaign in Languedoc, a region of southern France, where in absence of a strong central power, no one had successfully put a halt to the Cathars excessive power. During the Council of Verona in 1184, Emperor Frederick Barbarossa (1122-1190) pressured Pope Lucius III to make the Church pronounce itself against this heresy. Thereafter, in Verona, the episcopal inquisition was born, that is, the mandate for bishops to actively seek out the heretics. Until then, the Popes had limited themselves to sending their best and most credible preachers into those areas which had a high concentration of heretics, especially to Languedoc: the Cistercians, then Saint Bernard and finally, at the turn of the 13th century, Dominicans and Franciscans, that is, the mendicant orders which had just been established. The intervention of the Franciscan Anthony of Padua (1195-1231) is of great renown. Called to preach the Gospel in Rimini, a city which at the time was filled with Cathars, he was blatantly rejected. Nobody was willing to hear his words. So Anthony, one of the saints who worked the greatest number of miracles in all of Church history, went to the seashore and preached to the fish, the only creatures which the Cathars ate because they were deemed less impure than the others. The fish swarm to hear Anthony's words and swimming shoulder to shoulder manifested their approval by splashing and moving the waters as if they were clapping hands.

The Inquisition

In Languedoc, Cathars had enjoyed the protection, among others, of the Count of Toulouse and of the Viscounts of Carcassonne and Béziers. Numberless churches and convents had been destroyed, the bishop of Carcassonne had been thrown out, the bishop of Lodève killed together with many other priests, Dominic assaulted while he went to preach poor and defenseless. How was one to defend the majority catholic population from violence? The Church tried by all means possible to resolve the issue peacefully: preaching, public debates... But on January 15, 1208, an assassin hired by the Count of Toulouse killed the pontifical delegate Pierre de Castelnau. It was the final proof that every boundary had been crossed and that all bridges with Rome had been torn down. The Cathar doctrine is a cancer against which society needed to react. Innocent III (1198-1216) excommunicated the Count of Tolouse and by so doing freed the Count's vassals from their oath of loyalty to him: the crusade began; the crusade against the Albigensians.

From Northern France, ten thousand (sources disagree on the exact number) mobilized against the Cathars. In four years' time, city after city, the heresy was temporarily overcome. In Béziers, the first of the conquered centers, all inhabitants were killed. Elsewhere, they were forced into exile. Innocent called for the crusade to come to a halt because he did not want to exterminate the sinners, but to give them a chance to convert. But war raged on because King Phillip Augustus of France and his Barons wanted to take advantage of the situation and increase their lands. Nevertheless, the Cathar affair did not come to a close. The heretics reemerged under the leadership of the Count of Toulouse who cut off prisoners' hands and ears and poked their eyes out. Violence spread like wildfire and in 1233, Gregory IX entrusted the inquisition work to the Dominicans and two years later also to the Franciscans. The Pontifical or Legatine Inquisition was thus placed side by side with the Episcopal Inquisition.

"I have no pleasure in the death of the sinner, but that the sinner turns from his ways and live," wrote Ezekiel. By the middle of the 13th century, the Church launched a large-scale mission to all corners of the region to convert the Cathars: the friars of the Mendicant Orders, Dominicans and Franciscan, by their great poverty and holiness led the effort. Thrust forth by preachers, civil society began to organize itself in brotherhoods to assist the poorest in their needs. Life itself was returning to civil society by means of good works and mercy. In tandem with the popular missions and the friars, the Church invented a defense against heresy. The Church established a tribunal to seek out those who hid their revolutionary doctrine, that is, their death-loving doctrines: the tribunal of the inquisition (from Latin *inquirere* means to seek out).

Born in response to the particular necessities of the Languedoc region, the modus operandi of the inquisition process was defined in local councils: the Council of Toulouse in 1229, of Narbonne in 1235 and of Béziers in 1246. Later on, the same inquisitors, starting from their experience compiled the best courses of action in manuals called *Directories* or *Practice*; likewise, in the following centuries, the Spanish and Roman Inquisitions enacted during the Lutheran Reformation. The establishment within the inquisition procedures of a popular jury constituted an absolute novelty: a jury composed of competent lay people and clergymen representing the local community, which worked side by side with the inquisitorial fathers. The jury participated to each step of the process starting from the deposition of the accusation and interrogation.

If not always, the accused had a lawyer that would defend him, could always produce witnesses in his defense and even reject the same judges by appealing to Rome. Sometimes the accused were not allowed to know the names of the accusers because these needed to be defended from the Cathars' vendettas. The jury instead knew all the names. At the start of the process, the accused was called upon to give specific details about who were his enemies and why they were so. Such information would then be taken into account during the investigation. The authors of false accusations would be punished just as harshly as the heretics. In cases deemed especially hard to solve, torture was used. It was authorized by Pope Innocent IV, "however, without allowing them lose any body part or without putting their life in jeopardy." Moreover, in order to use torture, the inquisitor needed explicit permission of the bishop. Often, the punishments dealt out were penances or pilgrimages, or sowing a cross on one's garments or as it also happened, having to support a poor person for a year. Sometimes, the most severe sentences were commuted into lesser punishments since general pardons were often granted. Before the start of the inquisition process, a "grace period" was granted so as to give accused a chance to repent and if so receive only penitential punishment.

In times when no one ever doubted the need for the death penalty, the inquisition, only in some cases, passed sentences which included capital punishment executed by the "secular arm" (from the local authorities). In times when no one doubted torture's usefulness, the Church authorized it only in special cases and moreover, obliged the inquisitor to obtain the bishop's explicit permission. Did the Popes make a mistake by authorizing and organizing inquisitorial procedures? What about when towards the mid-16th century, these took place at home even, in Rome, where the Pope-King himself, as holder of temporal power, was responsible for the execution of the condemned? Whatever judgment is passed over the pontifical inquisition, one must keep in mind that in Rome, the Pope is also the head of state. As such, he had the obligation of defending the local population from anarchy and the violence which necessarily flows from it. It must also be kept in mind that any historical judgment on the inquisition is subject to centuries of anti-Catholic propaganda which went so far as to systematically fabricate facts.

Thus said, the drama surrounding the mystery of evil is profound and the attempts made to counter it are themselves hard to understand and painful.

Beauty by analogy

That same society which to follow the will of God went into Palestine, to give glory to God also built cathedrals, convents, beautiful cathedrals and beautiful convents in all corners of Europe. In the late Middle Ages, the monk Rodulfus Glaber described the architectural enthusiasm of the time as follows: "It happened that throughout the world, but especially in Italy and in Gaul, an effort began to rebuild churches, though many were still in good shape and did not need such restoration. It was as if a race began between one people and another; the common belief was that the world, after shaking off its old rags wanted to put on the white robe of new churches everywhere. All in all, almost all cathedral churches, a great number of monastic churches and even village oratories were restored by the faithful." By the faithful, wrote Rodulfus. Literally, that is how it took place because cathedrals were the people's concern. The craftsmen behind medieval cathedrals were common folk. In the measure they could and to the extent of their know-how, everyone played a part. Rodulfus wrote during the mid-11th century, but his description could very well be extended to the following two centuries.

Romanesque cathedrals are a living Bible: covered in frescoes and colors, each wall taught the people who could not read, and reminded those who could, of the Bible stories. Starting with Christ, his triumph and his judgment at the end of times. The majestic stone portals all speak of this: Jesus, true God, true gateway into life. To overcome death one need pass through him just like during any liturgical time, to enter the church, an anticipation of heaven, one must pass through him. Above the portal, above Christ, a rose window: a grand circular opening, as if it were a colored stone and glass lace in the shape of a rose. In catholic liturgy, the true rose is Mary, the "mystical rose." Can we exclude that the Romanesque rose window is a homage to Mary?

Another style began to spread starting from 12th century France. This style, thanks to its pointed-arches and ribbed vaults resting on grand stone pillars managed to transform massive Romanesque walls into an almost aerial space, perforated, and filled with glass, windows exploding with color. Stained glass windows are to the Gothic style as frescoes are to the Romanesque style. The role stained glass windows play in the Gothic style is played by frescoes in the Romanesque style. Biblical stories, about Jesus, Mary and the saints are all told through the splendor of glass lit up by the sun in different ways throughout the day, thus telling a story with a thousand facets of lights. The light is Christ. The light is also the splendor of creation and of Christ's Church.

Cathedrals are just as splendid as the miniatures employed to decorate holy books, the book of life which is the Bible and with the Bible, all liturgical texts. Then the paraments for bishops, abbots, priests, monks, magnificent vestments crafted so as to cover in gold, silver, precious stones and silk embroidery whoever is to impersonate Christ, his majesty, his beauty, his mercy. All full of colors. Many colors. In the most various shades. Different colors for the year's different liturgical times, for the many feasts which cadence the Christian liturgical year. What fantastic imagination would choose to dress in pink, an intense and full pink, the priest who solemnly walked in procession on Laetare Sunday, the fourth Sunday of Lent, after thirty days of the gloomy purple which cadenced the time of penance, fasting and almsgiving, a seemingly never ending time along the "quadragesima", that is, the forty-day period which precedes and prepares the Paschal victory?

Praising God demands beauty because man is made in the image of his creator, "the most beautiful of the sons of men." In that time period, disparagingly named the age in the middle, "medi-eval,"

Middle Age, by enemies of the Church in order to underline the total nothingness separating the first pagan pre-Christian from the second pagan post-Christian worlds, beauty is something for everyman. Not only for the few rich and knowledgeable. For everyone. Albeit the beauty of buildings, stones, cloth, frescoes can never compare with the splendor of God, nor can they compare with the incarnate beauty of His saintly men and women, true temples of the living God. Rich and poor, powerful and humble, knowledgeable and ignorant. Kings and queens. To say a few: Anselm of Aosta (1033-1109), bishop of Canterbury, who strenuously defended God's rights against those of the crown; Thomas Becket (1118-1170), Lord Chancellor and bishop of Canterbury, martyr, who defended the *libertas ecclesiae* from Henry II's abuses of power; Homobonus Tuchenghi, a merchant from Cremona (died in 1197) patron saint of merchants and tailors who spent on the poor the large sums of money he earned; Dominic of Guzman, who founded the Mendicant Order of Preachers, to whom our Lady entrusted the rosary prayer; Princess Elizabeth of Hungary (1207-1231), mystic and third order Franciscan; the Franciscan Bonaventure of Bagnoregio (1221?-1274), *Doctor Seraphicus*, philosopher who made use of his reason without making an idol of it, conscious of sin which always ensnares it; Bridget of Sweden (1303-1373), noble woman and pilgrim who received detailed revelations from Jesus and Mary.

Beauty in art, beauty in the life of saints, beauty in the institutions of the Christian people which, organized in countless brotherhoods, prayed and praised God by taking care of the poor in all their infinite needs. The thirst for beauty filled medieval times: "What is beauty, that beauty which writers, poets, musicians, artists contemplate and translate into their languages if not the reflection of that splendor of the eternal Word made flesh?" asked Benedict XVI in the catechesis dedicated to medieval cathedrals. "*Via pulchritudinis*, the way of beauty is a privileged and fascinating way to approach the Mystery of God," he answered.

Faith and Reason are in agreement

Western Monasticism, since its beginning, placed faith and reason at the service of work. The results are visible: swamps dried up and transformed into farmland, rearing and selective breeding, improvement of farming techniques, channeling of irrigation water, use of hydraulic energy and of fertilizers, tanneries, iron ore extraction. Monks were industrious and designed machines to improve and streamline work in the fields and workshops. Monasteries made products of the best kind: beer, wine, honey, parmesan, fruit, and medicine. Even Champagne, a few centuries later, had father Dom Perignon, a Benedictine abbot. The roman world, based on slavery, never saw such a systematic employment of intelligence. Enhanced working conditions in every area allow us to speak for the first time of capitalism as a monastic invention.

The collaboration between science and faith in the Christian world produced unheard of novelties of absolute importance. Amongst others, the invention of the university: communities of professors and students formed in the 12th century, whose autonomy with respect to the pressures of local powers was guaranteed by the Holy See. "Antiquity and the East never knew such corporative bodies, free associations of teachers and students – with their privileges, their fixed programs, their diplomas and their degrees – as the universities during the middle ages," wrote Maurice De Wulf. Knowledge fostered in universities was finalized to a greater and better knowledge of God, of creation, of the nature of man and society; ultimately it was aimed at the evangelization. Such knowledge was needed to convince atheists and non-Christians about the goodness and rationality of Christian principle. It was not by chance that the Mendicant Orders were the protagonists of those kinds of studies. The main centers were Paris and Bologna. Universities formed the best youth of all Europe without distinguishing between rich and poor: a new social class, that of teachers and intellectuals who later played a key role in the social and political development of Christian civilization. The knowledge fostered in universities was based on the dialectic born from confrontation: students practiced finding the best answers to questions, to *questiones*, intellectual conundrums posed by their teachers. At the end of the discussions, of the debates, after having analyzed all possible solutions and confuted the wrong ones, they reached the final answer, the true answer then given by the teacher.

The thirteenth chapter of the *Book of Wisdom* reads: "For all men who were ignorant of God were foolish by nature; and they were not able from good things that are seen to know him who exists, nor did they recognize the craftsman while paying heed to his works." Paul took up the reflection from the *Book of Wisdom* in the first chapter of the *Letter to the Romans*: "For what can be known about God is plain to them [to men], because God has shown it to them. Ever since the creation of the world his invisible nature, namely, his eternal power and deity has been clearly perceived in the things that have been made. So they [atheists] are without excuse; for although they knew God they did not honor him as God or give thanks to him."

Nowadays, in the midst of the scientist age, these words seem to have lost their meaning because by definition, science cannot express itself on anything non-quantifiable or non-verifiable by experience. This follows from the basic conviction that human reason cannot formulate metaphysical truth. In a Christian environment, instead, these words are the basis of the collaboration between faith and reason.

In the second Millennium, rational research on God and man, until then dominated by platonic thought as mediated by Augustine, began to confront Aristotle as rediscovered by Arab thinkers. Albert the Great (1206-1280), who took this step despite a clear incompatibility between many Aristotelian claims and Christian thought, amongst them, the belief in the eternity of matter. Below we quote a long passage taken from Pope Ratzinger's catechesis on Albert because as it is often with this Pope, his prose is unequalled in clarity and profoundness: "Saint Albert the Great, reminds us that there exists friendship between science and faith, and also that men of science, by means of their vocation to study nature, may find an authentic and fascinating path to sainthood." His "extraordinary openness of mind" enacted a real cultural revolution which welcomed and gave value to Aristotle, whose works, "display the strength of reason, explain with lucidity and clarity the meaning and structure of reality, its intelligibility, the value and goal of all human action." The discord between Aristotelian philosophy and Christian thought posed a question, continued Ratzinger: "A problem arose: faith and reason are in contrast or no? Here lays one of Saint Albert's great merits: he studied Aristotle's works with scientific rigor in the conviction that all that is truly rational is fully compatible with faith as revealed in Sacred Scripture."

The disciple of Albert is Thomas Aquinas (1225-1274), the *Doctor Angelicus*, the undisputed star of medieval thought. Thomas is the most perfect example of the great trust Catholics place in the good exercise of reason. His most renown work, the Summa, in which he raised and answered thousands of philosophical and theological questions, and which is constantly referred to by the magisterium, today, is still an unequalled model of Christian thought.

Pontifical hierocracy

Most literature, including the historical, described the Middle Ages as a time filled with superstition, obscurantist, a tunnel at the end of which came humanism, the triumph of objective reason. This is false. The Middle Ages, and this is undoubtably true, was a time in which the thought of God was ever present. This does not mean superstition. The Middle Ages were rather the time of logic, a confidence in reason which may seem even exaggerated. In fact, theologians, also Thomas, made a strenuous effort to describe with great precision each and every movement of thought in order to analyze it and confute it if it failed to lead to God. They proceeded meticulously, objectively, sometimes even pedantically. In such a way they meant to prove the truth of those propositions that reason distilled as true. Incontrovertible truths because passed through the sieve of confutation: thesis, antithesis, synthesis. We need not wait on Hegel to see dialectic appreciated. Likewise, with very clear language, Thomas offered readers of all levels proof for God's existence, taken up again from Aristotle; elsewhere the perfect, unconfutable, proof developed two centuries earlier by Anselm who analyzing language itself, proved the impossibility and intrinsic contradiction of atheism. In tandem with the construction of the splendid and increasingly daring cathedrals, medieval thought-built cathedrals of thought, theological cathedrals. The same doctrine of Pontifical Hierocracy is shaped upon the logical spirit which constitutes the distinctive feature of medieval philosophy: the spirit of logic's omnipotence.

For centuries, Popes defended themselves from the presumptuous attempt by emperors to intervene in the life of the Church by choosing bishops, abbots and even Popes (although, as a merit to emperors, we should say that churchmen accepted political offices without much fuss and that therefore they could not but expect some imperial control on their persons and actions). In order to push back and keep the claims of secular authorities in check, the Church developed doctrinal antibodies meant to clarify the prerogatives and duties of each according to the will of God, that is, according to justice. This is the context wherein starting from Pope Gregory VII and the reform he enacted, theological thought developed a linear and logic conception of pontifical prerogatives which led to the formulation of a new concept: *plenitudo potestatis* (fullness of power). Such concept identified the Popes as the rightful holders of this perfectly fulfilled power. To shed light on what is meant by the phrase *plenitudo potestatis*, we shall turn to Innocent III (1198-1216): "Peter is the only one who has been called to enjoy fullness of power. I have received the miter for my priesthood and the crown for my kingship; I was appointed by the Vicar of He about whom it is written: 'King of kings and Lord of lords, priest forever according to the order of Melchizedek.'"

The conceptual framework named Pontifical Hierocracy is extremely schematic and therefore simple. The starting point is the belief that all powers come from God. God the Father handed all power over to the Son Jesus Christ: Jesus transmitted his power to his vicar on earth, Peter; Peter transfers all power entrusted to him to the various Peters who follow him in time. These, in their turn, delegate the power they hold to both temporal and spiritual authorities. Every power on earth, from the greatest to the smallest, depends directly or indirectly from the Pope: *plenitudo potestatis*. What premise could possibly justify such an exorbitant claim to power? The belief that the whole of the west constituted a single well-formed and ordered body built on Christ. In other words, the belief that there are no differences between civil society and the Church: both are part of one single whole, one single reality named *Christendom*. Not by chance Boniface VIII (1294-1303) held that Christ gave the Church (Peter) the power "to govern with free dominion over all faithful people in order that as a mother over her children she should have power over each and all, with filial piety should honor her as universal mother and lady."

In abstract, from a theoretical point of view, the *plenitudo potestatis* doctrine is logically perfect. However, in practice it is an entirely inadequate scheme to describe reality. Let us set aside viewing Pontifical Hierocracy simply as a way of exalting oneself and one's role; let us suppose that Popes, jurists and theologians who thought it up did so in good faith. If so, the impression is that Popes tried to relieve the children God had given them of the burden of injustice and suffering. It almost seems as if, by drawing the boundaries of an ordered and perfect world, their thirst for fatherhood led them to hope they could save men from having to carry the weight of the cross. As if this were possible; as if this were the will of God.

"Be perfect, for I, the Lord your God, am perfect" (Leviticus 19): during the celebration of the Jubilee year which opened the third millennium, John Paul II solemnly asked God forgiveness for all those times Christian men and women, in two thousand years of history, failed to keep faith to his Word. The Pope quite sternly asserted the need for a purification of memory so as to enter the third millennium with a renewed missionary impulse. During the general audience held on September 1, 1999, he stated that the request for forgiveness, however, must not be understood "as a denial of her [the Church's] two millennia of history, certainly filled with merits in the fields of charity, culture and holiness. Instead, she responds to a vital need for truth, which next to the positive aspects acknowledges also the human limits and weaknesses of various generations of Christ's disciples."

Between Pope and Emperor, a king emerged

First the battle for the struggle over the investitures, then the conflict with Frederick I and the antipopes elected by him; then the violent clash with Frederick II, an emperor which didn't really seem to have much that could be called Christian; then Frederick's sudden death; then the long interregnum distinguished by the power struggles between Guelphs and Ghibellines in Germany and Italy. The Popes came out of centuries of struggle with the empire, a weakened empire at that, by increasingly leaning on the strongest and most stable monarchy of Europe: the first daughter of the Church who in those times was governed by King Louie IX of France (1214-1270) declared saint a few years after his death.

A few facts clearly show the hegemonical role assumed by the French starting from the second half of the 13th century. Innocent IV spent various years in Lyon to escape Frederick II, emperor of the Sacred Roman Empire and king of Sicily who risked viewing the Church as a useless nuisance within his lands; in less than twenty five years (1261-1285), four Frenchmen were made Popes; in 1266 Clement IV, French Pope, called Louie IX's brother, Charles of Anjou, to take the seat as King of Sicily[13], thus giving rise to a new dynasty bound to respect the Pontifical state' integrity and independence and thus putting an end once and for all to the Swabian plant to unify Germany and southern Italy; since the numbers of French cardinals increased, conclaves became never-ending: it took the cardinals twenty seven months to elect the monk Celestine V.

In Rome the situation was all but peaceful. Rome was dominated by a power struggle between the Ghibelline nobility, led by the House of Colonna, and the Guelph nobility, led by the House of Orsini, the latter favorable to the House of Anjou. The city was prey to such insecurity, that of the fifteen Popes enthroned between 1243 and 1303 only three were elected in Rome and only four died in Rome. When Celestine V abdicated after few months of government, the situation was so delicate that the new Pope Boniface VIII, a renowned jurist, was elected after a conclave lasting one single day. From the election of Benedict Caetani as Pope in 1294 to his death in 1303, nine years passed; nine years which would change the course of history and put an end to the Middle Age.

---

[13] After the Eastern Schism in 1054, the Pope entrusted the Standard of Saint Peter to the Normans so that they might conquer all Byzantine and Muslim lands in southern Italy and Sicily: thus the Norman kings were the Pope's vassals and that is why it was Clement IV who deliberated over the Sicilian crown (Frederick II was king of Sicily because he was the son of Constance, the last descendant of the Norman House of Hauteville).

If at home, the Pope had many enemies, first and foremost the House of Colonna, outside, the Pope had an implacable enemy, willing to go to all lengths to destroy him: the king of France Philip IV the Fair (1285-1314). What was it that ruined the relationship between France and Rome to the point of unleashing a battle to the bitter end between Philip and Boniface? The king wanted to tax the clergy without first asking for the Pope's authorization. It was not uncommon that Rome, in times of need or for the crusade, allowed monarchs to keep the tithes destined to the Pope. In this case, the king not only did not submit any request, but simply took possession of what was not his. On the other hand, Philip, who was always looking for money, not only attacked the Church, but also Lombards and Jews by expropriating and expelling them from French grounds and later on, by suppressing the Templars, squared off all debts he previously owed to the order.

Boniface's multiple attempts to give the king of France juridical explanations, even in paternal tones were useless. There was no arguing with him. Moreover, when the Pope threatened to excommunicate him, he answered with a violent smear campaign aimed at demonizing and bringing about the total character assassination of his enemy: the Pope was called illegitimate (because Celestine had abdicated), a heretic (he supposedly denied the soul's immortality and transubstantiation), a simoniac, an incorrigible sinner (a sodomite, idolater and author of shameful dealings with the devil). The king wanted to convoke a council to condemn and depose Boniface. The fact that only the Pope could legitimately convoke a council was a small detail for Philip. The king was interested only in having the support of the whole nation and so he convoked the Estates General (clergy, nobility, third estate) for the first time. In the meanwhile, he tarnished the Pope's position to smooth out the way so that the French nation could side with him closely. Boniface responded with the papal bull *Unam Sanctam*[14], a perfect example of *plenitudo potestatis*.

---

[14] This is the text of the papal bull published on November 18, 1302:
Unam sanctam

a) Urged by faith, we are obliged to believe and to maintain that the Church is one, holy, catholic, and also apostolic. We believe in her firmly and we confess with simplicity that outside of her there is neither salvation nor the remission of sins, as the Spouse in the Canticles: "One is my dove, my perfect one. She is the only one, the chosen of her who bore her," and she represents one sole mystical body whose Head is Christ and the head of Christ is God. In her then is one Lord, one faith, one baptism. There had been at the time of the deluge only one ark of Noah, prefiguring the one Church, which ark, having been finished to a single cubit, had only one pilot and guide, that is Noah, and we read that, outside of this ark, all that subsisted on the earth was destroyed. We venerate this Church as one, the Lord having said by the mouth of the prophet: "Deliver, O God, my soul from the sword and my only one from the hand of the dog." He has prayed for his soul, that is, for himself, heart and body; and his body, that is to say, the Church, He has called one because of the unity of the Spouse, of the faith, of the sacraments, and of the charity of the Church. This is the tunic of the Lord, the seamless tunic, which was not rent but which was cast by lot. Therefore, of the one and only Church there is one body and one head, not two heads like a monster, that is, Christ and the vicar of Christ, Peter and the successor of Peter, since the Lord speaking to Peter Himself said: "Feed my sheep," meaning, my sheep in general, not these, nor those in particular, whence we understand that He entrusted all to him [Peter].

b) Therefore, if the Greeks or others should say that they are not confided to Peter and his successors, they must confess not being the sheep of Christ, since our Lord says in John "there are one sheepfold and one [unique] shepherd." We are informed by the texts of the gospels that in this Church and its power are two swords; namely the spiritual and the temporal. For when the Apostles say: "Behold, here are two swords," that is to say, in the Church, since the Apostles were speaking, the Lord did not reply that there were too many, but sufficient. Certainly the one who denies that the temporal sword is in the power of Peter has not listened well to the word of the Lord commanding: "Put up thy sword into thy scabbard" (Mt 26, 51; Jn 18, 11). Both, therefore, are in the power (at the behest) of the Church, that is to say, the spiritual and the material sword, but the former is to be administered *for* the Church but the latter *by* the Church; the former in the hands of the priest; the latter by the hands of kings and soldiers, but at the will and sufferance of the priest. However, one sword ought to be subordinated to the other and the temporal authority, subjected to spiritual power. For since the Apostle said: "There is no power except from God and the things that are, are ordained by God" (Rm 13, 1-2), but they would not be ordained if one sword were not subordinated to the other and if the inferior one, as it were, were not led upwards by the other. For, according to the Blessed Dionysius, it is the law of the divinity that the lowest things reach the highest place by intermediaries. Then, according to the order of

On September 7, 1303, hand in glove with the House of Colonna, Philip sent his own chancellor Guillaume de Nogaret to the town of Anagni to arrest the Pope and force him to resign. With the help of a few traitors who opened the gates for him, stealing into the city by night, Nogaret found himself standing before a Pope which was all but yielding and who instead confronted him saying: "Behold my head, behold my neck. By the faith of Our Lord Jesus Christ I wish to die." He was freed by the people and returned to Rome where after a month he died.

---

the universe, all things are not led back to order equally and immediately, but the lowest by the intermediary, and the inferior by the superior. Hence we must recognize the more clearly that spiritual power surpasses in dignity and in nobility any temporal power whatever, as spiritual things surpass the temporal. This we see very clearly also by the payment, benediction, and consecration of the tithes, but the acceptance of power itself and by the government even of things.

c) For with truth as our witness, it belongs to spiritual power to establish the terrestrial power and to pass judgment if it has not been good. This is accomplished the prophecy of Jeremiah concerning the Church and the ecclesiastical power: "Behold today I have placed you over nations, and over kingdoms" and the rest. Therefore, if the terrestrial power err, it will be judged by the spiritual power; but if a minor spiritual power err, it will be judged by a superior spiritual power; but id the highest power of all err, it can be judged only by God, and not by man, according to the testimony of the Apostle: "Their spiritual man judged of all things and he himself is judged by no man." This authority, however, (though it has been given to man and is exercised by man), is not human but rather divine, granted to Peter by a divine word and reaffirmed by him [Peter] and his successor by the One Whom Peter confessed, the Lord saying to Peter himself, "Whatsoever you shall bind on earth, shall be bound also in Heaven" etc. Therefore whoever resists this power thus ordained by God, resists the ordinance of God, unless he invent like Manicheus two beginnings, which is false and judged by us as heretical, since according to the testimony of Moses, it is not in the beginnings but in the beginning that God created heaven and earth. Furthermore, we declare, we proclaim, we define that it is absolutely necessary for salvation that every human creature be subject to the Roman Pontiff. Signed in the Lateran, in the eight year of Our Pontificate.

The Pope is not in Rome anymore

While Rome, the city which is a world by itself, is unequalled, the French people attempted to make their origins as ancient and noble as that of the Romans and so fabricated an intricate set of genealogies. The 7th century French historian Fredegar traced the origins of the Merovingian dynasty all the way back to Aeneas' cousin, Priam the Younger. Alexander the Great and Francus, Clovis' ancestor, supposedly also descended from Priam. Others even identified King David and Emperor Constantine as the ancestors of Charlemagne.

While Philip II Augustus (1165-1223) clearly stated that in his home not even the emperor surpassed the king in authority (he loved to say, *rex imperator in regno suo*), during the reign of Philip the Fair, jurists, theologians and court scholars went so far as to claim, just as Pierre Dubois did, that France, because of its climate and a particularly favorable alignment of the stars, was absolutely the best place in the world for hosting the highest living authorities, that is king and Pope. Besides, Avignon's central position was an objective fact measurable in kilometers. Moreover, Philip was aware that the House of Capet to which he belonged enjoyed a particular privilege, that is, a kind of infallibility in spiritual matters (*"semper diretrix veritatis extiterit regia domus nostra"*).

No one at court doubted that the French people were the new Israel; the new chosen people. The idea of transferring the seat of the Pope to France seemed by consequence the most obvious solution. The Pope could even choose to forego all worries about government because the King of France, new roman senator, would have provided to solve all temporal matters. In brief, France and its king, though not even emperor, presented themselves as candidates for becoming the new imperial power.

Benedict XI, the successor to Boniface VIII, did not reign for more than a year. Upon his death, the conclave seemed to never end. Philip never stopped pressuring the assembly by threatening to convoke a council that would condemn Boniface postmortem. His threats were quite credible. It took the cardinals almost a full year to give in to the French king's will and elect Bertrand de Got, bishop of Bordeaux, 195th Roman Pope. Clement V, despite the many promises, never set foot in Rome: elected in 1305, by 1309 he had already transferred the pontifical residence to Avignon. From 1309 to 1377, the seat of the Pope stayed in Avignon. All Popes were French. Among the 134 new cardinals made in Christendom's new capital, 111 were French, 14 Italian, 3 from Castile, 2 from Aragon, 2 from England, not even one German.

The plague of nationalism appeared. Avignon is not Rome. Avignon is not the world. Though the Pope may have been formally proprietor of both the Venaissin County and the same city of Avignon, yet it is France, and all other catholic nations could never understand why their tithes should go to enrichen one of the many nations of Christendom. They could never understand why the most prestigious ecclesiastical offices should be entrusted to French clergymen. Therefore, throughout the 14th century, the English crown published multiple decrees in defense of its national treasure and of the English who might have been penalized in the religious offices they were awarded just because of their English origin. The role of the emperor, on the other hand, who had been completely set off balance by the Pope's transfer to France, lost the very reason for its existence, that is, to be roman emperor, meaning universal, and protector of the Roman Church. Thus Ludwig the Bavarian (1282-1347) attempted to confront the situation by surrounding himself with heretics and in Rome, by having the captain of the people, Sciarra Colonna, crown him emperor: power comes not from above but from below, from the people. This was the theory of Marsilius of Padua (1275-1342), excommunicated, who identified in the emperor the *Defensor Pacis* and who viewed the total submission of the spiritual power to the temporal as the condition for keeping the peace. Dwelled at court also the English Franciscan William of Ockham (1288-1347), he too excommunicated, who put in shambles the hierarchical, ordered and rational world of scholasticism. He said that between faith and reason there is no collaboration but rather total autonomy: universals do not exist, one cannot even speak of substances, only individuals exist and only these can be known. He brought about the triumph of Nominalism which deprived reason of its ability to know truth beyond the senses or metaphysical truth. It deprived reason of the power to know the truth. Regarding the Pope, this English Franciscan asserted that no such primacy belonged to him because it was neither wanted by Christ nor was it at all necessary.

Infallibility is not the Pope's competence but the Church's, maybe even in the person of a little old lady. Some years after Ludwig's revolution, Charles IV of Luxemburg, by the Golden Bull of 1356 established who the Prince-electors were (four laymen and three clergymen), thus separating the empire from the papacy. Since then, at least in principle, the Holy Roman Empire ceased to exist; the Empire of the German nation was born.

To go back to Avignon, Clement V was constantly blackmailed. In 1312, he convoked a council in Vienne to resolve the issue of the Templars raised by Philip who wanted them suppressed in order to confiscate all their goods. In 1307, in just one night, Philip had all the French Templars accused of heresy and treason, arrested and tortured, even though since they were members of a religious order they were subject only to the Holy See's jurisdiction. Clement V, alas, too late, took judgment of the Knights of the Temple upon himself, but the only thing he obtained, after the order's dissolution in Vienne, was to avert the passing of all the monks' many goods into the hands of the king.

In Avignon, pontifical absolutism reached a climax because the Pope reserved the appointment to the major benefices for himself. As a consequence, the cathedral and conventual chapters ceased to elect their own bishops and abbots; now they were all chosen by the Pope. Moreover, the Pope was in urgent need of money because the pontifical state was in constant turmoil. Moreover, the city of Avignon needed to be equipped with buildings worthy of the most important court in the west. From a pastoral point of view, the solution was devastating he decided to place a tax on every ecclesiastical act. To the fiscalization of the Church the Popes added the *commendam*[15] and the cumulation of ecclesiastical offices: whoever was charged with covering any office had to anticipate one year's worth of the annexed benefice's income as down payment to the Holy See[16]. Consequently, only the wealthy had access to ecclesiastical

---

[15] *Commendam* is the awarding of temporary control over a benefice to a clergyman who has already been awarded permanent control over another benefice.

[16] Before the Protestants, Jacobines and Liberals had expropriated the Church of all its goods, the Church was accustomed to assign a benefice to

offices. And since someone able to anticipate a year's benefice of a certain office is generally also able to anticipate the benefices for many other offices (sometimes tens of them, if not hundreds), a single prelate found himself charged with an infinite amount of duties. The solution to the obvious impossibility of performing all the pastoral duties assumed was to appoint vicars and vicars' vicars.

Nationalism, centralization of power, tax regime, *commendam*, cumulation of offices: this was the burdensome heritage of the "Avignon captivity."

Twenty-fourth daughter

Co-patron of Rome, Patron of Italy, patron saint of Europe, doctor of the Church, her body venerated in Rome's basilica of Santa Maria sopra Minerva, her head in Siena's basilica of Saint Dominic: Catherine of Siena (1347-1380) was the twenty-fourth daughter of a family of dyers and had a life full of ecstasies and mystical revelations. In the first, which happened when she was seven years old, she saw Jesus who gave her a beautiful nuptial ring which only she could see. She had a life full of penance, a life virtually without sleep, spent many years eating only the body of Christ, was a tireless nurse who cared for those struck with the plague with indomitable courage, an illiterate woman who asked the Holy Spirit to teach her to read and write and who dictated without hesitation a perfect theological treatise about the *Dialogue on Divine Providence*, a saint who five years before dying received the stigmata.

She was a Dominican tertiary who was put under trial because of her excessive discrepancy from common life. Her humble and hidden life was turned completely upside down by her obedience to the Lord's command. After having shown her paradise, the Lord told her: "You shall not lead the life you have led until now, your cell shall not be your normal dwelling place; instead, for the good of many souls, you shall have to leave even your own city"; "I shall place in your mouth a wisdom which no one can resist. I shall lead you before Popes, the leaders of churches and of the Christian people so that by

---

each ecclesiastical office, that is, an income meant to allow a clergyman to support himself and perform the duties entrusted to him.

means of the weak, as I am used to doing, I may humble the pride of the strong." Catherine obeyed and from that moment onwards she led a life of untiring witness before Popes and cardinals, captains and lords, kings and queens. From a historical point of view, Catherine's greatest merit was to successfully convince Gregory XI to put an end to the scandal caused by the Avignon papacy and return to Rome. "And do not delay anymore," she wrote to the Pope, "for because of your delay many inconveniences have occurred, and the devil has risen up and is putting pressure to stop this from happening"; "I pray you, be manly in carrying out what you must, and have fear of God"; "Come, come, now. Do not pose further resistance to the will of God who is calling you"; I tell you, on behalf of Christ crucified, "rip out from the Holy Church's garden all the smelly flowers, full of garbage and greed, bloated with pride, that is to say, the bad pastors and rectors which are intoxicating and putrefying this garden"; " Throw them out, that they may never govern"; "Plant flowers that are full of scent, pastors and governors that are true servants of Jesus Christ"; "Be a virile man and do not be fearful. Answer God who is calling you to come to take and possess the place of the glorious and holy pastor Peter, whose vicar you are"; "And look, though you fear for your life, do not come with the strength of people, but with the cross in hand, like a meek lamb. By so doing, you shall do the will of God; but if you come in any other way, you will trespass it"; "Come on Father, be a man! I am telling you that there is nothing to fear. If you were not to do what you should, then you should fear! You must come. Come then." These were some of the expressions Catherine used to address Gregory XI, thereby exhorted to imitate the courage of the great Pope whose name he carried.

Catherine's presence in Avignon, the letters, the prayers, gave this man Gregory XI courage, of which he did not have much, overcoming all opposition posed by the prelates and the court which in Avignon led quite a comfortable life. On January 17, 1377, the Pope made his entrance into Rome. Little more than a year after, he died. What to do? Who should be elected Pope? For the sake of decency, the choice had to fall on a Pope which if not Roman, at least was Italian: this is what the people shouted at the cardinals gathered in conclave: "Romano lo volemo o almanco italiano" (We want him Roman or at least Italian). A prelate from Naples was elected, well known among the French cardinals because he had spent much time in Avignon: Bartolomeo Prignano, archbishop of Bari, who took up the name Urban VI. Once he became Pope, Urban decided to put things in order and to begin his pontificate with attitudes and provisions radically contrary to the expectation of his electors. The cardinals did not think about it twice and decided to proceed to the invalidation of Prignano's election on the basis that it was not free since it was conditioned by the roman people's unrest. The rebellious deposed the Pope and elected a military man in his stead, cousin of the king of France, Robert of Genevieve who took up the name of Clement VII. It's the year 1378 and the great schism began: the only schism in the history of the Church, which did not take place for theological reasons but exclusively for political reasons. Behind Robert there was France which did not want to lose the opportunity of having a French Pope residing in France.

In the last two years of her life, Catherine spared no effort to support the Pope and call the cardinals to perform their duty: "Now you have turned your backs as vile and miserable knights: it was your own shadow that gave you fright," she wrote *To Three Italian Cardinals*. You have abandoned truth and chosen deceit: "What was the cause? The poison of self-love which poisons the world. It has transformed you, the columns, into something worst than hay. Not flowers giving a good scent, but a stench and you have filled the whole world with your stench"; "you have taken the office of demons"; "You are worthy of punishment: in truth I tell you (and thus I unload my conscience), if you do not return with true humility to obedience, this punishment will fall upon you."

Western schism

The so-called Western schism or Great schism lasted for almost 40 years (from 1378 to 1417) and was a time of utter devastation. The Church was split in two for purely political reasons, alliances or enmities between states. On the one hand, all the enemies of France were allied with Rome, that is to say the empire, England, Flanders, central and northern Italy, Hungary, the Scandinavian kingdoms, Poland, Portugal, Ireland. On the other hand were those who sided with France and the Avignon papacy: the House of Savoy, Scotland, Naples, later on also Spain (the successor of Clement, Pedro de Luna, was a Spaniard) and Sicily. Not only the states, but the same religious orders also split in two following the juxtaposed obediences: Dominicans, Franciscans, Cistercians, Carmelites, and the Carthusians.

Two obediences, two Popes, two colleges of cardinals, two courts, the religious orders duplicated along two different leaderships, exorbitant taxes to wage war on each other and prevail over the enemy obedience. The Pope's leeway to move was quite reduced because he needed to obtain or keep the support of kings, princes and emperors. In this chaotic situation, when roman universality exploded and therefore pontifical authority was undermined, a conception prevailed which bordered on heresy, if it was not completely heretical, and it acquired increasing credibility and importance because of the absolute uniqueness of that historical moment.

The solution to the west's drama, now split in two, came from the intellectuals, the university students in Paris, the theologians and jurists. They were convinced that because of the knowledge they possessed, they were the only ones able to pull the whole of society, and the Church, out of the tangled situation it was in. It was in these years, that for the first time in history, a new power took center stage, that is the power of the organized intellectual world; the power of the university. Amidst general confusion, scholars developed solutions aimed to bring to an end the war that for decades juxtaposed France and England[17], and to bring the papacy back to normality. In blatant

---

[17] The Hundred Years War broke out between France and England (1337-1453) after the fall of the House of Capet. Intellectuals favored the idea of forming a strong state encompassing both sides of the English Channel, that is, a grand English monarchy which would swallow up the French monarchy. In 1420, the project inspired by the university almost came to fruition when the king of France Charles VI, a mad man, signed the peace of Troyes with the king of England. In this treaty, he subscribed to the effective end of the French monarchy: upon his death, kingship would have passed to England, whose king Henry V had married Charles' daughter Catherine. However, the plan these university students had set forth was upset by a seventeen-year-old shepherd, a young girl who heard the voice of the archangel Michael order her to lead the French army against

contrast to tradition, canon law and the authority of Peter which was established by Jesus himself, feigning that there was doubt as to which obedience was the true one, the jurists in Paris took into account only the exceptional nature of the moment and by this reason developed a revolutionary theory: the schism can be resolved convoking a general council. Is the Pope's consent necessary to do so? This issue is blatantly disregarded because the council's authority not only is superior to the Pope's but only it is also truly infallible. Behold the birth of a new doctrine: Conciliarism.

To solve the issues generated by the schism, many cardinals belonging to both obediences in 1409 met in Pisa. There they excommunicated the two enthroned Popes as "manifest schismatics and heretics" and proceeded to elect a new Pope. The single result they obtained was that instead of two, now they had three obediences. The only way out of this chaos came through the ability and determination of Sigismund of Luxemburg. The son of Charles IV, he took up the proper function of the emperor as protector of the Church once again. He did so by obtaining the abdication of all three Popes and the convocation of a council in Constance (1414-1417). Here Oddone Colonna was elected, Pope Martin V. The Church's unity was finally restored. However, the Avignon experience and the schism which lasted 40 years were not all useless. In Constance, the voting method changed from per capita, as was the custom, to by nation (Italian, Franch, German, English, and Spanish). In Constance, almost everybody had the right to vote independently of their ecclesiastical office: even the university doctors and representatives of princes could vote. Two decrees were approved, both manifestly

---

the English and the Burgundians. Joan of Arc convinced a reluctant Charles, son of Charles VI, to go to war. She led the army to victory and thus made it possible for the new king, Charles VII to receive the crown in Rheims. The reward which awaited Joan was the stake. Submitted to harsh interrogations, the Maid of Orleans was unshakable. She was only 19 years old, she was alone, despised and ridiculed, but not once did she contradict herself. Nonetheless, her condemnation was merciless: death for heresy. Her last words were for the person to whom she dedicated her life and whose call she faithfully followed: Jesus. She was canonized in 1920 by Benedict XV and now Joan is the patron saint of France.

heretical and never acknowledged by Popes: *Haec Sancta* and *Frequens*[18]. At the close of the council, Martin V signed individual accords with each nation. The start of this custom was an acknowledgement of the Church's need to take note of the differing features of each national Church subject to different kings. The nations had won.

Renaissance papacy

While the Council of Constance came to an end, in Florence, Brunelleschi had begun building the dome of Santa Maria del Fiore and the Spedale degli Innocenti in the Annunciata square. The world turned the page; the perspective changed: man must be the starting point. Man. Not God. A new way of perceiving life burst through aggressively, bringing new styles, new priorities, and new aesthetic canons. It meant the return to Classic Greco-Roman art models, their elegance, sobriety and measure; a stark contrast with Gothic art viewed as barbaric. Brunelleschi always used perspective in his paintings, that is, the technique that places the human eye's point of view at the center. Philology, Philosophy, the recovery of ancient texts all became a real mania, favored by a massive exodus towards Florence and other parts of Italy of a flood of scholars in flight from the imminent fall of Byzantium. The Age of Humanism was beginning; an absolute novelty, a different way of life that from Italy spread to all Europe.

Meanwhile, the drama of a crumbling Roman Empire in the East came to its final consummation. The Muslims placed Constantinople under siege a first time in 697 and by 1453 it was finally vanquished. The empire had held off for seven hundred and fifty years. Mohammed II, who, "in order to guarantee world order," had commanded each sultan to kill all his brothers, ultimately conquered,

---

[18] The decree *Haec Sancta* also reads: "This synod, legitimately gathered in the name of the Holy Spirit, is indeed a General Council, represents the Catholic Church and receives power directly from Christ which whoever, of any state or condition, including whoever is raised to papal dignity, must obey in matters of Faith and for all that has to do with the eradication of the schism." The decree *Frequens*, instead, obliged the Pope to convoke councils in regular and frequent time intervals.

plundered and destroyed the second Rome. After the death of George Castriot, known as Skanderbeg (1405-1468), "Christ's athlete," the genius and heroic military commander who, despite the vast military disproportion, starting from Albania, for over twenty years held back the Islamic invasion, the Turks overran the Balcanic Peninsula and threatened Hungary. By 1516 they conquered also Hungary and from there launched the first siege against Wien. The fall of Wien opened the way to Rome, the eagerly yearned seal on world conquest.

However, while in the East there was nothing but defeat, in the West there was victory: the whole of the Iberian Peninsula was freed from Islam. In Portugal there was a singular man. Though he was not king, he exerted a greater influence than the king, his nephew: Prince Henry the Navigator, Grand Master of the Order of Christ, a military order established in 1319 to incorporate the goods of the recently suppressed Templar Knights. Henry was vastly resourceful and ambitious: he established the very first naval school in the world and planned the exploration and occupation of the African coastline. The inspiring motivation was to surround Islam from the south and overcome the Turks through alliance with the mythical "Prester John" who was thought to reign in Ethiopia.

In this context, the first humanist Pope, Nicholas V in 1454, a year after the carnage of Bysantium, addressed a bull to the Portuguese King and his uncle Henry, the true holder of Portugal's power. The Bull *Romanus Pontifex* which was written "without any entreaty on the part of King Alphonse," legitimized all present or future conquests made in Africa against Saracens and pagans, and sanctioned their enslavement. The document is unique not only because it gives witness to the great power still held by the papacy despite all past issues, but above all for its content. Besides the desire to spread the faith, what is most striking is the longing to pay back the Saracens in kind, without in the least taking account of the kind of love imposed by Christ upon his friends. Moreover, it put pagans and Muslims on the same plane[19].

---

[19] Without even accounting for the development in Canon Law. Starting from the middle of the 12th century with Gratian, it excluded infidels from the Church's jurisdiction. The thesis of the *Decretum Gratiani* was confirmed a century later by the jurist Sinibaldo de Fieschi, or Pope Innocent IV (1243-1254): the Church has no jurisdiction over the infidels because they are not

Below are some excerpts from this bull: "The Roman Pontifex, successor of he to whom the keys of the heavenly kingdom were entrusted, and vicar of Jesus Christ, looking with fatherly interest over all regions of the world and on the particular characters of all people dwelling therein, yearning and exerting every effort for the salvation of each one, wisely orders and sets forth after careful consideration that which he knows is pleasing to His Divine Majesty, by which he can lead the flock entrusted to him by divine command, the Lord's only flock, and thus acquire for it the merits of eternal happiness and also obtain forgiveness for their souls. And we believe that, with God's help, this may more surely obtained if, through special favors and privileges, we reward those catholic kings and princes who we are sure, as athletes and fearless defenders of the Christian Faith, will not only blunt the fierceness of Saracens and other faithless enemies of Christians, but also conquer kingdoms and lands, though these be located in the most remote and unknown of places, placing them under their temporal dominion for the defense and greatness of the same Faith, without caring for hardships and riches. Thus removing every possible obstacle, those kings and princes, may be ever more encouraged to continue carrying out such a praiseworthy and salvation-bearing cause"; thus said, Nicholas granted King Alphonse, "Full and complete power to invade, search out, capture, conquer and subdue all Saracens and all pagans and all other enemies of Christ, wherever they might live, together with their kingdoms, dukedoms, principalities, seigniories, estates and whatever other movable or immovable properties in their possession, to place them in perpetual slavery and occupy, take possession, use and turn these kingdoms, dukedoms, counties, principalities, seigniories, estates and goods to profit for themselves and their successors"; "The same persons, King Alphonse, his successors and the Enfante, may establish, have established and build churches, monasteries and other sacred places in all provinces, islands and districts conquered in the past or future; they may also send any clergyman, such as volunteers, lay people and also regular members of some mendicant order (granted their

---

baptized. Innocent was the Pope who promoted the evangelization of the Mongols by the Franciscans (Giovanni da Pian del Carpine) and Dominicans.

superiors' permission), and these may dwell there for all their lives, receive confession from any indigenous or foreign person dwelling in those districts, after which they may proceed to granting absolution for all cases except those reserved to the Holy See as well as deliver a beneficial penance and therefore give out the Sacraments."

Besides the lands, Nicholas granted patronage over conquered lands to the king of Portugal and his heirs: by pontifical delegation, they will be responsible for handling all issues related to the Church and its organization. This was the style of the renaissance papacy. Often, the papacy was held by members of great Italian families, patrons, lovers of luxury, of beauty and of culture, who filled their lives with beauty and luxury not only for their personal pleasure and family prestige, but also, or at least so they say, to give glory to God through art's magnificence.

The case of Enea Silvio Piccolomini, Pius II (1458-1464) is emblematic. His family, on his mother's side, boasted of being descendants of the gens Iulia, whose ancestor was Aeneas, son of Venus; hence the peculiar baptismal name. Once Pope, Aeneas took on the name of Pius, the name by which he is remembered. A cultured man, a courtesan, a diplomat, his activities included also literature. He transformed Corsignano, his town of birth, into Pienza, one of the first experiments carried out to build the ideal city. While he attempted with scarce success to unite the forces of the Christian west against the Turks, he wrote a letter to the Sultan Mohammed II persuading him to convert so that he could be crowned emperor of the Eastern Roman Empire.

Spain is ready

In order to comprehend how a nation so scarcely populated conquered, colonized, taught the language (Spanish) and converted to the faith (Catholic) men of so boundless and far-off a continent (America), one should ask oneself what kind of men were those who carried out this endeavor. To do so, we'll turn to Theresa of Avila's (1515-1582) biography. Theresa is known as "the great." Therefore, the events of her personal life cannot be taken as an example of a normal existence. Well, maybe not her life; what about her family's? Absolutely.

"My father loved to read good books and kept some in the common language so that also his children might read them. This reading, together with the great care my mother placed in making us pray and nurturing devotion toward Our Lady as well as towards some saints, began to awaken my devotion around the age, it seems to me, of about six or seven years. It was a great help to me that my parents favored nothing but virtue. They possessed many. My father was a man full of charity towards the poor, pity towards the sick and even towards the servants: to the point that no one ever managed to make him have a slave." The difference between this family's father and Nicholas V could not be starker. Theresa continues: "Once, having to keep a slave at home which belonged to his brother, he treater her with the same affection he used towards his own children and said that, that creature deprived of freedom inspired in him an irresistible pity"; "We were three sisters and nine brothers: by the grace of God, in virtue, all resembled the parents except for me." Theresa loved all of them but had a special care for one brother, "almost of my own age whom I loved more than the others and with whom I often read the lives of the saints. Seeing the torments the saints suffered for God [...] I intensely longed to die as they did [...] And so I took counsel with this brother so that together we might find a way to reach this our objective. We planned to go begging to Moorish lands so that there, they might cut off our heads."

One night, Theresa and her brother put their plan in action and escaped from home. They did not get very far because the next day they were captured just outside Avila, where a boundary stone memorializes their escape: "Since it became impossible for us to go where they would kill us in the name of God, we decided to become hermits. So, we tried as best as possible in our home's garden to build some hermitages by piling up some small stones, but they would tumble over immediately."

Theresa and her brother had a dream: to die as martyrs and quickly go to heaven with Jesus. Though only a child's dream, it speaks volumes about the environment they grew up in. A holy home, where what really mattered was to be pleasing to God. In fact, since 711, a date which marked the beginning of Islam's invasion, to 1492, for many centuries, Spain, the Spaniards had one mission for which and by which they were forged: to kick out the Islamic invaders. To bring Spain, the whole of Spain back to the faith. Spaniards reached their objective with great resolve and heroic perseverance. In fact, the persecutions unleashed against them periodically were bloody. We must also keep in mind, that Spain is the only instance of a land, at one time Roman, which managed to keep the faith and reconquer its freedom despite centuries of Islamic domination.

Let's take a step back. During the 15th century, after Avignon, the schism, the whole issue of the tax regime-*commendam*-office cumulation, if the Church had not reformed, it was destined to disappear. But it did in fact reform itself. The reform began in Italy, to be more precise, in the monastery of Santa Giustina in Padua where a group of Venetian patricians, following Ludovico Barbo, in 1419 began a profound renewal of the Benedictine observance which then spread to the rest of the peninsula. The other pole where the reform took foot was Spain: here, the profound change took place under the impulse of certain exceptional personalities, first amongst them was Queen Isabella of Castile (1451-1504) who married Ferdinand of Aragon in 1469. The "Catholic Kings," title conferred by Pope Alexander VI, the Spaniard Roderic Borgia, united Spain which had been divided into various kingdoms and completed the *Reconquista* in 1492 with the fall of Granada. Isabel and Ferdinand anticipated by a century the reform which the Council of Trent (1545-1563) extended to the whole Church: they chose bishops who were irreprehensible, learned, who dedicated themselves to the preaching; they imposed on them that they should reside in their own diocese; they eliminated all tax regimes, cumulation of church offices and *commendam*; they promoted university and cultural foundations.

Isabel's right hand man was the cardinal primate of Spain, Francisco Jimenez de Cisneros. He was a Franciscan, an anchorite, with no ambitions of ever holding any position of power, and once he was called to cover the vertex of the Spanish church, was inflexible in imposing the reform on the clergy: he put an end to concubinage, set up residence in the parishes, made the Sunday preaching mandatory. The entire Spanish Church was regenerated. Conscious of the importance of culture, Cisneros established the Complutense University of Alcalà and financed the compiling of the Polyglot Bible which contained Hebrew, Latin, Greek and Aramaic texts in adjacent columns.

Isabel financed Columbus' expedition and when in 1492 the three caravels touched land in Santo Domingo, setting foot ashore, Columbus planted the cross. Spain was ready: forged by centuries of battles for freedom and for the faith, Spaniards channeled their missionary zeal, their resourcefulness and their strength into the administration and evangelization of the pagan peoples whose existence had just been discovered.

Inter Caetera

While Portugal was setting off on its first colonial ventures, not having yet completed the reconquest, Spain lagged behind. By the end of the 15th century when the whole of Spain was freed and Columbus discovered America, this rapidly changed. To avoid conflicts between Spain and Portugal, the problem emerged about how to mark the boundaries of their respective areas of influence. What to do? Alexander VI solved the problem in 1493 with the bull *Inter Caetera*. After commending the kings for their faith and their accomplishments ("you have set yourself the goal, by the favor of divine clemency, to place said continents and islands with their residents and inhabitants under your influence and to lead them to the catholic faith"), the Pope guaranteed possession of all lands discovered or to be discovered to the south and west of a particular meridian to the Spanish crown: "If one of your envoys and captains were to find any of these islands, this forever gives, ensures and assigns to you and to your heirs and succeeding kings of Castile and León all the islands and continents – with all their dominions, cities, fields, places and villages as well as all rights, jurisdictions and connected privileges – found and yet to be found west and south, tracing a line from the Artic pole, that is, from the north, to the Antarctic pole, that is, to the south."

Alexander's idea worked because ultimately, Spain and Portugal respected the Pope's decision. With this bull, the Pope guaranteed for Spain the very same patronage privileges that Nicholas V had granted to Portugal: we command you, in virtue of holy obedience, "for said islands to appoint men who are brave, fear God, are educated, resourceful and expert in order to instruct said inhabitants and residents in the catholic faith and to educate them in good morals."

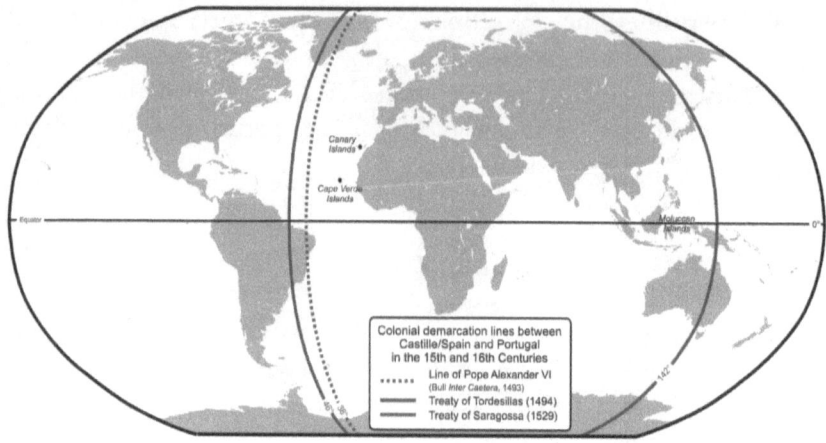

What was the situation the Spaniards found upon their landing in America? One particular aspect of Native American life really caused them to shudder to the bone: entire groups of people dominated by the terror of being captured and sacrificed to the god sun that was believed to need their hearts offered in sacrifice in order to continue shining. The amazing Mayan and Aztec temples served this purpose exactly. At the top of the Ziggurat's enormous steps was the altar where victims were sacrificed. Their chest was cut open with a knife designed to extract the heart while it was still beating. Around the altar was a drainage channel designed to allow the vast quantities of blood to flow downwards. The spectacle of these human sacrifices is represented in pre-Columbian artifacts: the hacking, the carnage, the blood spraying everywhere. In our times, some have tried to justify this world of horror by offering as an excuse that the lack of proteins typical of the Native American diet necessarily imposed the use of human flesh[20].

---

[20] It seems incredible but that is exactly what Professor Aldo Rullini wrote on November 25, 1998 in *La Stampa*, a newspaper renown for its seriousness. Mexico and its surroundings, reads Rullini's full-page article with title *Maya, cannibali per necessità (Maya, cannibals by necessity)*, "lacked

The figures show, that the total number of Spaniards who arrived in America between 1509 and 1559, were 27,787, decidedly few in contrast to the size of the continent. However, though they were so few in numbers, the Spanish successfully accomplished the prodigious endeavor of colonizing the whole continent, convert it, and teach Spanish to practically everyone. Certainly, the Spaniards were very clever to exploit the rivalries existing among the different peoples. But above all, they preached everywhere the good news of a God who does not demand human victims and who instead offered himself as a victim for our iniquity.

The catholic kings took the task entrusted to them by the Pope very seriously and they sent the best forces available: the most zealous Dominicans, Franciscans and in turn, Jesuits. Kings and religious orders made a gargantuan effort to spread the faith and culture among the Indios: it would suffice to say that in Mexico alone, at the end of the 16th century, more than three hundred convents had been built and that each monastery ran a school where hundreds of Indios were instructed; suffice it to say that the university in Mexico City was established in 1552, only thirty years after the Spaniards' arrival. Just as the Roman church had evangelized and Latinized all barbarian peoples, likewise the Spanish church evangelized Latinizing. Latin America is what it will be called.

---

proteins", because "there were very few domestic animals that were eatable." Therefore, Mayans and Aztechs, "to satisfy their physiological need had no choice but to sacrifice many prisoners and to do so needed to organize incursions and wars. [...] The end of every raid was celebrated with great popular feasts in which hundreds or even thousands of prisoners were killed on the altars placed at the top of the pyramids." The decapitated bodies would then be "dismembered, distributed and eaten." Rullini stressed that, "these mass sacrifices, as frequent and numerous as they were, were not able to satisfy the entire people's protein demand," and so he even dared to give further detail: "What mattered was that the leading social class, the priests and military men could benefit from these proteins." This quote, from such a shameful article, published shamelessly by a serious newspaper, gives the measure of the enormity of the hate surrounding the history of catholic Spain. A hate, so great, that it makes the intellect obtuse.

Theodor de Bry (1528-1598), a Belgian engraver and editor, continued the Lutheran propaganda against the Church of Rome, telling of some supposed crimes committed by Spanish Catholics in America. This is how, from the 16th century, the black legend against Catholic Spain began.

Spanish preaching had some help from heaven which made it very credible. Mary, the *morenita*, as she was called because of her skin color, appeared to the Indio Juan Diego in Guadalupe in 1531. Only fourteen year after Suarez's landing in Mexico. Mary had him ask the local bishop to build a basilica on the place of the apparition and as proof of her real presence there, she impressed the image of her face and body on Diego's *tilma* – the Native American robe. As in the book of Revelation, Our Lady is depicted "dressed with the sun and with the moon under her feet," while a splendid dress hides a bloating underneath her hands to show that the Virgin is pregnant with her American children. The liberation, the happiness produced by the encounter with the Savior and His mother; these were at the origin of that completely novel artistic phenomenon which was art in Latin America. The Queen from heaven appeared dressed with delicate pastel colors full of light. These are the colors which since then are the distinctive feature of popular Latin-American art.

Our Lady Of Guadalupe

Do Indios have a soul?

When Europe found out about the religious customs of the newly discovered peoples, the reactions were of horror. From the university, the learned even asked themselves whether or not such barbaric people had a soul. Consequently, they also asked if such people could be legitimately reduced to slavery according to the famous doctrine of Aristotle about natural slavery. Among those who believed the Indios did not have a soul were also some religious, and among these, the renowned Scottish philosophy professor in Paris, John Mair. Obviously, the divine revelation made in *Genesis* which defines man – every man – as made in the image and likeness of God, in certain university circles and in certain religious circles was deemed unreasonable or even an exaggeration.

It was not until Isabel intervened commandingly that the problem was solved. When Columbus, quite pleased with himself, brought back a load of the continents' produce, including a sizable representation of young Indios reduced to slavery, Isabel reacted with gross indignation, and though the admiral was full of honors and merits, she had him incarcerated and sent the ship back with her human cargo richly compensated for the pain endured. In 1504, when writing her last will and testament, Isabel reaffirmed her will to protect the Indios: I command "it is not to be tolerated or allowed that the indigenous people of the islands or the mainland, conquered or to be conquered suffer the least wrongdoing in their persons or in their goods, but it is to be commanded instead that they be treated with justice and humanity. Moreover, any wrongdoing they might have suffered must be repaired." Isabel had faith, and it was her faith that made her side without hesitation in defense of the Indios: No one must be enslaved just as no one is to be deprived of their property. In obedience to Isabel's will, the Spanish crown kept faith to this commitment for centuries to come.

Alas, the official church, that is, the Popes took action all too late. We saw Nicholas V's bull already. It was only after Paul III became Pope and wrote the brief *Pastorale Officium* in 1537, that there was a clear condemnation of slavery: "Because [the Indios] are men, and therefore capable of faith and salvation. They must not be brought to the destruction which slavery is." Reality is often not how one would like and certainly many Spaniards took advantage of the situation by harshly oppressing the indigenous population. However, the Spanish crown was always ready to hear the religious who returned home from America to denounce the abuses perpetrated against the Indios and never stopped trying to find way to limit the damages. Ferdinand I, after appointing a commission of theologians and jurists, in 1512 published the Laws of Burgos and the following year, those of Valladolid. These provided measures of tutelage over the work of children and women as well as guaranteed the right to retribution. In 1542, Charles V did the same. To fathom the unique nature of these provisions, one need only think that Europe itself, and not some far-off isle, waited until 18th century England to witness any attempt to curb the exploitation of the poorer population reduced to misery by the protestant reformation and the industrial revolution.

In Spain, the American continent's colonization was accompanied by an intense cultural debate over the legitimacy of the conquest. This is also a unique feature because all other present and future colonial powers never behaved in the same way. Universities, convents, the most influential people, all questioned themselves about the moral permissibility of the war fought beyond the ocean; about the proper behavior with respect to the American "barbarians"; about whether or not human sacrifices should be tolerated. Among the differing positions, one is of extreme interest because it was decidedly groundbreaking in how it viewed the proper powers of the Pope and the emperor: it was the view of the Dominican Francisco de Vitoria (1492-1546), the founder of international right. A thinker of supreme clarity, de Vitoria established that Christian princes cannot fight against barbarians (*etiam authoritate papae*: not even under the Pope's authorization) just because they commit sins against nature (Christian emperors, in fact, never waged war on pagans only because they did not want to convert); he claimed that the Pope had no jurisdiction over the infidels (the people of Israel never waged war on other people because of their infidelity or because of sins committed against nature); that war may never be justified by reason of the evangelization; and that weakness is never a valid reason to deprive someone of freedom or of the right to hold property because every man is "by nature the image of God."

With regards to human sacrifice, the view held was quite different. For de Vitoria, in this case, the Spaniards had the obligation to intervene because God would ask each one to give account of his neighbor (*"Unicuique mandavit Deus de proximo suo"*, *Sirach* 17,12) and also because one had to prevent the innocent from being condemned to an injust death ("Rescue those who are being taken away to death; hold back those who are stumbling to the slaughter," thus the *Book of Proverbs*). De Vitoria was quite convinced that barbarians were not in the least free to hand themselves or their children over to death (*Non ita sunt sui iuris, ut possent seipsos vel filios suos trader ad mortem*). For the rest, de Vitoria supported the right to free commerce, to free navigation, to the occupation of uninhabited lands and once colonized, to the right of defending them.

One final episode shows God tenderness towards the Indios: at the turn of the 17th century, a few religious tried to evangelize the tribes dwelling in northern Mexico but they encountered a very violent reaction; so the wonder was truly great when in 1622, a group of especially hostile Indians showed up at a convent to ask the priests there to administer the sacraments to them. They told of a "lady, dressed in blue" who catechized them and convinced them about the truth of the Gospel by means of many miracles. The lady in blue was the Spanish mystic Maria de Jesus de Agreda (1602-1665) who never ever, except through bilocation, moved out her convent.

Martin Luther

Mid-way through the second millennium lived a man who changed the course of history: Martin Luther (1483-1546). The Church's reform in Italy and Spain progressively spread throughout Europe. In Germany, however, it did not have a real impact on society. The leaders of the Church, bishops and abbots were all part of the nobility. Moreover, the riches accumulated in time were truly great: according to certain estimates, about 1/3 of the nation's riches were handled by the Church. In the 10th century, Otto I had established a new institution, the Count Bishop, and the praxis of having Prince-electors appoint three bishops (for the dioceses of Cologne, Mainz and Trier) who had the right to vote in the emperor's election. This caused the German church to play a pivotal role in the civil, economic, cultural and spiritual order of the nation; a nation which kept the roman imperial tradition; a nation, therefore, which constituted the heart of the west.

The implicit nationalism hidden behind the choice of Avignon, in Germany produced a unique type of humanism in that it itself assumed a nationalistic color. In fact, the humanist Ulrich von Hutten, a poet and knight, to exalt the German peoples' heroism, which he claimed had been constantly undermined by Rome in both its pagan and pontifical versions, wrote the *Arminius*, the name of the hero who in 9 A.D. annihilated the roman legions led by Publius Quinctilius Varus in the midst of the Teutoburg forest. Germany wanted to become the imperial nation again; it wanted to be first again. To do so, a part of Germany chose one man to be the nation's father, a man who in the name of the Bible and of the Gospel's purity spread loathing and hate against Rome. This man was Luther, an Augustinian monk. Luther's revolutionary life began in 1517: from that moment until his death this "German Moses" did everything possible to instill loathing for Rome and its history into the German people. We will quote some texts to illustrate the violence by which Luther conducted his campaign aimed at dismantling the German nation's Roman Catholic roots.

- In 1520 he wrote *To the Christian Nobility of the German Nation*: "Let us wake up, my dear Germans," he wrote. Let us awake and take conscience of the fact that Rome wants only to exploit us and makes demands which have no foundation in the Bible. Let us take conscience that Rome is the city of the Antichrist. That Satan is he who reigns in Rome: "They are cheating us"; "They have filled kings and princes with fear"; "Most of the Popes had no faith"; "Did not the Pope in many instances make mistakes?"; "In this battle, it is not men we are fighting, but the prince of hell." Luther addressed the princes because he wanted them to spear on the Church's reform. That same reform which clergymen never carried out, "because they have become completely unworthy." Why should it be the prince's prerogative to reform the Church? Because God and Luther so willed it: "Therefore, I hold that, since temporal authority has been preordained by God to protect the good and punish the evil, it should be left free to exercise its duty, so that it may penetrate undisturbed in the whole body of Christendom, without having to face anyone, neither a Pope, a bishop, a priest, a friar, a monk or anyone else"; "his [the prince's] office and his work, which he has received from God above anyone else, must proceed freely where it may be useful and necessary to intervene."

By the stroke of a pen, Luther erased centuries of battles fought by the spiritual authority to keep itself free of the temporal authority. The *Libertas Ecclesiae* was undermined at its very root because suddenly, "Give back to Caesar that which is Caesar's and to God that which is God's," became give to Caesar that which is Caesar's and give him also that which is God's. Luther gave princes boundless power. Yet, he never ceased to proclaim and write the word "freedom" like a mantra. What did he mean when he spoke of freedom? Freedom from Rome. Freedom from the Pope's spiritual authority: "We must become daring and free and not allow the Pope's false words to mortify the spirit of freedom." Freedom for the princes. Freedom only for the princes.

- In 1521 he published the *Passional Christi und Antichristi*: a series of twenty-six woodcuts created by one of the greatest German painters, Lucas Cranach the Elder. By means of simple and clear images, it was meant to show the poorly educated people who the Pope was, that is, the antichrist. Luther and Cranach's collaboration lasted for decades and contributed significantly to the Reform's success. If on the one hand Luther destroyed icons, frescoes and statues venerated by Catholics because he deemed them superstitious and impure, on the other hand, he was well aware of the value of images. Therefore, he created a new model of icons, which served to effectively and incisively teach people about the true nature of the Pope and the Roman Church: "These images are my last testament," he told his friend Wanckel;
- in 1522 he published the German translation of the New Testament enriched with illustrations: the dragon with seven heads and ten horns from the *Book of Revelation* was identified

with the Pope and his court while Babylon's fall was sketched as the destruction of Saint Peter and Castel Sant'Angelo;
- in 1523, together with Melanchton, he published the pamphlet *The Pope-Ass Explained*;
- from 1534 all editions of the German Bible were published containing images illustrating *Lutheran theses about Rome and the papacy*;
- in 1545 he published *Against the Papacy at Rome Founded by the Devil* with annexed a new series of caricatures created once again by Cranach entitled *Depiction of the Papacy*.
- Protestant iconography was so effective that the French Revolution took it as a model for its own.

Lucas Cranach, *Birth and Origin of the Pope*

Lucas Cranach, *The Pope, God of this World, is Worshiped*

The greatest revolutionary of the Second Millennium

These were the main features of the reformed creed:

- Luther stressed the equality of all faithful. The sacraments are three (Baptism, Penance, and Eucharist), therefore the Holy Orders is not a sacrament. Within the Church there are no privileged functions, all Christians are equal: universal priesthood;
- salvation comes only through faith, not through works. The will of man is enslaved, he wrote in 1525 in *De Servo Arbitrio* in a debate with Erasmus who one year earlier had written *De Libero Arbitrio*. Being a slave, man is not responsible for his actions. By what criteria then does God send some to hell and others to heaven? By double predestination: by his unquestionable

power, "by his universal action, God moves the will and thus man is compelled to want this or that, as God determines he should want and as he, by his power, drags him to carry out.";
- though Luther was a monk, he forbade the profession of religious vows (chastity, poverty, obedience) as they had been made until then, that is, forever. If someone really wanted to profess them, he should do so *pro tempore*. By so doing, Luther denied man the possibility of making any absolute choices. Choices made forever in view of heaven. On the contrary, the Church always encouraged these choices with respect to both marriage and the religious vocation: man is indeed able to carry out absolute choices because the divine grace connected to the sacrament plays in favor of his free will;
- the hierarchy was reduced to naught and all religious orders were erased. Thus the Church's goods suddenly lost their legitimate owners and by Luther's bidding, they were awarded to the princes. Luther's choice to privilege the princes in awarding the Church's goods unleashes civil war. Why princes (that is the first-borns) yes, and the others no? And the cadets? It was the Knights' war (1522-1523) in which, in the name of "German evangelical freedom," they claimed the right to share in the division of the Church's goods. Once the knights had been routed, princes had to face the peasants, that is, the people, who also mobilized in the name of German evangelical freedom. Pressed on both fronts, ultimately Luther decidedly embraced the princes' point of view and thus wrote a text of uncommon violence against the peasants: *Against the Murderous, Thieving Hordes of Peasants*. He called them "mad dogs," who had, "impiously looted convents and castles which did not belong to them," had covered "these crimes with the Gospel," and had wanted that "the goods of others would be held in common, all the while keeping their goods to themselves." Coherence is not one of Luther's strong points: the very same behavior which he reproached as distinctive of the peasantry, he strongly claimed as the God given right of princes. The war against the peasants lasted for two years (1524-1525) and caused the death of about 100,000 people. Chatting at table in the January of 1533, Luther claimed: "Preachers are the greatest murderers. In

fact, they exhort the authorities to use their office resolutely and at will in order to punish the harmful elements. During the uprising, I killed all the peasants, all their blood is on my head. But I throw it all on our Lord God because it was he who commanded me to speak as I did";
- "free interpretation": the magisterium should not exist as everyone may read and interpret Scripture with the assistance of the Holy Spirit. Sectarianism is inevitable;
- without a magisterium it makes no sense to speak about tradition: *Sola Scriptura*. But *Sola Scriptura* ignores all those passages that are in conflict with the Lutheran interpretation: the *Second Letter of Peter* is typical. The apostle seems *ante litteram* to deny the possibility of interpreting scripture individually: "Firstly, let this be known to you: no prophetic scripture should be subjected to private explanations, because no prophecy was ever created from the human will, but rather those men were moved by the Holy Spirit to speak on behalf of God";
- who were the princes who supported Luther? Mainly two: the prince-electors of Saxony and Phillip I, Landgrave of Hesse, called by Luther the "new Arminius." Phillip I was a man dominated by lust. At a point in his life, he tried to make his relationship with a young court damsel official by marrying her. However, Philip I was married to Christine of Saxony who was by no means at the bottom of the German social ladder. What could he do? The Landgrave of Hesse asked Luther to authorize a second, public wedding. The situation was quite delicate, and Luther's response was cautious: to make the second wedding public is out of discussion because it would be too great a scandal. Yet, considering the "needs set forth by his conscience," Philip I the Landgrave, "with his pastor's advice, may take another woman" and obtain a dispensation for a "supplementary marriage." However, Luther placed a condition, namely that the marriage should remain secret because the authorization was granted as "an opinion given in confession." Philip I married in the presence of Melanchton, but the marriage became public. The scandal was enormous. What did Luther do? His advice was to deny everything: "To say a necessary and useful lie that is helpful to you is not to go

against God, who on the contrary, quite willingly takes it upon imself." Luther didn't stop there; he transformed lying into a virtue: "It is a virtue if its aim is to achieve a goal that opposes the devil's evil, may save the honor, the life, and the benefit of a neighbor."

The Landgrave of Hesse case illustrates how Luther believed that the end justified the means. The enemy who must be annihilated is the Pope and roman court. Everything is allowed in order to achieve this goal, lies and slander included. We have already mentioned Leo XIII's opinion on history: "The science of history seems to be a conspiracy of men against the truth." From Luther onwards, protestant historiography is committed to assign all possible violence and iniquity to the Church of Rome (and to those who defended her such as, first and foremost, Spain): Protestantism aspired to win and build a new type of universality on the ashes of the roman world.

Lutheran doctrine brought the princes such enormous benefits, that Albert of Brandenburg decided to adhere to the reform. Albert was the grand master of the Teutonic Order, a military order established during the crusades and later charged by Frederick II to evangelize the Slav lands of Prussia and the Baltic Sea, in a way, these lands could be easily submitted to German domination. Albert of Hohenzollern, once a Lutheran, secularized in his favor all goods of the order, which he commanded and took up the hereditary title Duke of Prussia. This is the Prussia we are well acquainted with, the same Prussia which unified Germany and played a role of global importance from the 18th century until today. This same Prussia was born from the grand theft of all the goods which belonged to the Order of the Teutonic Knights performed by their very own grand master, Albert of Hohenzollern.

An abominable sin

It would be important here to discuss Luther's position with respect to Judaism because he is the father of the German nation and language and also because his thought deeply influenced German philosophy from Kant to Heidegger. In the first years of his ministry,

Luther was convinced that the Jews would have adhered to the pure Gospel he preached and would have converted to Christ. When this did not come about, Luther turned towards the Jews with the same hate he had for the Roman Catholic world. In 1543 he wrote *On the Jews and their Lies*: "Bloodthirsty bloodhounds and murderers of Christians everywhere for more than fourteen hundred years in their conscience and in their will, and they would undoubtedly prefer to be such with their deeds"; "Be on guard against the Jews, knowing that wherever they have their synagogue, nothing is found but a den of devils"; "As barbarian and cruel other people may have been, non-ever acted so criminally and sacrilegiously. No human being, no creature ever acted thus except for Satan, or whomever he possesses."

Luther asked himself: "What could we Christians do for the hateful and cursed Jewish people?" The answer came in seven articulate points termed as "beneficial counsels" (salutaria consilia in the Latin version):

- first: "It would be a useful thing that all their synagogues were burnt down, and if some ruin should be spared from the blaze, let it be covered with sand and mud in order that no one may ever again see a rock or a roof tile of those buildings";
- second: "Let their private homes also be destroyed. Indeed, what they do in synagogues, the very same they do at home";
- third: "Let them be deprived of all their prayer books and Talmudic texts wherein they teach idolatry, lies, stupidities and blasphemies";
- fourth: "Rabbis should be removed under pain of death from all teaching positions";
- fifth: "Throughout all provinces and dukedoms, Jews should be denied the public's trust and safe conducts." In this respect, as he had done many years before with the peasants, Luther promoted private vendettas: "If you princes and lords do not take the initiative to bar these loan sharks as is usual from public roads, then perhaps, some among the knights [...] could treat them as wildfowl in one of their horseback hunting outings";
- sixth: "By the most severe of decrees, the lords should forbid the Jews' usury and confiscate all the money they hold in cash,"

since "Everything they own is the fruit of their robberies and looting perpetrated by usury at our expense";
- seventh: "Jews, young and strong, men and women, must be subjected to labor; they must earn their bread with the sweat of their brow."

On the Jews and their Lies was nearly forgotten until it was printed again in 1936 by National Socialists. In his last sermon three days before dying, Luther took up the Jewish issue again: "We must not tolerate them," he said, because was cannot be made accomplices of their sins. The Jews are our "public enemies," and, "if they could kill us all, they would quite willingly do so; actually, they already often do so, especially those who pass themselves off as doctors." These were his last instructions: "Be therefore firm towards them for they know naught but to blaspheme our beloved Lord Jesus Christ in a most monstrous manner and wish to deprive us of our body, our life, our honor and our goods." And he concluded, I have wanted to warn you, "as a German."

Luther was defined *Hercules Germanicus* and *Propheta Germaniae*. He opened a new chapter in Germany's history: an anti-Catholic and anti-Roman chapter. A chapter filled with tragedy.

Charles V, Holy Roman Emperor

On his father's side he was the nephew of Maximillian I of the house of Hapsburg, Roman Emperor and of Mary of Burgundy, the last descendent for the duchy; on his mother's side he was the nephew of the Catholic kings Ferdinand and Isabel; the son of Philip, known as the Handsome and of Joanna known as the Mad, Charles V (1500-1558) was the king of Spain from 1516 and emperor from 1519. He held a boundless power: he reigned over Germany, Flanders, Burgundy, Southern Italy, Milan, Spain, America and even the Spanish estates in Northern Africa. He was Catholic and held a universal power almost like that of the Pope. After many centuries, he was the only one who held a power comparable to roman emperors and he was one of the few who wanted to use the power he wielded in defense of the Church from enemies internal and external, as the Edict of Thessalonica set forth in 380. During his reign, his enemies and those of the Church were many: Turks, Barbary pirates, Protestants. To these, we should also add Francis I of France. Though he was not an enemy of the Church, he was a fierce enemy of the emperor whose very existence threatened to make France irrelevant in the balance of power.

Among his adversaries were also some Popes. When he was elected emperor in 1519, the Pope was Leo X, the son of Lorenzo de' Medici belonging to the house of Medici, the powerful family of Florentine bankers who governed Florence and were traditional allies of France. Upon his death, Adrian VI was elected, a Flemish Pope and the last Pope who was not Italian until John Paul II. He had been the tutor of Charles V, led an ascetic life and as a strong proponent of Church reform, he identified most of the problems that the Church faced as stemming from the papacy and the roman curia. Unfortunately, Adrian died only a year after his election and was succeeded by Clement VII, another Medici and cousin of Leo X. For almost twenty years (1513-1533) the papacy was held by members of the richest and most influential family of the age. It was a renaissance papacy which distinguished itself by acting as a great patron of the arts, housing in its courts the greatest artists of the age. It was the kind of papacy which kept the family's interest very much at heart. Thus, the papacy was suspicious of Charles' power, though he was undoubtedly Catholic, and instead was quite in tune with Francis I, who in order keep Charles in check, did not hesitate to ally himself to the Church's enemies, namely, Turks and Protestants.

In 1520 Luther was excommunicated. The following year was called upon by Charles to go to Worms so that he could retract the heresies for which he was accused. Luther did not give in ("I cannot and will not retract because it is neither just nor beneficial to go against one's conscience. May God come to my aid. Amen"). The emperor, who was only twenty one years old, solemnly declared before the Imperial Diet: "You well know that I am the descendent of a long lineage of Christian emperors of this German nation, of the Catholic kings of Spain, of the Archdukes of Austria as well as the Dukes of Burgundy. They have all remained faithful to the Church of Rome even to death and have defended the Catholic faith and God's honor. I have chosen to follow in their footsteps. A single friar who goes against the whole of a thousand-year Christendom must certainly be in error. Therefore, I have chosen to risk my lands, my friends, my own body, blood, life and soul. And not only I, but also you members of this noble German nation; eternal shame would befall you if by your negligence, not only heresy, but the mere suspicion of heresy was to survive."

From then onwards, forced to stay away from Germany by the many wars he was fighting, Charles unceasingly asked the Popes to convoke a council that would address the Lutheran issue, make peace in Germany and so allow Germany to fight the Turks who had already occupied the greater part of Hungary and who in 1529 put Wien under siege. Francis I was staunchly opposed to calling a council because for him anything was better than a stronger Germany, and the Popes dreaded conciliarism. In the meanwhile, Rome's curia was very involved in politics, greedy for money, and made up of princes who spent their lives in sheer luxury, in hunting outings and pleasures of all sorts. The world-famous roman carnival is just an instance. The Popes refused to crown Charles emperor and so the emperor let the Landsknechts, soldiers who had passed to the reformation, rob, plunder and destroy Rome, killing and raping its inhabitants. It was the "Sack of Rome" of 1527. A real tragedy. An emperor who defended the Church and yet left Rome at the mercy of a band of enemy brigands. It seems to be an apparently irreconcilable contradiction. It is said that the papacy learned its lesson and that since that moment onwards, the curia began to change its habits. However, many years had yet to pass before the religious became the preeminent, if not exclusive, dimension in the life of the Popes and their court. The Palazzo Farnese is a perfect example: it was a palace commissioned by he who was to become Pope Paul III, built by the greatest architects of the time, including Michelangelo; though its construction was interrupted by the sack of Rome, it was immediately taken up again in 1541 and became the most beautiful building of the 16th century, has all its ceilings rigorously frescoed with pagan mythological scenes.

Despite the constant wars (four against the uncommonly treacherous Francis who right after signing a peace treaty would start fighting again), despite his efforts to stop the Turks and the Barbary pirates, Charles never managed to bring peace to Germany and put an end to the looting of Church possessions. In 1555 he signed the Peace of Augusta, by which he gave legal approval to protestant worship, decreed that all subjects should follow the religion of their princes (protestant absolutism won the day), and established the year 1552 as the *annus normalis*, that is, the year after which all looting of Church properties became forbidden. In 1556 he abdicated the throne: he gave the empire to his brother and everything else to his son Philip. In this way, the emperor officially acknowledged that it was not possible to serve as Holy Roman Emperor anymore. The reason was simple: once the unity of the faith was lost, the premises which made it possible were simply not there.

From 1556 to his death, Charles lived in a monastery in Yuste not far from Madrid. Of his own initiative, the most powerful man on earth gave away all of his boundless power. A truly unique case in history.

Contemplatives in action

Revolutions, civil wars, pauperism, nationalisms, the crisis of morality, the Turkish danger, the end of the European continent's religious unity, the pontifical court streaked with paganism: in the midst of such upheaval, God raised up a multitude of saints, men and women who started over from scratch; who started over by taking new and never before treaded paths. In a time where all seems bound for war and ruin, what is needed the most? Faith is needed. Hope is needed. Charity is needed. What is needed is to remember the reasons for faith, that is, culture is needed. Hatred's assault, which rewrites and bends history under power hungry and scrupleless men, needs to be stopped. Jesuits are needed, Camillians, the Comaschi, the Ursulines, the brothers of Divino Amore, the Theatines, the Barnabites, the Scolopi, the Somascans, the English ladies, the Oratorians, the Dascalced Carmelites, are all needed. Martyrs are needed. What is needed is a crowd of "contemplatives in action," as the many members of the new religious orders established during the 16th century were referred to. The Church, before and during the Council of Trent (1545-1563), resumed its work from the most diverse group of charisms the Holy Spirit could inspire. Amongst the many novelties, the most renown, the most opposed, but also the most successful was the Society of Jesus, a kind of militia trained in the heroism produced by faith as well as the wisdom produced by study. Protestantism was spreading like wildfire unimpeded and devastating all catholic lands and needed to be stopped. There was need to bring the Gospel anywhere in the world, to America, Asia and Africa, from the court of the Celestial Empire to the Guaranì Indios who were under attack by Portuguese slave merchants. The best suited for the task were the Jesuits because their charism was universal and hence designed to adapt to every situation. The sons of Ignatius of Loyola (1491-1556), a Spanish noble, who converted from the quest for glory on earth to the quest for the "greater glory of God," were the most culturally prepared men that the Church had. In fact, for the most part, they were in charge of running colleges which offered learning of absolute excellence at no cost whatsoever to a great number of youths from all continents. In 1556, upon Ignatius' death, the Society was in charge of 39 colleges. By the year 1600, these were 245 and by 1626 they were 444: a truly prodigious success. In its own colleges, the Society formed men who knew how to respond to the slander spread as propaganda and who knew how to answer the challenges posed by the protestant world in all areas of cultural and civil life. These men were conscious of the importance of Greco-Roman tradition, a *unicum* inherited by the Catholic Church. Among the many saints and martyrs which came out of the Society, Francis Xavier (1506-1552), merits a special place. He is the patron saint of missions and one of Ignatius' first companions. In 1541, he was sent in mission to Portuguese India and he was really a tireless faith pilgrim because in little more than ten years he evangelized India, the Maluku islands, Japan, and then decided to pass to China where he had good chances of becoming a martyr. But he never got to China because he died of pneumonia, poor, alone and exhausted on an island off the coast of Canton. The letter he wrote in 1546 to the Jesuits who remained in Europe is a touching witness of the sufferings he faced out of love for Christ: "I would have you know, dearest brothers, that in order to never forget any of you, so that I could recall you to mind persistently and each in a special way and for my consolation, I have cut out your names written in your own hands from the letters that you sent me and placed them with the vows of my profession. I carry them always with me because they give me great consolation"; "I will not say more because we will see each other soon in the next life with much greater rest than here... Your smallest brother and son."

As the Jesuits, also the Scolopi were dedicated to education and specialized in running schools for children that would be both free of charge and open to all social classes: these were the first public schools in all of Europe. The Scolopi's apostolate was moved by the firm belief that, if one were to educate children to study and religious practice early on, upon adulthood, they would be much better men and would have a much happier life. A profound change took place in the religious life of women: girls who wanted to offer their life to God but did not feel called to cloistered life, were now allowed to make their vows, continue to live at home and did not need to dress with a particular uniform; thus they brought to fulfillment the perfection of secular Christian life. Camillus de Lellis (1550-1614) introduced many innovations in the work of helping the sick: the brothers who cared for the sick needed to be prepared professionally. Camillus was a pioneer of professional education. The proverbial joy of Philip Neri (1515-1595), the absolutely modern character of his life bereft of external ties or vows, the oratory structure he created, the many miracles attributed to him and his charity towards all, deeply permeated corrupt roman society and influenced all social classes. His disciple, Caesar Baronius (1538-1607), a cardinal, dedicated his life to a scientific study of Church in order to respond to the protestant onslaught of slander depicting the Catholic world as superstitious and ignorant. His most memorable works were two: the compiling of the *Annales Ecclesiastici* which recounts the history of the Church from the very beginning until 1198 (upon his death Baronius had completed the twelfth volume) and the revision of the *Roman Martyrology*.

The Church is not an army in retreat. It is an army in movement.

Anglican England

The faithful island, full of monasteries and charism, the island that evangelized Germany was infected by Germany's apostasy. The end of the Hundred Years' War against France, lost to the French, backlashed violently in Great Britain. A terrible civil war exploded between two opposite factions of the nobility: the War of the Roses (1455-1485). Captured by Shakespeare in his tragedies, the war was so devastating that the nobility virtually self-destroyed. Peace returned with Henry VII of the House of Tudor. His son Henry VIII (1509-1547), described by Leo X as *Defensor Fidei* because of his anti-Lutheran writings, eighteen years after his marriage to Catherine of Aragon, the daughter of the Catholic kings and aunt of Charles V, demanded that the Pope grant him his marriage's annulment. He had fallen in love with Anne Boleyn and was determined to marry her to obtain a male heir. Blackmail and threats earned him his country's support, including that of bishops and universities. Clement VII tried to buy some time though there were obviously no grounds for annulment. But the sack of Rome was still very fresh in the Pope's memory and so it is comprehensible that he was cautious. In 1531, the clergy declared the king "protector and supreme head of the Church of England," though with the added restriction suggested by Bishop Fisher: "As far as it is allowed by the law of Christ." Nevertheless, his marriage to Anne Boleyn forced Clement to excommunicate the king of England.

From that moment onwards, the situation precipitated. In 1534, Henry passed the Act of Supremacy which made him supreme leader of the Church also in matters of doctrine and discipline. England was forced to bear with a 'Pope' who married six women and who had two of them killed, including Anne Boleyn. All subjects were forced to swear loyalty to the state religion. And so the persecution began. Too disaccustomed to watchfulness, one by one the bishops all gave in. Except one: the erudite humanist John Fisher (1469-1535).

Once again, the great host of English martyrs chose to be faithful out of love for Christ. A short time before he was decapitated, Fisher wrote to his sister Elizabeth: "Holy martyrs, men and women, whose number cannot be counted with certainty, out of love for him shed their blood and suffered with fortitude and zeal all torments, no matter how great and cruel. No man-made threat could ever frighten them, nor could the bitterness of any torment ever hold them back from following that love." The torments Henry reserved for those who did not recognize him as head of the Church were horrific: they were hung, drawn and quartered. A few days after Fisher's execution, it was the turn of Thomas More (1478-1535). He also was a great humanist, a friend to Henry, and for a time, even his Lord Chancellor. Probably, in virtue of their old friendship, at the very last minute, Henry decreed that he be decapitated.

The English Church was very rich because it owned over a quarter of the national wealth: in 1536, the king decreed that the so-called small monasteries be suppressed and that their respective assets by confiscated. The main beneficiary was the *gentry*, that is the petty nobility and bourgeoisie, which from this moment onwards became the chief supporters of the monarchy. The catholic people rebelled. They organized the Pilgrimage of Grace, a great host of knights who descended from the north towards London. Though Henry's army was much smaller, he managed to deceive Catholic military leaders with promises he never kept and so stopped the rebellion. The theft of ecclesiastical goods continued, and even great monasteries were suppressed. As in Germany, a succession of violence, looting, injustice followed leading to the loss of an immense artistic wealth and the spread of poverty everywhere, a natural consequence in England as everywhere else when ecclesiastical assets are privately managed.

Corruptio optimi pessima: the apostasy of the English Isles had a devastating effect all around, including in the culture. One tragic example is historiography: a systematic falsification of history was carried out in defense of Anglican England's 'good' claims. Good claims against Rome and all Catholic powers. English history remembers Mary Tudor, the daughter of Catherine of Aragon, a Catholic queen (1553-1558), by the derogatory name "Bloody Mary", while Elizabeth (1558-1603) was acclaimed with the noble yet completely false name of "Virgin."

In Anglican England, Catholics were sent to their death for treason. To help Catholics keep their identity, priests were needed who cared not for the looming martyrdom. This was the intention of the future cardinal William Allen, who in 1568 established a seminary in Douai. Though it started with only 4 young men, many more followed and between the XVI and XVII centuries, 438 missionaries from various seminaries crossed the Channel. From 1580, also the Jesuits began to land in England. They well knew that in a very short time they would all be arrested, tortured and killed. A month after his arrival, Edmund Campion addressed a manifest known as *Brag* to the Queen's Privy Council. In it he described the scope of the Society's mission on the island: "As regards our Society, be it known to you that we have made a league – all the Jesuits in the world, whose succession and multitude must overreach all the practice of England – cheerfully to carry the cross you shall lay upon us, and never to despair your recovery, while we have a man left to enjoy your Tyburn[21], or to be racked with your torments, or consumed with your prisons. The expense is reckoned, the enterprise is begun; it is of God; it cannot be withstood. So the faith was planted: so it must be restored." Almost a century passed from the martyrdom of Edmund Campion (1581) to that of David Lewis (1679), the last Jesuit executed in Great Britain. From the gallows Lewis wanted the crimes for which he was executed to be clear: "A Roman Catholic I am, a Roman Catholic priest I am, a Roman Catholic priest of that religious order called the Society of Jesus I am, and I bless God who first called me, and I bless the hour in which I was first called both unto faith and function. Please now to observe; I was condemned for reading Mass, hearing confessions, administering the Sacraments."

Under Elizabeth's rule, between 1570 and 1603, 189 Catholics were murdered after cruel torture (126 priests, missionaries, 59 laymen, 3 women); without counting those who died in prison nor those killed during the ruthless repression carried out in Ireland.

John Calvin

Luther was a revolutionary. Henry was a lustful and violent man. Calvin, instead, was an austere reformer. He brought to completion, or at least this is the impression many have, what Luther began. In

---

[21] Tyburn was a village near London where in 1537 Henry VIII had the leaders of the Pilgrimage of Grace executed. In this place a tree was planted called the Tree of Tyburn, a new type of gallows used to torture and kill in various ways. At present, Tyburn has become part of the city center, near the Marble Arch, where a plaque in the ground remembers the many Catholics executed there between 1535 and 1681. A few steps away lay the Tyburn convent where perpetual adoration is held in defense of the English nation.

the founding text of Calvinism, *Christianae Religionis Institutio* dedicated to Francis I in 1536, Calvin explained the idea of double predestination: "By predestination we mean the eternal decree of God, by which he determined with himself whatever he wished to happen with regard to every man. All are not created on equal terms, but some are preordained to eternal life, others to eternal damnation; and, accordingly, as each has been created for one or other of these ends, we say that he has been predestined to life or to death." Calvin, like Luther, held that Scripture is the only source of faith, since it was dictated by the Spirit and interpreted by the Spirit to each individual believer. However, such exegetical subjectivism was limited by the Calvinist reading of the Bible as taught in the Accademy established in Geneva in 1559. In opposition to Luther, Calvin discerned only two sacraments: Baptism and Eucharist. The latter excluded the physical presence of Christ which instead Luther firmly upheld.

Calvin viewed mankind as radically corrupt, but he was convinced that his doctrine would bring the primitive purity of the apostolic times back to the Church. By turning drastically to the spirit of the Old Testament, he gave great importance to the law: no games, no cards, no luxury, no elegant dresses, no balls, church elders periodically visited private homes to makes sure that the guidelines set by religious authorities were being followed. All needed to work a lot and reinvest their profits. Besides, money could not be spent for futile reasons or in luxury goods. As strange as it may seem given Christ's repeated claims ("blessed are you poor..."), Calvinists believe that riches were a sign of divine favor.

Worship had to be pure: no religious symbols; away with crosses, blessings, prayers for the dead ("a terrible and despicable practice"), fasting, abstinence, and devotion to Mary or the saints. His definition of the Catholic Church illustrates the sense of superiority and self-consciousness which distinguished Calvin: "A perverse clique of priests filled with countless superstitions: the public assemblies are schools of idolatry and impiety." In adherence to this belief, in Geneva where Calvin was called to enact the reform, it was the desire to "live according to the Gospel" which by 1536 officially forbade Catholic worship.

Calvin inaugurated the kingdom of the elect: a theocracy with an iron discipline. From 1536 to 1546 (excluding two years during which he was sent away for excessive rigidity) 67 people were condemned to death in Geneva alone, including some as witches and some because they were thought to spread the plague. The true Church of God must triumph throughout the world because the truth cannot be constricted to Switzerland. Thus, the Calvinists carried out an intense missionary work and assumed different denomination wherever they went: Huguenots in France, Presbyterians in Scotland, Puritans in England.

Here are some the main features of Calvinism in these countries:

- in France, in only 40 years, the Huguenots caused the unleashing of eight civil wars. In order to make their Church triumph, they called German and English Protestants to their aid, an act of treason against their own country: they repeatedly called the Germans to devastate, plunder and invade Catholic regions of central and southern France and struck a deal with Elizabeth for the help of men and arms in exchange for ceding Calais[22]. The French crown was not strong enough to resist the Huguenots. It was full of ambiguity, immorality and duplicity. So the burden of defending the French people, spontaneously organized in the Catholic League of France led by the House of Guise, fell on the finances and efforts of the Holy See and Philip II of Spain. Very little is known about the French Wars of Religion, which lasted from 1560 to 1598, the year in which the Treaty of Nantes was signed. The only certain fact is that in 1572, on the night of St. Bartholomew, Catholics organized a massacre of Huguenots who had come to Paris for the marriage

---

[22] At the beginning of the anti-Catholic campaign, Huguenot hatred struck the same body as Francesco di Paola (1416-1507), buried in Tours, whose bones were burned and dispersed in 1562. Hermit, founder of the Order of Minims, friars who live in humility, prayer and penance, Francis was a saint to whom God grants an infinite number of graces. Famous is the crossing of the Strait of Massina on board – so to speak – of its mantle. The fame of the prodigies he performed was so great that Louis XI, hoping to be healed by his intercession from a deadly disease, convinced the Pope to impose on the reluctant hermit the transfer to France. Francesco never returned to Calabria and was the origin (with the life, miracles and convents he founded) of the spiritual renewal of the court and of the French people.

of Princess Margaret to the Huguenot Henry of the House of Bourbon-Navarre;
- in Holland, the Calvinists rebelled against Philip II who aimed to reform the Church – just like his great grandparents had already done in Spain – depriving the nobles of their privileges and influence. The local leading social classes decided that it was more convenient to rob the Church of its assets, become rich without any obstacles and launch their colonial ventures;
- in England, the Puritans unleashed an era of revolutions by judging, condemning to death and decapitating king Charles I of the House of Stuart in 1649. Regicide is a crime which the Puritans carried out with a light heart. The anointed of the Lord is not the king. The pure are the anointed ones, the puritans guided by Cromwell towards the founding here on earth of the kingdom of heaven. They followed the eternal ambition of making "all things new" so typical of revolutionaries in all times. Cromwell led a new type of army ("new model army") which brought down the monarchy in the name of equality. At the same time, however, he had himself named Lord Protector and tried to perpetuate his office by handing it over to his son Richard. A new dynasty to substitute the old;
- conscious of their own superiority, in North America, Calvinists knew that they could not come to terms with the Native Americans. In fact they were exterminated. In the United States, Presbyterians and Puritans together were decisive in the formation of a national identity founded on the faith in freedom, work, entrepreneurship and wealth. The *WASP* kingdom: White, Anglo-Saxon, Protestants. In Boston Harbor there is a church whose features in the blink of an eye captures the soul of America as forged by the Calvinist ideal: in the Old North Church there is no space for the poor or for the community. The faithful are organized in private spaces, each owned by the different families, each furnished according to their own tastes and needs, each separated from the others by partitions which look like the walls of a home. The only difference between these liturgical boxes and small homes is the absence of a roof, which allows those present to see the pastor preaching from the pulpit.

Old North Church, Boston

The Jewish Question

In the *Letter to the Romans*, Paul wrote that God's election cannot be revoked and that the covenant made on Mount Horeb with the Jewish people is eternal. The Church believed that God made two covenants with men. The first was with the Jews, while the second was with Christians, sealed by the blood of Jesus on the cross. The relationship between peoples of the two covenants has been woven in difficulties because one often despised the other. Even though Jewish-Christian relations have been the cause of great suffering and are painful to describe, we cannot but do so here.

The whole of the first Christian generation is Jewish. Nevertheless, almost the entirety of the Jewish elite – Pharisees, scribes, the priestly caste – had Jesus condemned to death and persecuted Christians killing Stephen and James and trying to kill Paul. After the year 70, by the destruction of the temple and of Jerusalem, the Jewish people were deprived of a homeland and dispersed. The diaspora lasted until the establishment of the state of Israel in 1948. During almost two thousand years of pilgrimage from one side of the world to the other, two things seem to constantly accompany life in Jewish communities: success in business (chapter 15, verse 6 of Deuteronomy says: "For the Lord your God will bless you as he promised you, and you shall lend to many nations, but you shall not borrow; and you shall rule over many nations, but they shall not rule over you") and faithfulness to the covenant made with God through Moses on the slopes of the Horeb, which forbade Jews from assimilating the religions and uses of other nations.

Success and unyielding to the habits of the hosting people seem to be at the origin of that sentiment of loathing, if not all out hate, which surrounded the Jewish people wherever they went. No one likes to feel humiliated in his own home and many are willing to take advantage of any good excuse to take the goods of others. Plausibly, this is the reason why always, with lesser or greater violence, Jews were driven out from the nations where they made home. This is what happened everywhere with only one exception: Rome. The relationship that the Church established with Jews is complex and varied with the times and places. Yet, with regards to the Catholic world, one must refer to what is said in the magisterium, the only thing valid everywhere and for everyone. Keeping in mind all that was said above, with respect to Paul and the *Letter to the Romans*, and of Gregory the Great and the letter to the bishop of Naples, we shall analyze the most significant legal provisions issued by the Popes in regard to Jews.

First of all, a clarification: in the documents of the magisterium and in prayers, the adjective used in reference to Jews – *perfidus* – does not carry any moral connotation implying condemnation because according to the word's etymology, *perfidus* literally means without faith, incredulous. In the constitution *Licet perfidia Judaeorum* issued on September 15, 1199, Innocent III, wanting to be in continuity with the magisterium of the Popes who preceded him during the 12th century (Callixtus II, Eugene III, Alexander III, Clement III, Celestine III), wrote: since the Jews "request the aid of Our defense, in conformity to the meekness of Christian piety [...] we welcome their request and grant them the shield of our protection." What follows from this, is that Jews were never to be forced to receive Baptism and that no Christian "may presume in such unworthy a manner to offend their person or by violence take their goods." Moreover, "in opposition to the depravity and malice of evil men, we hereby decree that no one should dare to profane or damage any Jewish cemetery or remove the bodies of those already buried in order to gain money." Innocent inflicted excommunication on those who dared to disregard his decree. However, the level of detail used to describe the deplorable actions committed against Jews bears witness to the fact that those actions, though committed by "evil men," were not so rare after all.

In the 16th century, after one thousand and five hundred years, the magisterium suddenly changed with regards to Jews. The context was the revolution brought about by the reformation; there was a serious danger that the war unleashed against Rome could reach Italy; looting of the Church's goods was a very actual risk; Turkish forces were advancing. In this truly dramatic scenario, Gian Pietro Carafa, a noble Neapolitan man who was very hard with himself and others and an inquisitor with an iron will drive to reform the Church, became Pope as Paul IV (1555-1559). The Pope attempted with great strength and discipline to reform the Church by defending it, or so he believed, from the danger posed by heresy both external and internal. The result was that upon his death, the people rioted; they threw his statue in the Tiber and set fire to the inquisition palace. Meaning to mark a clear divide between the lives of Jews and Christians, on July 14, 1555, Paul IV issued the Bull *Cum nimis absurdum* ("it is truly absurd and inconvenient that Jews, submitted by their own fault to eternal servitude, with the excuse that Christian charity welcomes them and allows them to live side by side, would be so ungrateful towards Christians that they would return evil in exchange for good"). The bull commanded that Jews be confined to a ghetto, that they wear distinctive signs, barred them from buying fixed assets, from having Christian servants, from exercising any commercial activity that was not the sale of rags. Throughout the 16th century, many Popes issued provisions for the Jewish community, some to mitigate – such as Pius IV – the decisions made by Paul IV, while others – like Pius V – to make them harsher. Pius V issued *Haebreorum gens* in 1569 ("absorbed as they are in their sorceries, incantations, magic superstitions and evil spells, they induce many careless and weak people into Satan's deceits") which decreed the expulsion of all Jews from the Pontifical

State except for the communities of Rome and Ancona. Mostly abolished by Sixtus V in 1586, the anti-Jewish measures were restored by Clement VIII in 1593. We must await the beginning of the pontificate of Pius IX in order to see the ghetto walls torn down.

Though many were drafted to avoid the violence and disorder witnessed in all of Europe and which could have very well been extended to Rome, these bulls imposing limits so severe on Jewish life in the Pontifical State that they jeopardized the dignity of Jews as human persons, were responsible for grave injustice which indiscriminately befell the entire social group. The effects, as always, weigh most heavily on the weakest. The worry to defend the Christian people were so great that it induced the Popes to put the Word of God in brackets, as if the harshness of the times induced some to doubt the ability of Providence to guide history.

The Age of Mannerism and Baroque

While in England Queen Elizabeth profited on the slave trade, and financed and rewarded anti-Spanish piracy, Philip II (1556-1598) reigned from the Escorial, a convent near Madrid shaped as a grill which was the torture instrument used by the Romans to kill Lorenzo the deacon and patron saint of that monastery. Rome brought the council convoked in Trent to an end (1545-1563). The council confirmed doctrine and decreed reform for the whole Church: bishops were to be responsible for the religious life in their respective dioceses, they were to carry out modest lives, devoid of nepotism, caring for the poor and detaching themselves from temporal power, watching over the clergy, keeping at heart the people's religious instruction, carrying out regular visits to every parish; their stable presence was required, therefore the accumulation of benefices was suppressed; the clergy had to be prepared and morally irreprehensible and therefore seminaries were born; a list of prohibited books was established in order to protect the simple who had no weapons to answer protestant propaganda and thus were defenseless; the roman inquisition was reformed; protestant theories were starkly condemned but the reformers' names were not explicitly mentioned. Church architecture changed in function of the preaching and so church naves disappeared. The model of all Tridentine churches was the Church of the Gesù in Rome with central plan and side chapels for veneration of the saints and people's devotions.

Protestants unleashed an iconoclast campaign which annihilated the works of art spread for centuries throughout Catholic Europe. In Calvinist Europe, moralism and a pharisaical spirit enforced modesty and saving money in all styles of life. Meanwhile, in Rome and in catholic countries, an exuberant exaltation of life and its creator took place. Life itself moved and its presence danced even in the buildings. Shapes concave and convex, spirals, volutes, surfaces in motion and truncated: the Baroque. It was the scenography of processions, of liturgical feasts, of mysteries. It was the exultation in paintings of the saints in heaven and in statues with vestments that were rich and adapted with utter grace to the bodies of the blessed. It was the splendor of Titian's *Assumption* scene in the Frari church of Venice. It was the marble, warm, moved and alive in Bernini's Ecstasy of Teresa in the church of Santa Maria della Vittoria in Rome. It was the art of cupolas, of Saint Peter's colonnade embrace, of the ciboria's magnificence which guarded the tabernacle at the altar's center; it was the refinement of all liturgical objects; it was the splendor of polychromatic marbles.

It is the feast of the rosary and of the recognition of the power which flows from reciting the rosary: the miraculous victory obtained on September 7, 1571, in Lepanto against a Turkish fleet vastly greater than the Christian was proof. After Byzantium's conquest, Turkish Islam advanced by land and by sea. By sea, in 1571, the Turks defeated the Venetians in Cyprus. They took over Famagusta though it was heroically defended by Captain Bragadin: even after his nose and ears were mutilated, after he was put in a cage and left in the sun for twelve days, still refusing to convert to Islam, he was skinned alive starting from his head, his body was dismembered, his skin was filled with hay and then sowed back together so that after having circled the city riding on an ox, it could be placed on a ship's mast and triumphally return to Istanbul.

When the danger reached the highest levels, once again the Pope saved the west. Pius V united the forces of the pontifical state, the Venetians, the Spanish, and of various duchies and Italian republics in a Holy League. The fleet was commanded by John of Austria, the very young biological son of Charles V, to whom the Pope sent a banner with the image of Jesus crucified between the apostles Peter and Paul and the writing *In hoc signo vinces*. Next to the banner with the crucified Christ, they hoisted up a flag of Mary with the writing *Sancta Maria succurre miseris*. On the opposite front, Mehmet Alì Pascià waved a green flag on which the name of Allah was embroidered in gold 28,900 times. While the whole Christian world was praying the rosary, right before battle John ordered the whole army to kneel down and implore help from heaven. Victory followed. A victory filled with copious losses for the Turks in terms of both men and ships. It marked the end of the Turkish conquest of the Mediterranean Sea. While in prayer, the Pope saw the Christian triumph and from that moment onwards, October 7 became the feast of Our Lady of Victory which some years later turned into the feast of Our Lady of the Rosary.

It is the faith in the real presence of the body of Christ in the consecrated host; it is the adoration of the body of Christ in churches and processions; it is the devotion to the Sacred Heart of Jesus. In response to the gnostic attack repeated over the centuries, which questioned the real presence of the body of Christ in the Eucharist, the Church responded by celebrating with renewed solemnity the feast of Corpus Domini and practicing the devotion to the Sacred Heart of Jesus. The feast of Corpus Domini, which falls on the Thursday after the solemnity of the Most Holy Trinity, was instituted by Urban IV in 1264, a year after the miracle of Bolsena in which a priest who celebrated the Eucharist in doubting about the real presence, witnessed blood flowing out of the consecrated host onto his own corporal. The devotion to the Sacred Heart, also born during the 13th century and which further developed with time, received a decisive impulse after the revelations granted to Margaret Mary Alacoque (1647-1690), the nun who contemplated the heart of Christ "seated upon a throne of flames, radiant like the sun, with the adorable wound, surrounded by thorns underneath a cross." Jesus revealed his desire to Margaret Mary that the Church would celebrate his Most Sacred Heart on the Friday after the octave of Corpus Domini ("Behold that heart which so loved mankind"; "My heart shall dilate to release the fruits of its love abundantly on those who honor me"; "Those precious treasures which I reveal to you contain sanctifying graces to draw men out of the abyss of perdition") and so it was done starting from the year 1672.

A horrendous crime

Thanks to Christian preaching, the tragedy of slavery was significantly reduced. However, after the Muslim conquest, Western Europe's shores were scourged by constant raids of Islamic pirates wherein a great number of Christians were enslaved: slavery had come back in all its horror. At the turn of the second millennium, Islamic violence became a nightmare. Christians everywhere organized in order to try and redeem the greatest number of brothers who had been enslaved by the Muslims. This was the reason for the birth of the Order of the Most Holy Trinity. It was founded by two French noblemen, John of Matha and Felix of Valois, the latter being a relative of Louis VII. In 1193, while he celebrated his first mass, in a vision, John saw Christ freeing two slaves, one white and the other black. This vision gave birth to the Trinitarians who had only one goal: gather alms and use one third of them to redeem slaves. Upon their landing in Marseilles, those snatched out of slavery, as a solemn act of thanksgiving, went in procession to the cathedral singing Psalm 113, *In exitu Israel de Aegypto* (*When Israel came out of Egypt*), a psalm which had become flesh in their lives. In very few years, the Trinitarians multiplied: in over 600 homes, they gave hospitality to freed slaves who had no family or who were sick. In 1998, the eight hundredth anniversary of their establishment, John Paul II addressed these words to the Minister General: "The Most Holy Trinity, fount, model and aim of all existence: behold the heart of your spirituality. Your Rule begins with the words 'In the name of the Holy and undivided Trinity,' thus highlighting how it is faith in this fundamental Mystery which pervades the entire existence of people who, like your founder, choose to follow the Son of God radically. Your mission in favor of slaves and of the poor flows from this inexhaustible fountain of love, and you rightly live it as an extension of Christ's redemptive action."

A few years later, an apparition of Mary led to the foundation of the Mercedarians. Peter Nolasco (1180-1245), a wealthy merchant redeemed slaves with the profits earned from his trade. On August 1, 1218, Mary appeared to him. She invited him to establish a religious redemptive order to redeem Christians enslaved by Muslims. In ten days, Mary's project became a reality and in the first hundred and thirty years since their foundation, the merciful love of these redemptive brothers redeemed 52,000 people. When money wasn't enough and the slave was at the end of his strength, the brothers offered themselves as the price of redemption.

The discovery of America led to a truly tragic situation because the Christian world tarnished itself by committing a most abominable crime: they transported millions of black Africans to the new world as slaves. Although these were generally snatched away from their families by Arab Muslims they were transported on Christian ships: mainly Portuguese, English and Dutch. Millions of men treated like cattle. Such organized crime made all efforts to free them vain: another way was needed. The Jesuit Peter Claver (1581-1654), who called himself "slave to the Africans forever," over the course of 44 years tirelessly served and catechized the slaves who landed in the Colombian harbor of Cartagena and by so doing, baptized more than three hundred thousand. When slave-trading ships arrived with their cargo of desperate and terrorized men, most of whom were almost dead, Peter went to meet them. He brought "fruit, lemons, sweets," he wrote on March 31, 1627 to his superiors, making his way to the sick "who lie down on the wet ground, or rather muddy ground; so that the humidity would not be excessive, they tried to build an embankment with tiles and fragments of brick. This was their resting place. It was extremely uncomfortable not only for this reason but above all because they were naked having no protection or clothing." Peter wrote that among the sick, "there were two Negros, more dead than alive. They had already gone cold: not even their pulse could be felt. With a tile, we gathered some burning hot coals and placed them in the middle, near the dying. On the fire we threw some fragrant spices. We had two whole bags and we used them up completely. In this way, also thanks to our cloaks (they had nothing of the kind and to ask their taskmasters' aid would have been in vain) we tried to make them breath in those vapors. Really, thanks to that warmth, they seemed to come back to life. You had to see what joy we saw in their eyes as they looked upon us! By so doing, we could speak to them, not with words but with our hands and with our deeds: any other discourse would surely have been entirely useless. These people were deeply convinced they were brought there as food to be eaten. At the end we sat down, or rather knelt down next to them and began to wash their faces and their bodies with wine, making every effort to soothe them using all charms and displaying before them all natural things which in some way lead the sick to feel joy. Thereafter, we began to explain the catechism on Baptism and its wonderful effects on the body and the soul."

On February 22, 1992, the five hundredth anniversary since the discovery of America, while kneeling in silence, his head bent downwards, Pope Wojtyla prayed on the Island of Gorée in Senegal, in the "House of Slaves," there were a countless mass of desperate men awaited in chains to be shipped off to America: "From this African sanctuary which bears witness to the pain of the blacks, we implore from heaven forgiveness." It is "the tragedy of a society which called itself Christian"; "It is a human tragedy: the cry of generations demands that we free ourselves from this tragedy forever because its roots lie deep in ourselves, in human nature, in sin. I have come to give homage to all nameless victims. We do not know exactly how many they were. We do not know exactly who they were. Deplorably, our society, which called itself and still calls itself Christian, for a moment, even in our times, reverted to the practice slavery. We know what the death camps were. Here is one of their models. We cannot immerse ourselves in the tragedy of our civilization, of our weakness, of sin. We must keep faith to another cry, that of Saint Paul who said: "*Ubi abundavit peccatum, superabundavit gratia.*"

There was sin increased, grace abounded all the more.

The Galileo Case

"From the Englightenment to our days, the case surrounding Galileo has become a kind of myth. The image resulting from the reconstruction of its events was far from reality. In this perspective, the Galileo case was a symbol of a supposed rejection by the Church to scientific progress, or of a "dogmatic" obscurantism opposed to the free search for truth. This myth played a significant cultural role; it contributed to anchor many scientists who acted in good faith to the idea that there was an incompatibility between the spirit of science and its research ethics, on the one side, and Christian faith, on the other. A tragic reciprocal misunderstanding was interpreted as the reflection of an essential opposition between science and faith." This was the synthesis John Paul II offered on October 31, 1992, to members gathered in plenary session of the Pontifical Academy of Sciences.

The whole affair surrounding Galileo Galilei (1564-1642) was, according to Wojtyla, made into a myth. To try to understand why, we should briefly summarize the facts: Galileo supported the heliocentric theory, at the time quite revolutionary, yet did not support this hypothesis with any show of scientific proof (such proof would arrive some years later with Newton); in 1616, Galileo was called to Rome by the inquisition which forbade him to continue teaching and writing about the matter; in 1633 he was newly put on trial and this time condemned to retract his views for not having heeded to the prohibition of 1616. The scientist was placed under house arrest in his home in Arcetri where once a week for three years he had to recite the seven penitential psalms.

The Galileo case must be placed within the context of the protestant revolution and of the Council of Trent that, "prohibited the teaching of Scripture in opposition to the common approval of the Holy Fathers," said Cardinal Robert Bellarmine (1542-1621) in a letter addressed to the Carmelite mathematician Antonio Foscarini. The heliocentric theory could "harm the holy faith by making Holy Scripture appear as false"; this was the cardinal's reasoning. Things would be quite different, if for the heliocentric theory "there were true proof." In that case, "we would then have to very carefully explain those parts of Scripture which seem contrary and claim that we do not understand rather than claiming that what is stated is false." In the Catholic Church, science and faith are never in opposition: if Scripture seems to contradict a proved scientific reality, it means that

Scripture has not been rightly understood. This is what Bellarmine thought and this is what the Catholic Church upheld[23].

Let us come to Galileo. The great physicist held that when science and Scripture disagree, Scripture is undoubtedly mistaken. He believed this for the simple reason that when God inspired Scripture, he took the ignorance of the people he addressed into account (by speaking to "ignorant and undisciplined people," God had to "comply with the common people's incapacity"). This would explain, for example, why Joshua could have addressed such creative words to the sun: "'Sun, stand thou still at Gibeon, and thou Moon in the valley of Ai'jalon.' And the sun stood still, and the moon stayed, until the nation took vengeance on their enemies." Galileo had no particular esteem for the ignorant and base people and further, did not take God's thinking duly into account: God loves Israel, loves Israel as a father, as a mother, as a bridegroom. Galileo did not even stop to reflect on the fact that Moses (Moses!) was not allowed to enter the Promised Land because God did not forgive how he despised the people at the waters of Meriba[24].

When Bellarmine in 1616 advised Galileo to work as a mathematician and not as a theologian, Bellarmine was right. But Galileo, instead of committing himself to finding a proof in favor of the heliocentric theory, he preferred to vindicate a hermeneutic, which he deemed superior than that of theologians. Thus, he jumped headfirst into the well-known issue raised by Lutherans over the free interpretation of scripture.

---

[23] In this respect, Wojtyla quoted the opinions of Augustine and Leo XIII: "If, against the most manifest and reliable testimony of reason, anything be set up claiming to have the authority of the Holy Scriptures, he who does this does it through a misapprehension of what he has read, and is setting up against the truth not the real meaning of Scripture, which he has failed to discover, but an opinion of his own; he alleges not what he has found in the Scriptures, but what he has found in himself as their interpreter" (Letter 143, n. 7; PL 33,588). In 1893 Pope Leo XIII echoed this thought in his encyclical *Providentissimus Deus*: "Since truth cannot contradict truth, we may be sure that some mistake has been made either in the interpretation of the sacred words or in some other item of the discussion", Leonis XIII Pont. Max. Acta, vol. XIII, 1894, p. 361)."

[24] See Num 20,6-12 and 27,12-14.

Granted; in front of the insubordination of a famous and respected man like Galileo, though it always showed him respect, the Inquisition could have looked the other way. Actually, it could've done although he openly ridiculed his friend Maffeo Barberini, that is, Pope Urban VIII, in the *Dialogue Concerning the Two Chief Systems*; and moreover, although he did so in a book written in the common language, meaning, that it was destined for the general public; although, he not only went against the order imposed on him in 1616, but also obtained permission to publish the *Dialogue* by showing an obviously forged *imprimatur* of the Roman Court. But then again, the Inquisition could have looked the other way and not offer a plethora of novelists, movie directors and poets such excellent material for creating the myth of incompatibility between science and faith. Probably, the Inquisition thought that Galileo's philosophical and theological views would constitute a danger for mere mortals, seeing as they included a mythical view of science and consequently an inflated view of the opinion of scientists and finally an implicit vindication of the protestant belief about the free interpretation of Scripture.

To understand history one must keep philosophy in mind

In the 16th century, European courts and sovereigns were immersed in a cultural milieu that was being deeply influenced by Gnostic currents now given ample room for grow thanks to the Lutheran revolution. The Sectarianism which derived from the doctrine about the free interpretation of Scripture produced a lack of confidence in the possibility that theology could be scientific. Consequently, the burden of the search for truth fell entirely on philosophy no longer enlightened nor guided by revelation. Philosophy regressed to a sort of pre-Christian reflection. The aggravating result is that, after having come to know Christ and rejected him, reason is left to its own devices, loses its bearings and strays: this is the tragedy which follows apostasy.

With Pico della Mirandola (1463-1494), Humanism put sin aside, one of the key truths of revelation. In his *Oration on the Dignity of Man*, he supported the idea that people are indeed able to freely choose their destinies by selecting either to become angels or to become brutes. Machiavelli (1469-1527) separated politics from faith and de facto deemed politics the only art worth practicing. Truth is uninteresting; Power is what matters: how to conquer it and how to keep it. He who is powerful need not give account of himself to any God. England, Holland, two sister and rival nations, who launched a new type of colonialism which disregarded the evangelization, adopted the beacons of modernity from Italy: Bacon and the empiricists with Locke on one side of the Channel and Grotius with Spinoza on the other. Francis Bacon (1561-1626) was a philosopher and scientist who claimed science and power were equivalent: "Science is power." Power to change the world in order that every desire may be quenched, and every pain healed. Man's life is projected towards the future, a progress filled future in which the community of scientists, that is, of "apt and well-chosen geniuses," shall be able to free people from prejudice: "I want everything which aims to free the mind to spread to the multitudes." Bacon wholly condemned Greek and Christian thought because he viewed it as sterile and therefore immoral. The object of his philosophy is nature. Man is its "minister and interpreter," in the sense that he must discover its laws so that he may change them according to his needs.

In the 17th century, philosophical thought dwelled on nature. According to Huig de Groot (1583-1645), known as Grotius, the father of a certain modern understanding of natural law, God expresses himself in nature and reason describes nature by establishing the inalienable human rights that would be valid even if God were not to exist (*etsi Deus non daretur*). An action's morality is evaluated on the basis of its agreement to the natural rights set by nature. Society itself, in a certain sense, is the result of a rational choice because Grotius believed that the state is born from an original pact, a social pact which includes the right to rebel when the terms of the pact were broken. The times were over when there was a common consciousness recognizing that all authority came from God, and after having set aside the Pontifical Magisterium, inevitably, also the king's authority was set aside because it did not derive from divine right but from human consent: revolution is just behind the corner. The products of reason are not only law and morality but also the supposed existence of a universal religion common to all peoples.

Baruch Spinoza (1632-1677), an excommunicated Jew whose motto was *caute* (one must speak with caution keeping in mind that the majority of people are not yet able to understand the sublimity of one's thought), did indeed speak about God but only to identify Him with nature: *Deus sive natura*. Once God is put aside, and nature is fashioned into an idol, there is neither room for metaphysics nor for freedom because in a pantheistic universe, everything is God and so everything is good. There are latent totalitarian implications in this position; very soon they would have ample opportunity to manifest themselves clearly. The rejection of metaphysics led to a loss of interest in speculation about substance and quality. There was no talk of essences anymore. Once these were out of the picture, by definition, man, every man, ceased to be "image and likeness" of God. By so doing, an abyss was created between man and man: between he who is wise, enlightened, a scientist; and he is not wise, nor enlightened, nor a scientist. Between slaves, blacks, the poor, redskins, the needy, Irish and Catholics in general on the one side; and the white, the rich, the protestants, the enlightened and especially the scientists on the other. From the ashes of metaphysics, emerged empiricism. Empiricism denies human reason the ability to know truth. If so, everything becomes relative. It depends on experience and therefore it is in movement, in evolution. Without metaphysics, without the absolute, progress becomes the only dimension in which human life can hope to find any meaning. Progress becomes a substitute for faith and whatever is tied to progress becomes an undisputable dogma.

Progress. What a nice word. It is a fact, that some people have the pretentiousness of claiming to know which direction the world is moving in. Better yet: which direction the world should move in. They deny the existence of truth but are absolutely certain of embodying the true needs of man and society. In this way a self-contradiction is affirmed known as relativism. To say that truth is not knowable, is itself a truth. It is a type of negative truth, but truth all the same. Relativists are absolutely certain, without any chance of error or the shadow of doubt, that truth does not exist. This truth, as such, must be forcefully imposed on everyone for the excellent reason that it is better than that of others. It's better because it doesn't exclude from the outset any view about the world and thus it respects all of them. All of them, except for the view of those who publicly declare that Truth does in fact exist, obviously. These are by definition intolerant, and they must be completely disregarded. It is a blatant contradiction which they pretend not to see. This is Locke's empiricist position in *A Letter Concerning Tolleration*, which he wrote in 1685: everyone deserves to be tolerated except for Catholics and atheists.

Let's conclude these brushstrokes about philosophy by going back to Bacon. The English philosopher had a very noble opinion of himself because he described himself as a man whose nature was particularly in tune with the truth: "With regards to myself, I have understood that I am apt to the study of truth more than anything else," "I hate any kind of imposture," I am convinced to have "a certain familiarity and a certain affinity to truth." Bacon, the hater of imposture, Keeper of the Seal and Lord Chancellor, was condemned for corruption, imprisoned and banned from all public offices because in his service as judge he often accepted gifts from the parties in dispute. How can we reconcile his supposed truth filled spirit with his practice of corruption? Probably, Bacon drew a line between mere mortals and scientists like himself. The enlightened were allowed what the profane were not because, by definition, the wise attributed a high moral value to the guiding role they assigned themselves. In this way, intellectual and moral qualities coincided and moral law, which is distinctive of the learned, in reality is nothing more than an omnipresent and all-inclusive formula. Any content can be put in it. A moral person is not one who puts the Decalogue into practice anymore but on the contrary, very often a moral person is he who breaks the Decalogue.

It is the triumph of Gnosticism.

1648 Westphalia: A revolutionary peace

The years between 1517 and 1648 are often referred to as the Age of the wars of religion. The expression "wars of religion" is generic and implies that in Europe, the different churches fought each other. It was not so. Catholic peoples and their rulers fought, when they could, only and exclusively for the right to keep on living.

The Peace of Augusta established the year 1552 as the *annus normalis*: nonetheless, many deemed it useful and quite convenient to continue the work of dismantling ecclesiastical institutions by robbing the Church of the truly enormous goods accumulated with time. Princes and local authorities gained an additional profit by following this course of action: they got rid of church oversight and, as Luther used to say, became "free" to make any decision they wanted independently of its social and economic effects. This type of freedom was responsible for igniting war throughout the whole central part of Northern Europe. Such wars took up religion as a noble excuse to increase power, prestige, riches, and lands of those who promoted them. In this explosion of *libido dominandi*, the House of Habsburg in Spain and Austria tried to defend justice and faith. Especially Spain dried up its significant financial reserves by intervening a bit everywhere to help the Church (in Holland, France and England) and to promote the evangelization not only in America, but also in the Philippines. Not to mention, the Islamic front, which in Spain still had a fifth column, namely, the *Moriscos*. The attempt made by Philip II to integrate them failed and so in 1609, Philip III decreed their expulsion.

The last appalling episode of wars officially fought in the name of religion was the Thirty Years' War which for three decades disrupted the lives of the peoples in central Europe. The war began in 1618 because the Habsburgs of Austria demanded respect for the clauses set forth in the Peace of Augusta and could not stand the fact that reformed churches were built on Catholic properties in Bohemia. The first three phases of the clash (respectively the Boheme, the Danish and the Swedish) ended favorably for the Catholics and in 1626, Ferdinand II issued the decree of restitution by which the assets illegally taken from the Church after 1552 had to be returned. The Empire lost the last and most decisive phase of the fight against the France of Louie XIII (1610-1643) and of its ministers Richelieu and Mazarin. The latter fact proves, if such proof were still needed, how deceiving and improper the expression "wars of religion" is: in the first decades of the 17th century, no wars of religion were fought between Catholic France and the Catholic Empire. It was France who was fighting the never-ending battle for supremacy over the continent.

The war came to an end with the Peace of Westphalia in 1648. It was a revolutionary peace because it deeply altered the nature of Europe. Until then, Europe was the product of the evangelization and of faith, and therefore was kept united by faith. The absolute novelty was the approval of multiple clauses about the Catholic Church despite the Holy See's manifest opposition. In the Bull *Zelo Domus Dei*, Innocent X cried out in protest against the terms of Westphalia because they were blatantly unfair: behold people who look for "their own benefit rather than the glory of God," and since they care not that "any agreement or provision about church matters made without the approval of the above said Holy See, is null and its effects have no validity," they forever abandon illegally occupied church assets to the heretics and their successors.

Among the many clauses, the Peace made Calvinism legal and moved the *annus normalis* to the year 1624, thus opening the door for future adjustments. Germany came out in pieces from the Thirty Years' War, divided in hundreds of mini states each one with ample autonomy. Spain, the empire's closest ally, in 1643 was defeated in Rocroi and since it did not acquiesce to the Peace of Westphalia was forced in 1659 to make the Peace of the Pyrenees which marked the end of its great power. The undisputed victor was France, which became the ruling nation in Europe.

After Westphalia, the Holy See de facto lost all influence in the European arena. The values which the Church of Rome represented for over one thousand years became completely irrelevant. To deliberately ignore the appeals and the contribution of the Holy See during peace negotiations, to de facto accept the relativism which flows from the doctrine about the free interpretation of scripture, to pretend to believe that religious issues are per se divisive and at the root of conflicts, means to implicitly admit that on the political level, it is only the balance of power which matters. In the lay Europe which emerged out of Westphalia "free" of the Catholic Church and its magisterium, bullying, violence and the spasmodic thirst for power led to never ending wars and revolutions, all culminating in the two world conflicts of the 12th century.

A few words about France, the nation which for the time being won: some of her features and her history. In France, from time immemorial, the king ruled unchallenged over the Gallican national church, so called in opposition to the universal Roman Church. The king's primacy was established of old but with Charles VII, it assumed heretical undertones. His rise to the throne was due entirely to the courage and faith of Joan of Arc, that is, to the grace of God in the most literal sense. Nevertheless, Charles made himself the mediator between the "just" demands of the clergy in his kingdom and the Pope. It was the year 1438 and the Western Schism had just come to a close. In an environment reeking of conciliarism, the Pope attempted to take the situation back in hand by moving the Council, which became revolutionary, from Basel to Florence: this was the context in which Charles VII issued the *Pragmatic Sanction* of Bourges, inspired to Emperor Justinian I, by which he assumed the role of judge over religious issues. The Holy See did not underwrite the *Pragmatic Sanction* and some decades later, in 1516, Leo X of the House of Medici signed an agreement with Francis I which partially limited regal demands. In any case, the king's power was exorbitant: though formally the selection of churchmen was autonomous, practically it was the king who oversaw them because the electors had to hear his just pleadings; the bishop committed to defend the assets of the king and his children, supplied advice and guaranteed to keep these secret. From the death of the titular bishop until his successor was installed, the king profited from the income of vacant benefices and thus he would make sure long interludes of time passed. Many abbeys were ruined in this way. It was the king who convoked provincial and national synods; no law issued by the Church could contradict his ordinances and none were enforceable if they did not first receive his *placet*. The Church's judicial power was held hostage by the parliament of Paris and of the provinces: the Paris parliament, made up of clergymen and laymen acted as a kind of supreme court and intervened in all matters: excommunication, indulgences, bishops' attire, the assignment of benefices and the confirmation of appointments, the authentication of relics, overseeing the compiling of breviaries, overseeing financial administration. In France, *libertas ecclesiae* simply didn't exist because, when all is said and done, the church was an instrument at the service to the kingdom. Starting from the second half of the 16th century France became a ruling nation and so, even from a cultural point of view, it was the most perfect example of an absolute monarchy.

De Propaganda Fide

During the years of the Galileo affair, in the years of the Thirty Years' War, in the years when it gradually lost influence on an international level, the Holy See took an important step to recover those functions which for many years had been delegated to rulers but in reality were its own prerogative. It did so by claiming the primarily important task of guiding the evangelization which now reached the whole world. For a few decades, various attempts were hindered by the kings, who in virtue of the patronage granted to them, deemed it their prerogative to handle first-hand the spreading of the faith in their own lands as well as in those not directly controlled by them. However, in 1622, Clement VIII established the congregation *De Propagande Fide* which gradually managed to centralize the work of overseeing all catholic missions by coordinating a real army of missionaries unhindered by political, prestige, and power demands of colonial powers. The responsibilities of *Propaganda* were many: initiatives for the freeing of slaves, the establishment of local seminaries, the promotion of geographic exploration for better knowledge of mission lands but also for the purposes of science, health care, the building of all kinds of schools, the battle against the trafficking of women and opium. In 1626 a polyglot printing house was established which edited texts on all subjects, often at no cost; its archives were full of documents of the utmost interest, its library very rich, its palace, begun by Bernini and completed by Borromini, splendid.

At the turn of the 17th century, two significant events took place in Asia where the evangelization had arrived for some time now through the Portuguese and then the Spanish. Two important nations leaned in opposite directions: Japan began the persecution while China opened itself up to the Gospel. The preaching in Japan had begun with Xavier in 1549 and in very few years the faith took root and spread. However, in 1587 a persecution began that was ruthless for its intensity and length. With various ups and downs it lasted until 1889 when religious freedom was introduced. A unique instance in the entire world, the Japanese maintained the faith without priests, meaning without Eucharist and without Confession for over two hundred years until in 1865, a French missionary with incredible awe discovered their existence. The "hidden Christians" survived in the catacombs for a length of time almost as long as that of the persecution unleashed by the Roman Empire.

The history of the Gospel's preaching in China was quite different. It was begun in the final part of the 13th century with Franciscans led by Giovanni di Montecorvino (1247-1328) and it was taken up again thanks to the science and knowledge of the Jesuits which by their culture attracted the Empire's attention. In these circumstances, the leading role was played by a Jesuit from Macerata, Matteo Ricci (1552-1610), a learned mathematician, cartographer, astronomer and even painter. Ricci arrived in China in 1582 and followed a motto of Pauline inspiration to the letter: "Become Chinese with the Chinese."[25] Supported by Clement VIII he chose to present Christianity as the natural evolution of early Confucianism. He dressed as a Mandarin, took on a Chinese name, grew his hair and beard just like the Confucian scholars, and accepted ancestor worship typical of traditional religion. In a few words, Ricci adopted a perfect inculturation model by which he managed to reach the court in Beijing. A man of science, he put all his knowledge in the service of the Gospel and offered quite a tribute to the Chinese: he printed the *Map of the Ten Thousand Countries of the Earth* which was a world atlas of great accuracy and precision; he published *The Memory Palace*, an interesting treatise about mnemotechnies; with a Chinese colleague he translated Euclid's works; he built an automatic clock. All of this had such an impact, that in Beijing's forbidden city, that is, the most symbolic and meaningful place in the Chinese world, today, one can still marvel at the watercolor paintings made by Ricci exhibited next to traditional Chinese paintings. In the years which followed his death, Dominicans, Franciscans and Capuchins unleashed a violent debate against inculturation as enacted by the Jesuits in China and India. More than a century of controversies led Benedict XIV to condemn the Chinese rites in 1742 and the Malabar rites in 1744.

In 17th century Europe, when the Protestant assault moderated its hostility, the danger came from inside the Church. The Jansenist heresy reproposed a version of an essentially Lutheran

---

[25] "I have become all things to all men," wrote Paul in the *First Letter to the Corinthians*.

anthropological vision camouflaged as Catholic. Bishop Cornelius Otto Jansen, Jansenius (1585-1638), a teacher in the University of Louvain, which paradoxically was established to combat the protestant heresy, in his *Augustinus* offered a tragic view of a completely corrupt mankind. Moreover, he firmly asserted that divine grace was irresistible, denied free will and by promoting the idea of predestination, denied also the universal salvific value of Christ's sacrifice. Jansenist pessimism went hand in hand with burdensome rigor and exasperating religious scruples in opposition to both the common practice of official religion based purely on outward appearances and the laxity ascribed to the Jesuits whom he accused to be Semi-Pelagian. The acclaim gained in France by the followers of Jansen was directly related to the fame of those men who adhered to his doctrine: philosophers, logicians and mathematicians like Blaise Pascal (1623-1662), Saint-Cyran, Angélique and Antoine Arnauld.

For decades many pontifical reprimands were issued but the Jansenists strenuously defended the orthodox nature of Jansen's teachings and the sincerity of their personal adhesion to the Roman Church. Louie XIV's intervention put an end to Jansenism as a religious movement when in 1711 he decreed the destruction of Port Royal, the monastery run by the Arnauld sisters chosen as the movement's spiritual center. Since then Jansenism mutated and became a political movement.

The religious policies of Louie XIV (1643-1715), who was the most perfect embodiment of the absolute monarch, worked to unite the French people and strengthen them. After all, wars needed to be fought to consolidate the power and greatness of the nation. The French king's Catholic faith was never evident: in the fight against Jansenism, as with the Huguenots compelled by the abolition of the Edict of Nantes to abandon France in 1685, really at play was a never-ending conflict with Rome. In fact, Innocent XI secretly excommunicated the king who further widened the prerogatives of the Gallican church.

Through Margaret Mary Alacoque, Jesus asked Louie XIV to consecrate himself, his family and France to the Sacred Heart. One hundred and three years later, Louie XVI, while in prison vowed to fulfil the consecration requested of his grandfather if only he were granted the chance to earn his freedom. Too late, confided Jesus to Sister Lucia in Fatima.

Wien, September 11, 1683

On September 11, 1683, Wien was under siege by an enormous Turkish army commanded by the Grand Vizier Kara Mustafa Pasha and on the verge of starvation was ready for surrender. The Turks, who in 1571 had been shut off from the sea, continued their conquest on land. They seemed unstoppable and right behind Wien they fixed their gaze on Rome and St. Peter's. Everything was ready for what Islam had been working towards for a thousand years. A genius polish warrior, Jan Sobiesky and the Capuchin friar Marco D'Aviano made all the difference. Charged by Innocent XI to form a Holy League against the Turks, father Marco became councilor and confessor to Emperor Leopold I, around whom he successfully united Spain, Portugal, Poland, Florence, Venice and Genoa. From the French side, since Louie XIV was too busy with his own interests, only a few volunteers showed up.

On the vigil of the battle, Friar Marco entrusted Wien's fate to the Virgin Mary and turned to God with the following prayer: "Oh great God of hosts, Look upon us here prostrate at the feet of Your majesty to implore forgiveness for our faults. We well know that we the infidels rising in arms to oppress us is our just deserve, because the iniquities we commit every day against your goodness have justly provoked your wrath. Oh great God, we ask your forgiveness in the depths of our hearts; we loathe sin because You abhor it; we are afflicted because we have often excited Your most high goodness to anger. For the love of your very self, we prefer to die a thousand times over rather than to commit the smallest action that may displease you. Aid us with your grace, oh Lord, and do not allow that we, your servant, break the covenant which we have made with You.

Therefore, have mercy on us, have mercy on Your Church, for whom the infidels have already prepared their fury and power. Though it be our fault that they invaded these beautiful and Christian lands, and though all these evils which befall us are nothing more than the consequence of our malice, yet look favorably on us, oh good

God, and do not despise the work of your hands. Remember that to snatch us out of servitude to Satan, You have shed Your most precious Blood.

Will you allow that it be trampled over by the feet of these dogs? Perhaps will you allow that faith, this beautiful pearl which you sought with such zeal and redeemed with such pain, be thrown under the feet of these swine? Do not forget, oh Lord, that if you should allow the infidels to prevail over us, they shall blaspheme Your holy Name and will ridicule your power by repeating a thousand times: 'where is their God, that God who could not deliver them from our hands?' Oh Lord, let no one hold the unleashing of the wolves' fury against you right when we invoked You in our wretched anguish. Come and aid us, oh great God of battles! If you are for us, the infidel armies cannot harm us. Disperse this people who wanted war! [...]

Therefore, deliver the Christian army from the evils which threaten it; withhold the arm of your wrath looming over us and make our enemies understand that there is no other God besides You and that only You have the power to grant or deny victory and triumph when it so pleases You. Like Moses, I stretch out my hands to bless Your soldiers; sustain and support them with your power to the ruin of Your and our enemies, to the glory of your Name. Amen."

At dawn on September 11, while Wien is all in prayer, after having celebrated mass before the whole army on Mount Kahlenberg, Marco, turning to Sobiesky, shouted: *Iohannes vinces* (John, you shall win). The victory of the Christian army over the Turks is of incalculable and unforeseeable proportions. It was such, that Mohammeh IV sent his Grand Vizier a green silk chord and invited him to use it so as to put an end to his life. The following day, it is told that the pastry-cooks invented croissants, a pastry shaped like a crescent moon, while in the Church of the Madonna of Loreto a solemn *Te Deum* was celebrated in thanksgiving. Innocent XI, attributing the victory to Mary's intercession, decided to celebrate the deliverance from danger by establishing on September 12 the Feast of the Most Holy Name of the Blessed Virgin Mary.

Three hundred and eighteen years later, in memory and in redemption of September 11, 1683, on September 11, 2001, Muslim terrorists made the Twin Towers in New York collapse. In memory of September 11, 1683, John Paul II restored the Feast of the Most

Holy Name of Mary in 2002, which in the meantime had been suppressed. On April 27, 2003, Pope Wojtyla beatified Marco D'Aviano, the friar who came from the small province of Veneto and who is buried in the Capuchin church that holds the remains of emperors in its crypt. The emperors could not give a more solemn homage to the Capuchin friar's memory and to the role he played in forming the Holy League in support of Leopold I by patiently harmonizing the conflicting interests of those involved. With the Peace of Carlowitz in 1699, the League dealt a final blow to the Turkish threat in Europe: Hungary, Transylvania, Croatia, Dalmatia, and Podolia were finally delivered from Muslim domination. The Turkish conquest was over.

A Presbyterian Pastor at Work

In 1717, Modern Freemasonry was born in London. In 1723, the Presbyterian Pastor James Anderson wrote *The Constitutions of the Free-Masons*, the founding text of every lodge. Freemasonry's closeness to Protestantism is obvious since the very beginning.

The *Constitutions* is of great interest because it summarizes the main philosophical ideas developed in the preceding few centuries. Moreover, while previously they circulated only in exclusive circles and were the privilege of a very close-knit group of people, and though these theories were essentially elitist, this text made them available to a much wider public.

Dutch and English colonialism, which took the upper hand over the Spanish and the Portuguese (France is a special case), did not pursue any religious aim. The conquest of new territories for them had nothing to do with exporting the "true faith." Now, if there was no common faith what united the homeland and the colonies? What made them compatible? In absence of the religious element, the need arose to find a least common denominator of a cultural kind. The *Constitutions* can be read keeping this need in mind: colonial powers needed to find effective tools that could involve the leading classes of countries under their power; they did so by giving them the impression that they actually mattered through co-opting them into the exclusive, powerful and privileged world of the lodges. In fact,

The Constitutions say that "Freemasonry becomes the Center of Union and the means to foster sincere friendship among people who would have forever been distant."

The implicit content in the Peace of Westphalia became explicit in the *Constitutions*: the Catholic Faith was no longer regarded as the center of union but rather of division. Particular faiths are always a cause for conflict and therefore it would be advisable to put them aside and "force" the brothers to believe only "that Religion wherein mankind can all converge yet allowing people to hold their personal opinions." Anderson insisted on this point repeatedly: "Since we, as Freemasons, belong to the above-mentioned Universal Religion." In the initiation ceremony to the Royal Arch one can understand what the theory developed by Grotius about universal religion means for Freemasonry. In that step, the two names of God are revealed to the brothers: Jehova and Jahbulon, that is the synthesis between the God of the Jews (Jah-Jahweh), of the Chaldeans (Bul-Baal), and of the Egyptians (On-Osiris): Jahbulon precisely.

"A Freemason is required by his condition to obey moral law." "You must act as it would suit a moral and wise man," wrote Anderson. Morality is a most important issue for Freemasons. In fact, they insist that the brothers should be men who have a good reputation: "Those admitted to be members of a Lodge should be good and sincere men, born free and of a mature and reasonable age, not slaves, not women, not immoral or scandalous men, but those who enjoy a good reputation." At the same time, the *Consititutions* repeatedly forbid the brothers from revealing their affiliation. Thus they are forbidden from speaking about anything that has to do with the life of the Lodge to relatives, friends or acquaintances (and even with brothers who belong to a lower level): "You must be cautious in your words and behavior so that the more attentive outsider may never discover or find what is inconvenient for him to learn; sometimes you may have to deviate a conversation and carefully manipulate him to safeguard the honor of our respectable Brotherhood"; "Do not let your family, friends and neighbors come to know what regards the Lodge, etc., but rather wisely safeguard your honor and that of the ancient Brotherhood."

Not only Spinoza, but also the other brothers act *caute*, that is, cautiously, with much caution.

The need to keep the secret about everything which has to do with the lodge is tied to the need to defend the "honor" of the brotherhood. This excerpt is not clear: why must they use absolute discretion about one's affiliation in order to safeguard their honor and that of Freemasonry? In order to try and understand why, we will turn to a text written midway through the 19th century by a distinguished member of the French Freemasonry. Jean Mearie Ragon wrote: "Freemasonry is the universal morality which suits all men of all climates and cults. Just like the other cults, Freemasonry does not receive any law but rather itself establishes it since its morality, one and unchanging, is more extended and universal than that afforded by religions of other countries which are always particular."

Ragon claims that Freemasonry is charged with the task of establishing what is good and what is evil on its own, that is, of establishing moral norms. It would not be uncanny if, as in Bacon's case, that Freemasonry views those behaviors which the Decalogue and Christian people firmly condemn as good and just.

In addition, the importance of secrecy is stressed by oaths which go along with every step of Freemasonic life. This is the oath a candidate makes upon entrance into the order as apprentice: "I promise and swear to never reveal the secrets of Freemasonry, to never let anyone know about all that is revealed to me under penalty of having my throat cut, my heart ripped out, my tongue and entrails lacerated, my body turned into a corpse cut in pieces, then burned, reduced to dust and the dust thrown to the wind for the loathing of my memory and eternal infamy."

Freemasons are convinced that the definition of good and evil is their prerogative because they believe themselves the only ones who make use of reason eminently: "Freemasonry is a perfect and positive science; it is founded on a doctrine which springs forth from perfected human reason," wrote J.M. Ragon. The certainty of being better than the profane, that is, better than those who do not belong to the lodges, allows those of the order of Freemasons to define themselves as better: free. Almost exactly two centuries before, Luther had claimed freedom for princes (and only for them) by identifying freedom with independence from the magisterium of the Popes. Now, Freemasonic brothers, in virtue of the science dictated to them by perfected reason, which they believed to possess, made a claim on freedom (only for themselves) to choose what is good and what is evil, free from any ties to Revelation or the Decalogue.

However, though they are free, inside, Freemasons are under commitments to strictly obey: governors "must be obeyed in their respective fields by all Brothers according to the ancient duties and rules, with all humility, reverence, love and speed," wrote Anderson. To differentiate the deeply loathed Catholic obedience from Freemasonic, Ragon wrote: "The freedom of Freemasons is reasonable obedience as opposed to passive obedience, a sign of slavery."

In very few years, Lodges spread speedily throughout the world. The certainty of forming the best part of society, their reason enlightened, morality self-established, secrecy, obedience, all prepared the landslide of violent uprisings against those who were an obstacle on the road to triumph of the emerging new world.

Go, set a Watchman, let him announce what he sees[26]

From the 18th century up until today, the history of the Church is a narrative about a long and continuous series of more or less violent persecutions in all parts of the world. From the 18th century up until today, the Popes played a great prophetic role: they analyzed the features of secret associations, then expounded with clarity their main principles and described a long time in advance what their inevitable consequences would be. The first official condemnation of Freemasonry was issued on April 28, 1738, by Clement XII, in an apostolic letter *In Eminenti* published twenty-one years after the establishment of London's lodge. Keeping in mind that Freemasonry is a secret association and its ways of operating are also secret, it was issued at a truly surprising speed. Along the seventeen and 19th century, the Popes were like watchmen who kept their eyes open, saw and decried what they saw in a vast number of documents.

Freemasonry claims that it is tolerant towards everyone and therefore that it is not anti-Catholic. Moreover, each new sect assures its goodwill towards Catholicism. However the Popes never deviated from their firm condemnation of any kind of secret association no matter what its name was: "If they did not act wickedly, then they

---

[26] See Isaiah 21,6.

would not so decidedly hate the light," wrote Clement XII. Oaths, secrecy, "a kind of affected appearance of genuine honesty," religious indifference ("men of any religion and sect unite"), they are harmful "not only to the temporal peace of the Republic, but also to the spiritual health of souls." The pontiff's conclusion was final: "In virtue of holy obedience," let no one dare participate, "propagate or favor said Societies of Free-Masons."

Over time the Popes dealt out multiple excommunications and yet, Freemasonry took hold even within the Church. The Jesuit José Antonio Ferrer Benimeli made a list describing the clergy's participation to various lodges in the 18th century. This list, though it is "merely an orientation," and though it is "incomplete and provisional," furnishes documentary evidence about the affiliation of "all religious orders and of all the high clergymen, from bishops to the humblest rural parish priest." The Jesuit spoke of 2,000 Freemason clergymen amongst whom were 2 bishops, 5 archbishops, 5 metropolitans, 30 vicar generals, 300 secular canons, 157 Benedictines, 39 Capuchins, 35 Cistercians, 33 Minims, 32 Dominicans, 30 Franciscans, 30 Agustinians, 26 ex-Jesuits. Such involvement denotes a gross superficiality and guilty disobedience on the part of the clergy to the pontifical magisterium.

The Archive of the Congregation for the Doctrine of the Faith holds the correspondence between the cardinal of Rohan and Giuseppe Balsamo, self-named Count of Cagliostro (1743-1794) who founded an "Egyptian" Freemasonry. So, at least one cardinal appears to be in a lodge. Their correspondence is very interesting because the Grand Master addressed the prelate as if he was simply an executioner of his commands: if Rohan had not speedily obeyed, not long thereafter "he would have been dealt due punishment. You will be subjected to the penalty which our enemies are made to suffer. In few words, you will forever regret it." The oaths pronounced upon entrance to a lodge are in no way metaphorical.

If Freemasons thoroughly infiltrated all settings, at court their presence was quite relevant. From the first decades of the 18th century, it was obvious that something was off in the relationship between the papacy and the various European courts. The analysis made in 1737 by the Venetian Ambassador Alvise Mocenigo is remarkable: "It is an undeniable fact that there is something unnatural in the life of all Catholic governments. They are involved in such gross conflicts with the Roman court, that they ever even contemplate an agreement which would not harm the latter's vital principles. It may all be due to an increased cultural level, as many claim, or to a bullying spirit against the weak; however, it is certain that princes, in a few quick moves, have mobilized to snatch all earthly prerogatives away from the papal throne." At court, Freemasons inspired rulers to enact reasonable and enlightened religious policies which reduced the number of religious orders and set the pace of their days to prevent prayer from acquiring an exaggerated importance; for sure it cannot be done at night. That is how in France, from 1762 the midnight office was abolished because it was deemed prejudicial to a productive workday, cloistered life was limited and many convents were suppressed. Enlightened Despotism, they'll say, and the name itself is a program. Despotism: despotic powers, powers that do not grant the Church any freedom whatsoever. In the name of reason. In the name of progress. In the name of happiness. To be brief, in the name of the power of the lodges.

One by one, all European courts became favorable to enlightened despotism. But putting propaganda aside, anti-Christian philosophy seemed to not benefit the common good at all. Here are a few examples to appreciate the point. English Empiricism and the French Enlightenment, which divulged this philosophy, had two words in common: freedom and tolerance. Freedom? The most distinguished people from both schools, namely, in order, Locke (1632-1704) and Voltaire (1694-1778) made their fortune by trafficking in slaves. This is what Locke thought about the vast majority of people who did not enjoy a comfortable life like his own: "The greater part of humanity is not really capable of leading intellectual and moral lives because it is occupied with work and is enslaved by the needs that their mediocre situation dictates. So their lives are consumed only with providing for their needs." The English philosopher believed that a taskmaster rightfully has "absolute power" over the slave, a "legislative power of life and death," an "arbitrary power" which has to do with life itself. With regards to the poor, the idea is pretty much the same: children must be separated from their parents and sent to work at the age of three. David Hume (1711-1776), the very last promoter of English Empiricism, supported the idea of burning all books which did not contain analyses by numbers and facts; this same idea was what in 645, led Caliph Omar to destroy the Alexandria library since "either the books therein are in agreement with the Quran and therefore they are useless to us, or they are not in agreement with the Quran and therefore they are evil."

With regards to freedom, the "brother" Voltaire excluded black people. The following he wrote in his *Essay on custom*: "Negroes are by nature slaves of other men. Hence they are to be bought as cattle from the coast of Africa." Apostle of tolerance? In his *Philosophical Dictionary* he defined Jews as follows: "An ignorant and barbarian people who embody the most sordid kind of avarice with a most despicable superstition and the most invincible hate for all peoples who tolerate and enrich them." In the encyclical written in 1775, *Inscrutabili Divinae Sapientiae*, Pius VI spoke as follows about Enlightenment philosophers: "These perverted philosophers, after having spread this darkness and ripped religion from the hearts, try even to have men break all bonds that unite them to each other and to their rulers by their duty; they proclaim ad nauseam that man is born free and is not subject to anyone."

Dominus ac Redemptor

The fiercest and most prepared adversaries of Enlightenment philosophy and of secret societies were the Jesuits, the fathers who almost everywhere were in charge of educating the leading European classes. Directly proportional to their schools' success was the hate which surrounded them. Starting in 1614, a small anonymous booklet was circulated which bore the title *Monita Privata Societatis Jesu*. It spread to every country in multiple editions. It was a grand forgery which divulged information about a supposed command given within the Society by which it should not pursue the glory of God (*Ad Maiorem Dei Gloriam* was the Jesuits' motto) but rather the Order's power.

The Jesuits at court tirelessly countered the counsels given by neopagan philosophers who were the advocates of enlightened despotism: it's no surprise that Freemasons want them dead. In fact, this is how they refer to the Jesuit fathers in the initiation ritual to the

33rd degree of the Ancient and Accepted Scottish Rite: "HE OF THE TOMORROW, Hiram [Solomon's architect, the mythical founder of Freemasonry] foreshadows the Immortal man, raised from the ages, who shall rule the world after having annihilated all despotism, all fanaticism. To HIM fulfilment of the Great Work is due. Light against the black militia of Ignatius of Loyola: crusaders for Gnosis against the theocratic infidels; Knights of the unique and universal Temple against those who profane and usurp the Temple."

Those who "usurp the Temple" were expelled from all Catholic nations starting from Portugal where the Freemason Marquis of Pombal launched a defamatory campaign against the Society by accusing it of conspiring against the life of the king. In 1759 he successfully obtained their suppression, the seizure of all their assets, the brutal expelling of all foreign Jesuits, hard prison for those who were Portuguese, amongst whom, the elderly man Malagrida who instead was killed. The courts of France, Spain (where blame for a popular uprising was attributed to the Jesuits), Italy and Austria followed closely thereafter. The Enlightened Despots demanded that the Pope conform and suppress the Society. While the armies of France and Naples invaded the pontifical estate in Avignon and Benevento, Clement XIII did not give in to the princes' *dictat* and bravely defended the Jesuits. His successor, Clement XIV was not so brave and by Papal Brief, *Dominuc ac Redemptor*, on July 21, 1773, he suppress the Society of Jesus forever, or at least so he intended, and he condemned the Superior General Lorenzo Ricci to hard prison, meaning to a regime of bread and water, in the Castel Sant'Angelo prison. Such decision was made, the Pope claimed, for "the good of the Church and the peace of the people," but neither the Church nor the people benefited at all from this astonishing surrender to governments' tyranny. Giuseppe La Farina (1815-1863), a Freemason historian and one of the Italian Risorgimento's main players, commented on Pope Ganganelli's decision in his *History of Italy*: "With the suppression of the Jesuits, the rebellion of princes against the papacy was finally consummated and by the Papal Bull issued on July 21, the Pope cowered down before the princes."; "Never before did freedom have such enemies as the Jesuits, never before did the Papacy have such industrious and intrepid militia: Pope Ganganelli's Bull wasn't a reform; it was capitulation forced on him by the victor."

It's worthwhile to clarify that, when La Farina speaks about freedom, he is referring to Freemasons, the only free people by definition.

Anti-Catholic persecution continued despite the sacrifice of the fathers (some of whom, that is, the polish, were welcomed by Catherine II of Russia) and reached the once Christian heart of Europe, that is, the Roman Empire, ruled by the House of Habsburg. In the 18th century, the imperial family in its entirety entered Freemasonry and so Maria Theresa of Austria (1740-1780), her husband Francis of the House of Lorraine and their children, the Emperors Joseph II (1780-1790) and Leopold II (1790-1792), were all Freemasons. In theory, the Empire was still Holy, that is inspired to Catholic faith, but in 1785, Joseph II issued a decree which made Freemasonry legal: "In the past and in other countries, Free-Masons were outlawed and punished, their Lodges' meetings were disturbed and banned; that is why their mysteries were unknown. Though I am still ignorant about them, for me it is enough to know that such gatherings of Free-Masons may produce some sort of good with respect to humanity, poverty and education." Joseph II's religious policy removed every freedom from the Church within the empire and this legacy passed to history as "Josephinism": the emperor forbade communications of bishops with Rome, forbade all appeals to Rome, the religious could not be accountable to their Roman superior, seminarians could not study in Rome's Collegium Germanicum, he redrew diocesan boundaries, intervened in liturgical matters, reformed ecclesiastical studies by establishing which books needed to be adapted and which teachers could work, he suppressed about 300 convents, a third of the total, starting from enclosed religious orders and Mendicant Orders, he reduced the number of religious feasts. Pius VI tried to put a stop to the emperor's craving for modernity by going to Wien in person. However, despite the honor shown to him, Joseph II's anti-Catholic beliefs were in no way touched.

In support of his own religious policy, Joseph II took advantage of the theses of the auxiliary bishop of Trier, the heretic Febronius (Johann Nikolaus von Hontheim, 1701-1790) who challenged the universal mission of the Pope and his supreme jurisdiction over the whole Church. He proposed a return to some supposed primitive liberty of national churches that with time the Popes took over.

Further, he promoted reconciliation to the Protestant Churches by appealing to a council and the intervention of imperial powers.

The Habsburgs paid a dear price for their apostasy: the queen of France, Marie Antoinette was decapitated on October 16, 1793 and in 1806, after one thousand years, the Holy Roman Empire came to an end. In the first book of the *Aeneid*, Virgil lends his mouth to Jupiter to reassure Venus who was worried about the fate of her son Aeneas and the Romans: "To them I have not placed limits of time or enterprise: I have given them power without end." Francis II of the House of Habsburg put an end to the Roman Empire and nullified the history of his house by becoming just a simple? Francis I of Austria. Thereafter, he gave his daughter Marie Louise's hand in marriage to Napoleon, a noble Corsican who became the master of Europe and who proclaimed himself emperor of the French. La Farina made the following comment: philosophers "would flatter the prince in order to fight the priest"; the princes "did not understand that by rejecting the Pope as their judge, they had to accept the people as judge; they wanted freedom for themselves, not for their subjects; they rejected divine right but did not accept human right either: an impartial writing of history would claim it was they who were shortsighted, not the people who were ungrateful." By people, La Farina refers to the members of the lodges.

"Quanno nascette Ninno" – When the little Child was born

While the world proceeded with certainty towards dechristianization, at least of the leading classes, God took care of his Church by means of saints who were like magnets directing the life of the faithful towards the good. We will choose three, two French and one from Naples.

In the France of the Sun King, while the court amused itself in Versailles' luxury and in showing off the national greatness, the Holy Spirit raised up saintly men and women who cared for the normal people, for the poor people. They chose humility as the key to their evangelical mission. The more the world flaunted is pride, the more people of God do the opposite. Jean Baptiste de La Salle (1651-1719), the firstborn of ten children from a noble family of jurists, founded the Institute of the Brothers of the Christian Schools which helped withstand the impact of the gnostic attack on the Catholic world. De La Salle stood with the poor he wanted to educate and never abandoned them. That is why he founded free schools, some of which ran also on Sundays, primary and professional schools in which the youth had lay teachers who had consecrated themselves to God but who lived in the world, the so-called "little ignorant" because they were neither priests nor knew Latin. They were humble teachers.

The second of eighteen brothers who went by foot on pilgrimage to Paris and then to Rome, lived as a hermit in a cave, cared for the sick in hospitals, was a mystic, a tireless missionary who was thought to be overly eccentric and therefore opposed and repeatedly kicked out from where he went in mission; who was so zealous in his apostolate to the poor of the Vendée department, that Pius XII credited his pastoral dedication for the stark opposition this department made to the French revolution; the constructor of Calvaries with the help of crowds of people which were then destroyed because of some curious military needs: Louis-Marie Grignion de Montfort (1673-1716). He founded the Company of Mary and the Daughters of Wisdom. Grignion de Montfort opened the Age of Mary, the age during which the role and presence of Jesus' mother became a dominant and recurring theme in the history and life of the Church.

"I foresee many angry beasts will arrive in fury with their diabolical teeth to rip out this lowly writing and he whom the Holy Spirit used to write it, or, to enclose it in the darkness and silence of a chest so that He will not be known; actually, they will attack and persecute those men and women who read it and try to put it into practice." The book Monfort was referring to is *True Devotion to the Mary*. Though he wrote it in 1712, it remained lost until it was found by chance and published it in 1842. God revealed a secret to this mystic: to reach Jesus, the best and surest way is Mary. To Jesus through Mary: "Since the entirety of our perfection lies in acquiring the likeness, being united and consecrated to Jesus Christ, then the most perfect of all devotions, the one which most consecrates and conforms a soul to Jesus Christ the Lord is the devotion to the Holy Virgin, his mother. The more a soul consecrates itself to Mary, the more it will be consecrated to Jesus Christ. That is why, a perfect consecration to Jesus Christ is nothing other than a perfect and total consecration of oneself to the Virgin, which is the devotion I teach; in other words, it is a perfect renewal of the vows and promises of Holy Baptism." There is no miracle Jesus works that has not first passed through Mary: "She sanctified Saint John from the womb of his mother, Saint Elizabeth, by means of Mary's word; as soon as she spoke, John was sanctified and this was the first and greatest miracle of grace. In the marriage feast of Canaan, he changed water into wine after Mary made a humble prayer, and this was the very first miracle in the order of nature. He began and continued his miracles through Mary and, through Mary, He will continue them until the end of times."

Monfort's Company of Mary was a "small and poor Company of priests" who "under the banner and protection of the Most Holy Virgin Mary, went about in a poor and simple way to teach catechism to the poor in the fields and to incite sinners to practice devotion to Mary." Montfort had one exceptional admirer who was Pope Wojtyla. On his episcopal seal the motto *Totus Tuus* appeared which was "inspired by the doctrine of Saint Louis-Marie Grignion de Montfort. These words express total belonging to Jesus through Mary: '*Totus tuus ego sum, et omnia mea tua sunt.*' This is what Louis-Marie wrote and he translated it thus: 'I am all yours and everything that is mine belongs to you, my beloved Jesus, through Mary, your Holy Mother.' This is how Montfort summarized the family life of the Christian: 'Every son of the Church must have God as Father and Mary as Mother.'"

He was a prodigal child who registered for university classes when he was 12 years old. When he was 16, he was already a lawyer, later judge, and then doctor of the Church and bishop. He really lived a life full of miracles. Alphonsus Maria de' Liguori (1697-1787) lived in Naples during the Age of enlightened despotism and of the unchallenged rule of the all-powerful Bernardo Tanucci, the first minister under Charles III of the House of Bourbon and then under his son Ferdinand IV. The environment in Naples was very hostile. The same tyrannical laws employed in Bourbon ruled France had been implemented here: the Jesuits were expelled, many convents suppressed and the jubilee year pilgrimage to Rome of 1775 was strictly forbidden. Nevertheless, through his excellent legal training,

Alphonsus managed to obtain approval for the Redemptorist congregation which cared for farmers and shepherds: the poor people of the Naples area. How can one catechize a people of poets who had always expressed itself in song? Through song. That is why Alphonsus composed many hymns in Neapolitan dialect. From one the most famous, *Quanno nascette Ninno*, a beautiful song which is lengthy and full of catechetical content, came *Tu scendi dalle stelle*, the most beautiful and most famous Christmas song in all of Italy.

"Quanno nascette Ninno a Bettlemme\Era nott'e pareva miezo juorno.\ Maje le Stelle – lustre e belle\Se vedetteno accossí:\E a cchiù lucente\Jett'a chiammà li Magge all'Uriente;\Co tutto ch'era vierno, Ninno bello,\Nascetteno a migliara rose e sciure.\Pe 'nsí o ffieno sicco e tuosto\Che fuje puosto – sott'a Te,\Se 'nfigliulette,\E de frunnelle e sciure se vestette;\Che tardammo? – Priesto, jammo,\Ca mme sento scevolí\Pe lo golfo\Che tengo de vedè sso Ninno Dio;\Correttero i Pasture a la Capanna;\Là trovajeno Maria\Co Giuseppe e a Gioja mia;\Cercajeno licenzia a la Mamma:\Se mangiajeno li Pedille\Coi vasille – mprimmo, e po\Chelle Manelle,\All'urtemo lo Musso;\Po assieme se mettetteno a sonare\E a cantà cu l'Angiule e Maria;\"Viene suonno da lo Cielo,\Vien'e adduorme sso Nennillo;\Pe pietà, ca è peccerillo,\Viene suonno e non tardà"[27].

The love of saints for God has a boundless freshness and creativity.

---

[27] "When the little Child was born in Bethlehem it was night, but it seemed like midday. Never before were the stars so bright and beautiful: the brightest went to call the Magi from the East;\And though it was winter, sweet little Child, thousands of rose and flowers sprung up. Even the dry and hard hay placed underneath you, spouted up and dressed up in fronds and flowers;\Why do we tarry? Quickly, let us go that I feel faint from the desire to see this little Child-God;\The shepherds ran to the hut; there they found Mary with Joseph and my Joy;\They asked the Mother permission: first they ate up his baby feet with kisses and then those little hands, lastly his dear face; Then, together with the angels and Mary they began to play and sing;\Come from heaven oh sleep, come, make this little Child sleep; please, he is so small, come, oh sleep, do not delay."

From Enlightened Despots to Terror

There is every kind of evidence to show that the war unleashed in the name of reason and civilization against the Society of Jesus was the prelude to the war against all religious orders and against the papacy. Both the blind belief of being the better part of society and faith in one's own scientific recipes developed to bring progress and happiness to the world, bring about an environment where there is not the least respect towards those Catholics who continued to think that the only salvation is the cross of Christ.

The dynamic which governs revolutionary events was already implied in the essay Kant wrote in 1784, *Answering the Question: What is Enlightenment?* The philosopher in search of perpetual peace (this is also the title of one of his essays) attacked the Catholic Church directly without ever mentioning it: "A society of churchmen" has no right to "oblige itself by oath to any immutable symbol" because this would be equal to "a crime against human nature," distinguished by "progress." Kant believed that the Catholic Church had no right to exist because it neither was nor wanted to be enlightened: "To agree in order to keep an immutable religious institution alive [...] and by so doing to slow down humanity on its road to improvement [...] is absolutely forbidden."

In 1776, in the name of the God of Nature, the American colonies vindicated their right and duty to rebel against a prince who behaved like a tyrant and who, as such, "is not apt to govern a free people." In any case, the American "brothers" care to specify that by so doing they are in no way lacking "in consideration towards their British brothers." The year 1789 was the turn of the French people. "In the presence and under the auspices of the Supreme Being," they demanded respect for the "natural, unalienable and sacred rights of man" ("liberty, property, security and resistance to oppression," art. 2 of the *Declaration of the Rights of Man and of the Citizen*) and that the "Nation" be recognized as the source of all authority: "No body or individual may exercise any authority which does not proceed directly from the Nation" (art. 3); "Law is the expression of the general will" (art. 6); "No one shall be bothered on account of his opinions, including his religious views" (art. 10); "Since property is an inviolable and sacred right, no one shall be deprived thereof except where public necessity, legally determined, shall clearly demand it, and then only on condition that the owner shall have been previously and equitably indemnified" (art. 17).

Saint Paul's belief that all authority comes from God is turned upside down in the sense that the nation is considered to be the source of all authority and it expresses it through the general will. To understand what is meant by the phrase general will, we need to turn to Rousseau who defined it as follows: "The general will aims at the common interest" and therefore it is the will which "is, or should be, the true engine of the body politic." Who embodies the general will? In *The Social Contract*, written in 1762, Rousseau answered: the general will is the result of the unifying pact amongst equals which produces "the total alienation of each individual and all his rights to the community," thus producing "a moral and collective body," which receives from this original pact its unity, "its common Ego, its life and its will." And also: "Whoever dares endeavor to establish a nation, must feel himself capable of changing, as it were, human nature"; he must "take from man his own powers, and give him in exchange powers that are unfamiliar to him." From the moment that the "common ego" of which Rousseau speaks does not exist, the inevitable and logical consequence of his philosophy is totalitarianism: "All equally need a guide" (all, both individuals and the collective); in order for the social compact to not be "an empty formula," "whoever refuses to obey the general will, shall be compelled to do so by the whole body; this means nothing less than that he will be forced to be free."

Rousseau on the one hand, Kant on the other, and in between the enlightened together with the thinking of all lodges, altogether contributed in the name of liberty, equality and brotherhood (freemasonic trinomial), to shape an inhuman society wherein few individuals subvert the social, political, economic and religious life of the nation in an attempt to make all things new and better.

In spite of the principles solemnly set forth in *The Declaration of the Rights of Man*, in 1789 all Church assets were seized and handed over to the nation, in February of 1790, with few exceptions, all religious orders were suppressed, and in July of the same year, the clergy was forced to make the oath of the *Civil Constitution of the Clergy* with the obvious intent to put an end to the Catholic Church's existence. The

Constitution transformed the Church in a duplicate of the state, whose features it traces: the same number of diocese as departments (passing from 134 to 83), all religious offices become elective and the voters are the same who vote for the "members of the department assembly" (atheist, Freemasons, anti-Catholics included), the role of the papacy is abolished by law ("all churches and parishes in France and all French citizens are forbidden, under any circumstances and under any pretext, from acknowledging the authority of an ordinary or metropolitan bishop whose seat is in the territory of a foreign power," art. 4), and the authority of bishops is also abolished by law as they now must take into account the opinion of their associates.

Starting from 1790, the French clergy was divided among the Juring (those who obeyed and made the oath) and the Refractory (those who refused to make the oath). Whoever rejected the oath was incarcerated, deported, or killed. In March of 1791, Pius VI condemned the *Constitution* and from that moment onwards, Louie XVI refused to receive communion from Juring priests. When he tried to escape with his family, he was discovered and imprisoned. The situation suddenly worsened, France was on the verge of bankruptcy and the Jacobins planned to live off of others by invading the boundary state in the name of the liberal trinomial. When the Marquis La Fayette was about to enter Belgium, the Minister of Foreign Affairs Dumouriez wrote him a letter: "Put aside all thoughts about what you are lacking: enter into a promised land."

In 1792 the bloodbaths began, Vendée rose up in arms against the violence perpetrated by the revolution and in 1793 terror arrived: the king and queen were guillotined, the people of Vendée exterminated[28], catholic worship was forbidden, the millenary civil and religious life of France was abolished: the names of the saints were banished, the names of months and days were changed, the calendar was rewritten, Notre Dame was called the Temple of Reason personified by a

---

[28] In his *History of the French Revolution*, the liberal historian Jules Michelet wrote: "The impious war of the priests exploded in the west"; "We find a people who are oddly blind and bizarrely lost because they rose up in arms against the Revolution, their mother." The "mother" revolution planned the massacre of the "brigands" in Vendée. These were killed using various methods meant to maximize death at minimal cost: it was the first genocide of the modern age.

prostitute dressed in red. An internal passport was now needed, both male and female attire was determined by law, the law against suspicion was approved in order to make the death penalty legal without needing to prove guilt. The revolution consumed itself to the point that Robespierre himself, the main responsible for the Reign of Terror, was publicly executed.

Slaughtered lambs

In a very short time, over fifty thousand churches and chapels disappeared from France, monuments of singular beauty were destroyed leaving no trace, abbeys, convents and priories numbering over twelve thousand were demolished, over twenty thousand castles looted and set on fire.

Catholics, normal people and supporters of the monarchy were killed using a tool invented for this: the guillotine. A simple, quick, cheap and not so painful way to kill; or so they say. The streets of Paris turned into rivers of blood. If apostates, such as bishop Talleyrand, just to name one, were many and powerful, then the saints who confronted martyrdom by clinging to the cross of Jesus, slaughtered lambs like their Lord, were many more. Amongst them were sixteen Carmelite nuns of Compiègne butchered on July 17, 1794. The persecution in this case arrived in the name of liberty. The Jacobins broke into the Compiègne monastery's enclosure convinced to free some poor women locked up in a convent by who knows what violence or subterfuges. They gave absolutely no credit to the spontaneous declaration sent by the Carmelite prioresses to the National Assembly in which the monks described their lives as follows: "At the base for our vows is the greatest liberty; in our house reigns the most perfect equality; here we know neither rich nor nobles. In the world many people love to say that monasteries lock up victims who are then gradually consumed by remorse; but we confess before God that, if happiness is to be found on earth, we are happy."

After interrogation, all the nuns confirmed that they wanted to continue "to live and die in their monastery," but they were denied even this liberty. Instead, they were kicked out of their own home, supposedly, to make them free. From there, the road to bearing witness through martyrdom was short. They were accused of "slowing down the progress of the public spirit," transferred to Paris as seditioners who "in their hearts bear the criminal longing of seeing the French put in fetters again by tyrants and enslaved to bloodthirsty and lying priests" and so sentenced to capital punishment. While they were dragged on wagons to the guillotine, along the way, the nuns prayed singing psalms and hymns. Under the scaffold, they sang *Veni Creator Spiritus*, renewed their religious vows and then one by one, in peace, after having asked their superior for permission to die, they went up the steps of a high scaffold to the guillotine placed there so that all could enjoy the show: *Laudate Dominum Omnes Gentes*, is psalm 116 which, accompanied them in song to their encounter with God. It was a heroic death, moving, full of dignity, a death which enlightened reason lacks the categories to understand or explain.

While martyrdom was consummated in France, whose both lay and religious high classes for many centuries enjoyed the merits and responsibilities of the Gallican church separate from Rome, the Enlightened Despots decreed the end of Poland which was split up in three phases (1772, 1793, 1795) between orthodox Russia, Catholic Austria, Calvinist Prussia. At the end of the 18th century, Catholic Poland ceased to exist.

In the meantime, on the opposite shore of the Channel, in England, in the name of science, an Anglican pastor anointed himself prophet of reducing births. Robert Malthus (1766-1834) published in 1798 an anonymous work, *An Essay on the Principle of Population*, in which he proved that, unimpeded by any other factors, the growth rate of world population follows a geometric progression while the growth rate of food follows an arithmetic progression. "Be fruitful and multiply, fill the earth" (*Genesis* 1,28) is a meaningless expression for the Christian Malthus: to him, demographic growth is the "greatest evil".

From a scientific point of view, Malthus' theory is groundless. Nonetheless it had an astonishing and lasting success.

While anti-Catholic and anti-Christian hate growing in Europe precipitated civil nations into a state of barbarism, in the Far East, in Korea and in California, the other side of the world, the missions produced many fruits. The people of Korea converted when no missionaries had been sent. The Korean Church is truly a prodigious fact also because throughout the 19th century it was repeatedly and cruelly persecuted. On October 14, 1984, celebrating the Korean martyrs, Pope Wojtyla said: "In Korea, a case unique in all history, faith was brought by the Koreans themselves. In fact, Koreans embarked on the road to faith by the initiative of a few lay people. Their experience helps us understand how important to eternal salvation is human reason's natural aspiration to truth. We know that it was the loyal quest for truth that pushed those lay people – it was a group made up of scholars and philosophers – at great risk to themselves, to make contacts in Beijing where they had heard resided men, some of them Catholic, who could enlighten them about the new faith they heard about in new books. These lay men and women, rightly considered the "founders of the Korean Church, between 1779 and 1835, that is for over 56 years, spread the Gospel throughout their country without the help of any priests, except for the very brief stay of two Chinese priests. When French missionaries arrived in 1836, they had already offered and sacrificed their life for the faith in Christ."

In California, Charles III of the House of Bourbon sent Franciscans to take the place of the Jesuits who had been brutally expelled in 1768. The Spanish king chose to use the evangelization as a weapon against English and Russian colonial competition and found the missionary zeal of Junipero Serra (1713-1784), a learned Franciscan from Palma de Majorca, to be the best guarantee for the success of his political scheme. California's chief cities were all named after saints or angels (San Francisco, San Diego, Santa Barbara, Los Angeles, Santa Fe, and Sacramento) because of Serra and his genius as a missionary entrepreneur. Junipero planned and partially brought to completion the construction of 21 fortified convents, set apart by a one day's walk, starting from San Diego in the south all the way up to Monterrey and San Francisco in the North along a road called the *Camino Real*. This was the last Spanish enterprise in the new world: if you want to admire something ancient in California, you need to visit the chapels and convents of the Franciscan missions.

A New Empire

The French Revolution was followed by a transition period during which all European nations were invaded in some way. The Spanish and Italian people rebelled against the violence perpetrated by the Jacobins who were supported in every nation by members of the lodges. Besides all idealistic motivations (liberty, equality, brotherhood), the Freemasons were clearly very pleased with dividing up Church assets. However, the invading army was brutal, made thousands of victims and gained the upper hand. The very same revolution Luther started was advancing once again, this time not for the sake of the Gospel's purity. A young general of the Republic distinguished himself and climbed up the ladder at an extraordinary pace. Napoleon Bonaparte (1769-1821) was Consul, then First Consul, First Consul for life and finally Emperor. All obstacles seemed to yield before him, including all the kingdoms of Europe; except for Russia where the "winter general" decimated the Jacobin army. To guide the conquered nations, the so-called liberty that France brought, appointed the relatives and friends of the winning general.

One by one the kingdoms fell. Amongst them, one had a unique history and was the most coveted, the most prestigious, and the most ancient in the western world: the State of the Church. Napoleon played cat and mouse with the Pope: feigned peace treaties, offered only apparent cease fires, and made lightning quick invasions. The general scientifically and meticulously robbed all the greatest works of art he encountered (Rome and Italy are filled with them) and transferred them to France[29] which seemed to obtain that universal power which it craved since the time of Avignon. Rome, the "red harlot of Babylon" as Luther called her, the city loathed by the whole enlightened protestant world, had to fall. And Rome, at the end, fell. So, an endless procession was formed, pulled by camels and Maremmano Bulls that were meant to "give the convoy a singularly majestic aspect," in which the most splendid artistic and cultural riches of the world were transported to Paris, the new world capital.

---

[29] Napoleon appointed a mathematician, Gaspard Monge at the helm of the "Commission of the Sciences and Arts": every action, according to the modern myth, must be placed under the patronage of "science".

The singular most important jewel robbed because of its historical and symbolic importance was the Roman Archives, true symbol of the city's millenary power.

After looting, among many others, the Basilica of Loreto, and after the Peace of Tolentino, which Pius VI was forced to sign in 1797, while hundreds of *Madonelle*[30] spread throughout the Pontifical State cried (there is evidence of over two hundred cases of this phenomenon), Napoleon invaded Rome, proclaimed the Republic and imprisoned the Pope. Pope Braschi, a dying eighty-year-old, was transported from city to city until he landed in Valence, France, where death put an end to his Calvary.

With Pius VII (1742-1823) we start all over again. The future emperor needed the support of the Pope and of Catholics because to conquer Europe he needed to ensure social, civil and religious peace in France. That is why he coerced the Pope into approving a concordat signed in 1801 which established very harsh and unfair terms upon the Church. Though Catholic worship was permitted again, Pius VII had to substitute all bishops, including those who suffered wrongdoings, persecutions and the prison time under the revolution and its violence and yet had not caved in ("His Holiness shall request titular bishops of French episcopal seats whom he surely trusts will, for the sake of peace and unity, accept any sacrifice including that of their own seat," art. 3). Moreover, he had to accept that the First Consul should appoint the prelates and that once these were names, they should swear an oath of fidelity to the First Consul ("Upon the Holy Gospels, I swear and promise God to be obedient and faithful to the government selected by the constitution of the French Republic. I also promise to never, directly or indirectly, associate with, attend councils or have relations that are contrary to the public order; I promise that if I come to know that in my diocese some are plotting against the State, I will inform the government," art. 6). Finally, in exchange for a sum as settlement, he renounced to all confiscated Church assets (the Holy See shall not give "those who purchased alienated Church properties trouble of any kind," art. 13).

---

[30] *Madonelle*: these are the thousands of paintings and bas-reliefs of Mary installed on the corners of buildings and squares to place the lives and houses of a city's inhabitants under Mary's protection.

In 1804 Napoleon deemed the time was right for a new empire. It would not be Catholic but nonetheless a universal empire that could substitute that of Rome. The Pope was forced to go to Notre Dame in Paris to attend a farce: a coronation ceremony for the imperial couple wherein Napoleon chose to crown himself. The tyrant did not stop at this. Two years later he declared that the temporal power of the Pope was at an end, he imprisoned the Pope and transformed Rome into a French city.

After so much movement, so many carnages and continuous wars, so many injustices and robberies, Napoleon's time came to an end and in 1814, the Pope returned to Rome where his first order of business was to restore the Society of Jesus. In the meantime, national delegates gathered in a congress in Wien where the fate of Europe, distraught by the revolution's fury, was decided. To contain French power and avoid any future politics of conquest, they chose to hold fast the principles of legitimacy and balance. These were diplomatic principles, meaning they were not absolute. In fact, for the sake of balance, in some cases the principle of legitimacy was not honored. The most outrageous examples were Catholic Belgium and Catholic Rhineland: the former was united to Calvinist Holland while the latter was assigned to Calvinist Prussia though there was no excuse for this – as in the case of Belgium – because these were not even contiguous territories. The ecclesiastical principalities which for almost one thousand years governed the rich Rhineland disappeared. Bishop counts were substituted by the King of Prussia who was implicitly invited to continue his territorial expansion uniting the lands in his possession.

This fact proves how European leaders never renounced the ideals of enlightened despotism and its inspiring philosophy: "The rest of mankind, who were not killed by these plagues, did not repent of the works of their hands," reads the *Book of Revelation*. The only difference with the time preceding 1789 was that now rebellion to the commandments and the magisterium was not carried out in the name of reason (impossible seeing its results) but in the name of sentiment. After all, it is just the other side of the medal. The end of the revolutionary period gave way to another revolutionary period which used other means to reach the same goals. It is Romanticisms: in art, literature, historiography, painting, music, poetry; Romanticism which in politics meant Nationalism and Liberalism. When not openly rejected, God was ignored or put aside.

Napoleon-Sun-God

The Age of Restoration

After twenty-six years of revolution, what remained? A lot. The end of local autonomies that lasted for centuries, a kind of exasperating central concentration of power, burocracy, central state education, lodges which owed allegiance to France had been established everywhere the army passed; men of the military and the bourgeoisie who Napoleon put in power fought to stay there and were ready for periodic uprisings; according to the Egyptian tradition, cemeteries were placed far from sight outside the cities so that death would not disturb the life of the living; inglorious end to the Holy Roman Empire; end of ecclesiastical principalities; above all the impossibility for Spain, invaded and looted, to defend its colonial lands from the greed of the English, French and Americans who used the lodges to prepare uprisings in the name of independence and liberty.

The sects reorganized and in Italy they gave life to the Carbonari: "We must remember a society that was recently born and has spread throughout Italy and other regions [...] it is usually called the Carbonari," wrote Pope Pius VII in the Bull *Ecclesiam a Jesu* issued in 1821. The Carbonari "feign having a singular respect and a kind of extraordinary zeal for the Catholic Religion," however, their objective was to destroy the Church of Christ as the documents found by the Pontifical Police at the time of Gregory XVI (1831-1846) prove. The text known as *Istruzione Permanente* written in 1819 says: "Our ultimate goal is the same set by Voltaire and the French Revolution: the complete annihilation of Catholicism and even of the same Christian idea." To reach said objective, the Carbonari aimed to infiltrate the clergy, the seminaries and high schools and to corrupt moral customs: "Man loves to have long chats in cafes and to lazily watch shows. Entertain him, work him with ability, make him believe he is important, teach him little by little to feel disgust for daily work so that after having separated him from wife and children, and after having shown him how hard it is to live fulfilling one's duties, instill in him the desire for a different life." The member of the Carbonari known by the pseudonym Piccolo Tigre (Little Tiger) wrote: "The essential goal is to isolate man from his family and make him lose his habits"; "when you have managed to instill disgust for the family and religion in some hearts (one is almost always followed by the other), let some word slip which will make him desire to affiliate himself to the nearest Lodge"; "the unknown exerts such power on men, that one prepares himself in trembling for lofty trials of initiation and of the brotherly banquets. To become members of a Lodge, to feel oneself, without wife or children, called to keep a secret which no one ever reveals to you, to some natures, it represents a luxury and an ambition." The *Istruzione* also reads: "Squash the enemy, whomever he may be, squash him with the power and strength of badmouthing and slander"; "You must seem simple as doves, but you will be prudent as serpents. Your parents, your children, your own wives must always be completely in the dark about the secret you carry and if, in order to better deceive their probing eyes you should decide to go often to confession, you are rightly authorized to keep the utmost secret about these things"; "You must have all the appearance of the most serious and moral man. Once your good reputation is well established in colleges, high schools, universities and seminaries, one you have captured the trust of professors and students, try to have those who are enrolled in the clerical militia seek out your company"; "the issue is to establish the kingdom of the elect on the throne of Babylon's prostitute: let the clergy march under your flag without ever doubting that it is following the apostolic keys."

A final quote, lapidary and short: "We have begun a great corruption, the corruption of the people through the clergy and of the clergy through us; such corruption will one day lead us to bury the Church," thus wrote Vindice to his cousin Nubio (the Carbonari so addressed each other) chief of the Alta Vendita.

The Popes did what they could to oppose the hate from organized sects. They made concordats, wrote encyclicals, warned princes of the true goals of secret associations; but they were not heard. Often, the Restoration period is referred to as the time of alliance between throne and altar, but this alliance is only formal; it is a front used by princes as an instrument of social control; not a sincere return to faith and penance for the compromise made with the Enlightenment and the disasters it caused. Proof of this is the *Memorandum* sent to Gregory XVI on May 21, 1831. It was written by the Prussian envoy to Rome and it summarized the outcome of the work done in an international conference sponsored by France which gathered in Rome French, English, Austrian, Prussian and Russian diplomats (including a conspicuous representation of the Sardinian government) to discuss solutions to the problem of the Papal State.

The document taught the Pope how to govern his own state and identified the solution to all problems in the "general admission of lay people to administrative and judiciary offices." France, England, Austria, Prussia and Russia: who were the powers who, in the Pope's own home, carefully dealt with issues going completely beyond their specific competences? England, Prussia and Russia were not Catholic states and were not moved by any sort of benevolence towards Catholicism. All powers involved in this initiative, including those who officially were Catholic, had already persecuted the Church; in

France, the Freemason Louie Philip I of Orleans had just climbed the throne; in its own empire, starting from the Poles, Russia oppressed all its Catholic subjects; in Prussia, Frederick Wilhelm III succeeded Frederick II who being an enlightened despot had addressed a letter to Voltaire wherein he foresaw the steps to put an end to the Catholic anomaly: "We should think of the easy conquest of the Papal State to supplement extra expenses and then the pallium is ours and the show is at an end. All the powers of Europe, not wanting to acknowledge a Vicar of Jesus Christ that is subject to another Ruler, will make their own patriarch, each in his own state"; "In this way, little by little, all will distance themselves from the unity of the Church, and will end up having a religion in their kingdom just like having another language."

In 1831, not only the sects, but also the states decreed the death of the Papal State.

Caritas Christi Urget Nos

The Church that came out of the revolution was missionary. Now the missions had the added advantage that they were detached from any patronage and from the demands set forth by colonial nations. France was an exception because while from 1870 at home it persecuted Christians, abroad it supported the mission on account of its national prestige and the process of colonization.

When Peter asked, Jesus promised him: "There is no one who has left house or brothers or sisters or mother or father or children or lands, for my sake and for the gospel, 30 who will not receive a hundredfold now in this time, houses and brothers and sisters and mothers and children and lands, with persecutions, and in the age to come eternal life." Like Jesus prophesied, the Church was persecuted everywhere: the martyrs numbered in the tens of thousands in China, in Japan, in the Philippines, in Korea, in Indochina. In Oceania, the missionary zeal of Pierre Chanel (1803-1841) gives an idea of the liberation, the true liberty which the announcement of the Gospel brings to people terrorized by demons and by those who exploit this terror to oppress and dominate: "His preaching of the Christian religion destroyed the worship of evil spirits who the leaders of

Futuna (the island of his martyrdom) promoted to keep their people under their power. That is why they made him suffer a most excruciating death."

Daniele Comboni (1831-1881) began systematically evangelizing Sub-Saharan Africa. He was the founder of the Comboni Missionaries of the Heart of Jesus and of the Comboni Missionary Sisters (originally Pie Madri della Nigrizia). He wrote to his parents: "We shall have to labor, sweat, die; but the thought that we sweat and die out of love for Jesus Christ and for the salvation of the most forsaken souls in the world is really too sweet to stop us from so great an enterprise." Over Peter's tomb in Rome, Comboni had the great intuition to "save Africa with Africa" and hence made every effort to teach and form Africans so that they would themselves become doctors, teachers, nuns and priests. Comboni was a tireless apostle and never tired to go throughout Europe addressing all, rich and poor, the powerful of the earth and bishops to obtain donations and prayers in support to the mission in Central Africa. Next to the Comboni brothers worked the White Fathers, members of a congregation for the evangelization of Africa founded in 1868 by the bishop of Algiers Charles Lavigerie.

In a Europe, agitated by periodic revolutions, and under the influence of the industrial revolution which reduced men to machines, simple tools that produced wealth to profit factory owners, the social issue precipitated: people were no longer defended by Christian charity, now dismantled, nor by philosophical and moral Christian teaching, now ignored and despised. They had been left to themselves and to the sad influence of sects. In this context, the great Bishop Baron Wilhelm Emmanuel von Ketteler (1811-1877), bishop of Mainz, defended the people from the brutality of exploitation. He was a "Social bishop," was elected to parliament as a champion of the Center party, that is, the Catholic party, and was deeply aware that the social issue was first and foremost a moral issue. In 1864, he anticipated Leo XIII's magisterium and his *Rerum Novarum* by publishing *The Issue of Workers and Christianity*. He was a strenuous defender of the German church's freedom from the totalitarian power of the state. Such power found its highest legitimization in Hegel's theory about the "ethical state" which was developed in order to give an unquestioning "ethical" license to all provisions adopted by the kings and the leading classes. Ketteler anticipated the pastoral determination of another great personality, the bishop of Münster, Count Clemens Augustus II von Galen (1878-1946), who opposed Hitler with courage and frankness when terror risked taking the upper hand over moral conscience.

Though the Church lost many of its goods, its point of strength remained the care for culture, formation and information: to this end the Society of Jesus was reconstituted, in all European regions many orders of teachers were born, a network of Catholic publications was formed. At the top was the Jesuit magazine "La Civiltà Cattolica", born in 1850 by the initiative of father Curci. It was a top-notch formative publication which described all cultural, religious, political and economic aspects with a precious and detailed appendix with correspondence from all regions of the world. The newspapers were also important. Two were the most authoritative and strenuous defenders of the Church from the lies and attacks unleashed by the culture and by the European governments and parliaments: "L'Univers", edited by Luois Veuillot (1813-1883) from 1836 in France and "L'Armonia", based in Turin with Giacomo Margotti (1823-1887) as chief editor, one of the key personalities in Italy during the 19th century, though today he is practically unknown.

Jacques Paul Migne (1800-1875), a priest and foremost responsible for divulging Greek and Latin Patrology, in 1833 founded and was editor in chief of "L'Univers". He wrote: "In the last sixty years, the Church produced more religious congregations than the eighteen previous centuries of Christianity especially in France." The old orders which had been suppressed and deprived of their goods now came back to life with renewed strength, they found new resources and investments, and often they even managed to buy back their own convents. Next to the old orders, a countless number of male and especially female institutes were born. The apostolate of women was the true novelty of consecrated life in the 19th century as well as the lay people's commitment. Just in Italy, 183 new congregations were born, compared to the 43 born in the previous three centuries.

In Turin, the complex and contradictory capital of the House of Savoy, where next to the Holy Shroud was the leader of Italian Freemasonry and of the attack made on Catholic Italy, there were many saints who dedicated their lives to the service of the poorest, of homeless youth with no education, of the prisoners (as is the case of Giuseppe Cafasso, the "priest of the gallows" who escorted those sentenced to death to the gallows to prevent them from doubting the love of God), or of those with the gravest deformities. It was Giuseppe Benedetto Cottolengo (1786-1842) who took care of the latter through the establishing of the Little House of Divine Providence to serve those who had monstrous physical appearances or who were infected with such revolting sicknesses that no one wanted to care for them.

Liberal Catholics

To destroy the Church in Europe, that is in the continent which was first generated by the Church's missionary apostolate ad whose identity is entirely Christian, more time was needed. Not everything can be done, and it cannot be done immediately as the French Revolution had tried to do. Small steps were needed that would divide the faithful and almost inadvertently separate them from Rome. To do so, liberal Catholics were needed. Founded in France after the rise of the bourgeois monarchy of Louie Philip I of Orleans, liberal Catholics gathered around the newspaper "L'Avenir" and his editor in chief, the erudite priest Félicité de Lamennais (1782-1854). How could Catholics be favorable to the kind of conjugated freedom Luther advocated or the declined freedom the French wanted? Obviously, they could not. Gregory XVI (1831-1846) said it loud and clear in *Mirari Vos* issued in 1832: "Incited by the unhealthy and unbridled longing for unlimited freedom, they are completely engrossed with sabotaging, or better yet eradicating any right of princes which might, under the guise of freedom, lead people to the harshest of servitudes."

The Pope was right: the freedom of modern times, separated from truth, is always at the origin of the "harshest servitude." The facts stand there to say so. Yet, the word liberty is so beautiful that members of secret societies keep on using it in the hope that their "servitude" might end up convincing also the Catholics. In Italy, first among liberal Catholics was Massimo d'Azeglio (1798-1866), member of one of the most illustrious families of the state of Sardinia, Manzoni's son in law and friend to the highest rulers in Europe, with a rather restless personality he travelled, painted, wrote, and enjoyed living well and beautiful women. Freemasonry used d'Azeglio to prepare the destruction of the Pontifical State through the unification of Italy under the House of Savoy, docile executioners of the anti-Catholic schemes developed abroad. The same d'Azeglio recounted the facts quite sincerely in *I Miei Ricordi (d'Azeglio's Memoirs, My Recollections)*: on a Roman afternoon in the house of a friend he received a visit by the sectarian Philip who suggested he should become the advocate of Italian unification under the House of Savoy. His task was delicate because he was supposed to convince the brothers dispersed throughout Italy to trust the King of Sardinia Charles Albert who though he himself was a Carbonari, during the insurrection of 1821 had betrayed the leaders of the conspiracy.

D'Azeglio after a few days decided to accept. Why? "Not because I saw anything which could benefit Italy; but I felt the need to be occupied with something which would overpower the thoughts that tormented me in my soul," in order "to have some way to make my melancholy pass, and finally because of my taste for action and adventure." What were the arguments d'Azeglio employed to convince Freemasons into trusting Charles Albert? The following consideration did it: "If you were to invite a thief to become a gentleman and he were to promise it, you may doubt he will fulfil his promise; but to invite a thief to rob and fear that he should not keep faith to his word, actually, I really don't see why!"

Being an insightful and intelligent man, d'Azeglio knew that it was impossible to have a revolution: the Italians were too catholic. So, in order to bring about the revolution, he concocted a new type of conspiracy which he called an "open air conspiracy": it consisted in using the pen, flood the press with propaganda to divulge calumnies against the Papal State and its administration. Giuseppe Montanelli, a key player in the Risorgimento, hit the nail on the head when he called him the "philanderer lover." He became a statesman able to work on anything but specialized in the inner workings of the Papal State and by 1846 he had published *Degli ultimi casi* di Romagna. Some skirmishes organized by the liberal faction in Rimini offered him the right occasion. The uprising failed but d'Azeglio hit the bull's eye. The pamphlet immediately became a best seller and European public opinion came to know about the insurrections that took place in

Romagna, that is, the Papal States. A taste of the Marquis' prose: "In Italy and outside of Italy, not only Protestants and other adversaries of Rome but the same Catholics, her greatest devotees, when they are not moved by their own private passions, they undress of all esteem for the temporal power of the Pope, they preach that it is damaging to the faith and to religion and they would like it either to be completely removed, or at least to be restricted."

Though the Papal States were the oldest in the entire west, d'Azeglio's conspiracy questioned their very legitimacy with these words: "If the Pope has become a prince by the donations of Pepin and Charlemagne, of the Countess Matilde and others, why was this reason to keep him as legitimate ruler? Because universal opinion approved the belief that this mode of acquisition was legitimate and that the donors were legitimate owners of the thing donated; obviously, if universal opinion had believed the opposite, not only this acquisition but this principality could not have lasted; and it would have been inconceivable for the one to donate it and for the other to accept it. But the times have changed." This was his conclusion: "We must acknowledge therefore that the idea, upon which legitimacy for the Church's power was based, as that of many others, has ceased to exist." The Marquis d'Azeglio was not renowned as a Freemason. He is known for being Catholic from a Catholic family and the brother of a Jesuit. D'Azeglio's argument confused Catholics because it was meant to confuse. It was an open-air conspiracy. If Rome and Italy, for the first time in their millenary history, became colonies, it is also due to liberal Catholics.

In the meantime, in Rome a new Pope was made. Pius IX (1846-1878) was a man filled with energy, a reformer, full of charity towards all, including his enemies. As soon as he was elected, he followed the example of many of his predecessors by granting amnesty but extended it also to those imprisoned for political crimes. It was enough that they committed to not conspire against the state anymore and the rebels could go. Before the Pope's charity, the Fremasons' strategy was simple: make Pius IX seem like a liberal Pope. This is what Giuseppe Mazzini, a Carbonari, so clearly suggested when he wrote *Agli Amici d'Italia (To the Friends of Italy)* in 1846: "Take advantage of this crippling concession to gather the masses by feigning gratitude when it is convenient. Feasts, hymns, crowds gathering, the growing relation with men of all opinions, all these are enough to launch ideas, to instill a feeling of strength in the people and make him become demanding."

Without the shout, "Hurray for Pius IX," had he not been given up for a liberal Pope, that is, for a revolutionary Pope, the victory of the Risorgimento would not have been so easy. This was said by Don Giacomo Margotti: "When the Pope was sacrilegiously taken as a symbol of the revolution, there was no city or small town that was not in commotion inspired by the loftiest of thoughts"; "without feigned devotion to Pius IX, the libertines would not have been heard."

In Rome against Rome

In the name of freedom and independence, during the eighteen twenties, the lands of Latin America were taken from the Spanish motherland by *libertadores*. All of them were Freemasons: Simon Bolivar, José de San Martìn, Francisco de Miranda and the general Bernardo O'Higgins. The immense Catholic continent where Spanish was spoken was fully dismembered by an elite class of Creoles with no scruples who were kept far away from leading positions because the Spanish monarchy was still tied by the provision set forth in the Last Will and Testament of Isabella of Castile with regards to the defense of the Indios. Following a well-tested scenario, Church assets were left to public looting in the name of liberty: convents and churches religious orders had built everywhere were robbed, dismantled and destroyed while in 1975, Garcia Moreno, the Catholic president of Ecuador, was assassinated. With regards to the empire, which was Brazil, it was indeed autonomous from Brazil, but it was ruled by Dom Pedro di Braganza, the son of the king of Portugal and Grand Master of the order of Freemasons. In 1823, James Monroe, president of the United States of America said a key indicative phrase: America to the Americans.

In Spain, liberals organized periodic rebellions with violent anti-Catholic outbursts: they began in 1834 with the *Matanza de los Frailes* (The Slaughter of the Friars) and continued in their fury before and after the abdication of Isabel II in 1868 and the proclamation of the

Republic in 1873 carried out behind the motto, *Guerra a Diòs* (War on God). In Bismarck's unified Germany, transformed in 1871 into an imperial nation with its palace at Versailles (an insult to France in response to the humiliation received during the Thirty Years' War and in the Peace of Westphalia), the Calvinist Empire unleashed the *Kulturkampf* against the Church, a battle for culture which obviously Catholics are viewed as not having. It was a frontal attack which started in 1871 with the suppression of the Catholic section of the Ministry of Culture, followed by the arrest of bishops, the expulsion of Jesuits, the suppression of almost all religious orders, the interruption of diplomatic relations with the Holy See and a series of other provisions which aimed to make the very existence of the Catholic Church in Germany impossible. The *Kulturkampf* toned down a notch because the party of the *Zentrum* held its ground and because the social democratic danger was now serious, and two fronts could not be fought at the same time. In the meantime, in Paris, France, after the defeat against Prussia at Sedan in 1871, the revolution exploded once again, the so-called Commune, in which the bishop was killed, and indiscriminate violence was perpetrated in the name of an equal and anti-Christian society.

Pius IX described the persecution unleashed against the Church throughout the world in the encyclical *Etsi Multa* issued in 1873: "Some among You, Venerable Brothers, may be surprised that the war against the Church today is spreading so much. But whoever acknowledges the character, the objective and the intention of sects, whether they be called freemasonic or any other name, and compares these to the character, mode and amplitude of this war in which the Church is assailed on all sides, cannot certainly doubt that this calamity is due to the deceit and scheming of those sects. Satan's synagogue is formed by them, and he commands his army against the Church of Christ. He raises his flag and advances for battle. Our Predecessors, watchful in Israel, denounced these sects a very long time ago, from their very beginnings, to both kings and peoples. Later, multiple times they struck against them with condemnations. We have also failed in respect to this duty. Oh, if only the supreme Pastors of the Church were given more trust by those who could have put an end to this disastrous pestilence!"; "Having obtained what they so desired, that is, to decide everything everywhere, now they audaciously direct the power and authority they acquired in order to reduce the Church into terrible slavery, demolish the foundation upon which it stands, contaminate the divine imprints in which it shines full of light and even more, annihilate her completely throughout the entire world, if it were ever possible, after having struck her with frequent blows, defeated and destroyed it."

When the Pope wrote this, the Protestant and freemasonic hatred had arrived to Rome. To Rome because Rome is the *Urbe* and one cannot dominate the world without controlling Rome. In Rome, because the Pope is in Rome and because the Pope is the head of the Church and the Church must be destroyed. In Rome because it is believed that once the Pope lost his temporal power, he would have inevitably given up also the spiritual: "Each day it becomes clearer how true and just were what We declared and repeated so many times, that is, that the sacrilegious occupation of Our State aimed first and foremost to breaking the strength and efficacy of the Pope's primacy and destroy, if it were possible, the Catholic religion," continued Pius IX. In Rome, against Rome. Against her millenary and unique history and, despite all the sins of men and Popes, still beautiful city and civilization. Here, Catholicism is an essential part of the national identity and history. Not to mention the privileges which came to the peninsula from the presence of the Pontifical See, true heir of Rome's universality.

Philosophers, conquerors (Napoleon), liberals, protestants all view the Italians as slaves because Catholics. But the type of liberty which Freemasonry prepared to give Italians was well described in articles 3 and 7 of the *Constitutions* approved by Italian Freemasonry in 1864: article 3 explains that the "direct and immediate" goal of Freemasonry "is indeed to contribute effectively to the gradual enactment of these [freemasonic] principles in a united Italy, is indeed that these gradually become the enforceable and supreme law for all acts of individual, domestic and civil life," article 7 recalls the final goal of the order: "The ultimate goal of its work is to gather all free men into a great family which may and must little by little succeed to all sects that are founded upon blind faith and theocratic authority, all cults that are superstitious, intolerant and enemies amongst each other, in order to build the true and only church of Humanity."

The goal of all lodges is humanity. It is the world. The romantic myth of nationalism was broadcast in an instrumental way to destroy the existing order inspired by Catholic values (in Latin America and Italy and later also in all regions subject to the Austrian Empire) and also because in order to destroy the Catholic Church, Rome needed to lose its *status* as caput mundi and become simply *caput Italiae*. A Russian Orthodox composed a truly wonderful synthesis to describe this drama. In *A Writer's Diary*, published in 1877, Fyodor Dostoyevsky wrote: "Oh yes, he [Cavour] achieved his aim; he united Italy; and what was the result? For twenty-five hundred years Italy has borne within her a universal and unifying idea – not some abstract idea, not some speculation of a bureaucratic mind, but something real and organic, the fruit of the life of a nation, the fruit of life in the world: this was the unification of the entire world, first the ancient Roman unification, and then the Papal one"; "but what was it that ultimately emerged in its place? What do we have to congratulate Italy about now? After Count Cavour's diplomacy, what did she achieve that was better? What did appear, was a united, second-rate little kingdom that had lost every last one of its universal ambitions [...] a kingdom that is utterly satisfied with its unity, which signifies absolutely nothing, with its mechanical but not spiritual unity (not the former universal unity, that is) and, on top of this, that has debts it can never pay and, on top of this, that it is utterly satisfied with its own second-rateness."

Acherò

"I saw a Lady dressed in white: she wore a white dress, a veil which was also white, a blue belt and a golden rose on each foot": the first apparition of Mary in Lourdes to Bernadette Soubirous happened like this, in a cave near a river. It was February 11, 1858. The Lady – *Acherò* [that one], as Bernadette referred to her to the police commissioner – made the sign of the cross and then recited the rosary with me counting the beads of the rosary she held. Then she disappeared. On February 18, the date of the third apparition, besides the cross and the rosary, there was a small exchange between the Lady and the young girl in the local dialect: "Would you be so good as to write your name?" "It is not necessary," answered Mary, and she asked: "Would you be so kind as to come here for fifteen days?" "Yes," answered Bernadette. And the Lady continued: "I am not promising that you will be happy in this world, but in the next." On Mount Sinai, Moses insisted that God reveal his name to him. Also, Bernadette insisted: what is your name? During the eight apparitions, *Acherò* said: "Penance. Pray God for the conversion of sinners. Kiss the earth as penance for sinners." During the ninth apparition, Bernadette started digging the ground with her hands and dirtying herself with mud because *Acherò* told her: "Go drink at the spring and wash," although there was no spring in Massabielle. The Lady showed a spot at the end of the cave and Bernadette recounted that the water "was so dirty, that for three times I spewed it out, and at the fourth I could drink it." During the twelfth apparition, a farmer girl immersed her paralyzed arm in the spring and healed: it was the first miracle. On the thirteenth apparition, the Lady told Bernadette: "Go tell the priests that they should come here in procession and here build a chapel." The parish priest rejoined asking what her name was. Finally, on the sixteenth apparition, the Lady raised her eyes to heaven and with hands joined at the height of her chest revealed: "*Que soy era Immaculada Councepciou*", I am the Immaculate Conception. Bernadette did not know the meaning of that name, but the priest surely did. The apparitions, a total of eighteen, finished on July 16, the feast of Our Lady of Mount Carmel: "I had never seen her so beautiful," said Bernadette.

After centuries of lively discussion and uncertainty, Pius IX proclaimed the Dogma of the Immaculate Conception on December 8, 1854. Four years later, the Lourdes apparitions most solemnly confirmed the truth of the Marian definition and were a gift from heaven to the most slandered and vilified Pope in history. Newspapers all over the world had cartoons showing him with women, accusations claiming he was affiliated to an American lodge. The same Catholic historians qualified him as a man of faith but with poor political intelligence and therefore not fit to face the challenges that the modern world posed to the Church.

Following the same old screenplay enacted abroad and repeated by the House of Savoy and their leaders, the kingdom of Sardinia was described as the most moral in all of Italy because it was constitutional and liberal. Yet, the Savoy kingdom violated all the principal articles of the Albertine Statute, beginning with the first which defined the Catholic religion as the sole state religion. In 1848, right after the Statute was granted, the Jesuits were suppressed, the fathers were placed under house arrest and their goods were seized. In 1855 it was the turn of contemplative and mendicant orders suppressed on the basis of "free church in a free state." During the following years, all religious orders were abolished, and 57,492 people were expelled from their homes, often in the middle of the night to avoid being seen: they were literally robbed of everything that catholic piety had donated over the centuries. Beside the convents, also churches and properties, paintings, sculptures, archives, libraries, liturgical objects and paraments; everything was ransacked by the liberal elite, the only people who could acquire the goods of the church without fearing excommunication. After Italy's unification more than one hundred dioceses lacked a bishop while prisons were filled with religious and priests who refused to sing *Te Deum* in thanksgiving for the new triumphant moral order. In the name of freedom of the press, the Pope's encyclicals were not divulged, in the name of the right to property's inviolability, ecclesial properties were robbed. Priests who dared refuse sacrament to liberals who had been excommunicated were fined two thousand Lire (an outrageous sum) and sentenced to two years in prison (this was prescribed by article 268 of the penal code approved in 1859 right before the Italian states were invaded).

At the center of this tragedy stood Pius IX, the Pope who stayed thirty-two years on the throne of Peter (the longest pontificate in history) and who witnessed the dismemberment of the Christian people. Though defense of the Pope's temporal power for him was "a matter of conscience," the really pressing issue for him was "that all Catholic peoples may come to know the truth" (this he wrote in 1849 to the Great Duchess of Tuscany). On account of his desire to make the truth know, Pius IX did not retract from his duty to write tens of documents describing what was taking place in Italy in the name of liberty. Mastai Ferretti never tired to tell the facts though he was perfectly aware that liberals would do everything in their power to bury its? under the deluge of words of their rhetoric. So a few months after the proclamation of Italy's unity, during the secret concistory held on October 9, 1861, Pius IX minutely described the desolating panorama of Italy turned upside down by the tyranny of those who "call what is evil, good, and what is good, evil, replacing darkness with light and light with darkness": "Bishops [are] expelled from their dioceses and incarcerated, the clergy is persecuted, religious families suppressed, their members expelled from their own monasteries, deprived of everything, nuns forced to beg for bread, churches undressed of their furnishings, profaned and turned into dens of thieves, sacred goods looted."

The most sacred principles of private and public law were trampled upon, the just liberty of persons cut to pieces, property assaulted, the honor of Catholics ruined by false accusations: "The heart is still horrified at the recollection of so many centers set on fire and razed to the ground in the Naples area, of so many religious and Catholics of all ages, sex and condition thrown in prison without due process or cruelly murdered"; "Similar misdeed are perpetrated by those who are in no way ashamed to proclaim that they want to grant the Church freedom and give back to Italy its moral sense."

The Italian Risorgimento retraced the anti-Catholic provisions issued by Protestant and liberal governments. From this point of view it was nothing new. The Italian Risorgimento, however, was undoubtedly original because it denied the fact that its actions were guided by loathing and hate for the Catholic Church. On the contrary, Italian liberals were compelled to insist they were fervent Catholics. In fact, the very first article of the constitution they drafted pronouncing Catholicism as the state religion, established a connection between morality and the respect for the constitution that they could not fail to honor.

A Pope to defend liberty and truth

Pius IX was prophetic in the literal sense of the term because he denounced the communist threat as early as 1846, when he published his first encyclical *Qui Pluribus*. Two years before Marx and Engels wrote the *Manifesto*, Pius IX had already described "the vile Communist doctrine as adverse in the maximum degree to natural law; once it is admitted, the right of everyone, of things, properties, even the same human society would be deeply subverted." Decades before Communism rose to power in Russia, the Pope warned against the inevitable radicalization of the revolutionary process: "By abusing the names of liberty and equality," the masterminds of this conspiracy aim, "above all, to the following: to make the people familiar with the foolish and dangerous inventions of Communism and Socialism. It is also well known, since the teachers of Communism and Socialism, though by different roads and in various way, all have the same ultimate aim, namely, by means of sophism and vain promises of happier conditions, deceive, agitate workers and the people of lower classes with continuous commotion and have them little by little become accustomed to graver misdeeds in order to use them to invade, sabotage, dilapidate properties, first and foremost of the Church, and if needed of any other legitimate owner: ultimately, to violate all human and divine rights; and in this way to destroy divine worship and annul all order in civil society."

The Communist revolution continued the Pope, "will not bring people the slightest happiness, but rather a dreadful increase of misery and calamity. This is because it is not in men's power to establish new societies and communities that are contrary to the natural condition of human matters: that is why wherever these conspiracies unfortunately take hold, they cannot but weaken and demolish the *status* quo down to the very foundations through never-ending mutual aggression, theft and horrible carnages of brothers against brothers; ultimately, once the few have enriched themselves on the spoils of everyone else, they will start to lord them to everyone's ruin" (*Nostis et nobiscum*, 1849). Communism is not the best defense of the poor people; the Catholic faith is: "The poor and the other unfortunates who live amongst us Catholics live in much lighter conditions than in other nations. And the help given to them would be much greater if many institutes, which the piety of our elders brought to life, had not been so impoverished and even destroyed by the most recent upheavals"; "Moreover, let all the faithful know that the kings and leaders of all pagan nations abused their power more often and more gravely than those here; let them therefore acknowledge that they are in debt towards our most holy Religion if the Princes of the Christian age, because they were fearful, as Religion warned them, of that most severe account which those in power will have to give of themselves, and of that eternal torment by which the great shall suffer great torments (Wis VI: 6, 7), they established a more just and benevolent regime towards their subjects."

Pius IX warned against Communist propaganda and at the same time railed against the injustice, the duplicity, and the theft carried out by the state's liberal management. He inserted Liberalism among "the principal errors of our times" and condemned them in the *Syllabus* published on December 8, 1864, in tandem with the encyclical *Quanta Cura*. If some are scandalized by reading lay and catholic liberal historiography of a Pope who condemned liberty, then they are not taking the facts into account. The facts prove that by condemning Liberalism, Pius IX defended liberty from liberal tyranny which, besides, reduced Italians to utter misery and forced them into a massive immigration.

In 1870, right before the conquest of Rome, Pius IX convoked the Vatican Council I. In Rome and all of Italy, after a thousand years, a pagan view of life had returned to power and it deeply subverted the habits and institutions of the catholic people: not only were the people impoverished, but it was shocked, discomforted, embittered. As the enemies of the Church foresaw, the risk was real that the fall of the spiritual power due to distrust would follow the fall of the temporal power. The Pope comforted, reassured, gave courage: the word of Jesus is eternal and overcomes the world. The Pope is really infallible because Christ promised Peter. Faith in Peter's infallibility has always been a part of the deepest beliefs of the Christian creed. However, it was proclaimed as a dogma in the Constitution *Pastor Aeternus* issued in 1870 because the Church needed to respond to the presumptuous law of progress used to justify anti-Catholic violence and the adaptation of Christian truth to the times. Pope Mastai Ferretti protected the doctrine of salvation of which he was the keeper, fulfilled in Christ and needing no improvement. He defended the possibility man has to make absolute choices (he defended religious vows and the indissolubility of marriage), as well as the capacity of Christ' vicar to make infallible choices. Against everything and everyone, Pius IX defended catholic truth which the "ferocious hate against our religion of clear diabolical origin" (*Gravissimum supremi*, 1866) tried to destroy by all means.

The truth is the exact opposite of what the legend promoted by historians claimed: Pope Mastai Ferretti perfectly understood the gravity of the challenge posed by the anti-Catholic world to Christ's Church. He understood it so well, that he went straight to the heart of the problem, to the heart of the truth of faith attacked by the satanical hatred which dominated Italy.

Throughout his long reign, Pius IX never tired to confront and respond to liberal lies but he never forgot whose vicar he was. Therefore, together with the entire Italian Church, he literally offered the other cheek to his persecutors. From beginning to end, the line of action for his pontificate was that described in 1849 in *Quibus quantisque*: "Certainly, though we do not merit it, acting here on earth in the place of Him who 'When he was reviled, he did not revile in return; when he suffered, he did not threaten, with all patience and silence, we bore with the most bitter insults and never neglected to pray for those who slandered and persecuted us"; "we give infinite thanks to God, for having made us worthy to suffer injury for the sake of Christ's name and for having been made to resemble in part the image of his passion; in faith, in hope, in patience, in meekness, we are ready to suffer the most bitter trials and sufferings and to even give up Our life for the Church if by Our blood We were enabled to repair the calamities of the Church."

A priest acrobat, prophet and saint

An acrobat, juggler, an organizing genius, teacher of charity, founder, in his own way, of a vast empire, Giovanni Bosco (1815-1888) from Becchi, a little town in the province of Asti, was a giant of his time. A *monstrum*, a unique case. So unique, that when all religious orders were being suppressed, the statesman Urbano Rattazzi explained to him how to sidestep the law and have his order approved. Charm: Don Bosco had plenty of it. Many were his followers, enormous the sums received in donations, hundreds of youth saved from the streets, thousands of honest craftsmen and catholic workers were formed in the schools he founded; everything blossomed in Don Bosco's hands. Even miracles, even prophecy; and both miracles and prophecy make him a personality that needs to be treated with care.

Since his childhood, Bosco had dreams which became real. When he was nine years old, Jesus and Mary revealed to him what he would accomplish when he grew up: he saw a courtyard full of kids who played happily; some however were blaspheming and so he launched himself against them to silence them when suddenly a Man appeared who called him and told him to place himself at the head of those youth: "It is not through blows but through meekness and charity that you must win over these friends"; "Who art Thou who command me to do the impossible?" "It is precisely because it seems to you impossible that you must make it possible through obedience and through acquiring learning." "Where shall I become learned?" "I will give you the Teacher. Under her guide you will become wise; without her, all wisdom becomes folly."

Time passed, and in November of 1854, the Italian parliament discussed the law which would suppress enclosed convents and those of mendicant orders. In these circumstances, Bosco dreamt a servant dressed in pink uniform who shouted: "Announce: a great funeral at Court!" Five days later the dream returned and this time the servant shouted: "Announce: not a great funeral at Court but great funerals at Court!" Don Bosco wrote to King Vittorio Emanuele to keep him updated about his nocturnal visions and to beg him "to stop that law at all costs." But Cavour, after consulting with his official theologians reassured the ruler: "Your Majesty, do not be afraid of what D. Bosco wrote to you. The times of revelations has passed." At the start of the year 1855, work in parliament was interrupted by multiple very grave mourning which struck the Crown: on January 12, the Queen mother Maria Teresa died at 54 years old; on January 20, Queen Maria Adelaide died at 33 years old, on February 10, Duke Ferdinand of Genoa, the brother of the king, died at 33 years old; on May 17, Duke Vittorio Emanuele of Genovese, the youngest child of the king died with only 4 month of life.

When the government project reached its final approval in April of 1855, Don Bosco had a book printed written by the Baron Nilinse by the title: *I beni della Chiesa, come si rubino e quali siano le conseguenze; con breve appendice sulle vicende del Piemonte* (*The goods of the Church, how they may be robbed and what are the consequences; with a brief appendix about recent events in Piedmont*). On the cover he had written: "How! can anyone violate a private home for no reason, and you dare to lay your hands on the house of the Lord! St. Ambrose." The book discussed the "terrible punishment which throughout the centuries befell all those who, whether rulers or subjects, had removed, sold, bought any goods consecrated to God [...] making the terrible proverb true: The family of whoever robs from God will not reach the fourth generation!" Right before his signature, Bosco wrote to the king: "*Dicit Dominus: Erunt mala super mala in domo tua*" (The Lord says: evil upon evil shall fall upon your house), "If His Lordship will sign that decree, he will have decreed the end of the Savoy royalty." Vittorio Emanuele II signed the law which suppressed religious communities on May 28, 1855. Upon his death on May 9 1878, Umberto I succeeded him. Upon the killing of Umberto I on January 29 1900, Vittorio Emanuele III succeeded him. After Vittorio Emanuele III's abdication on May 9, 1946, Umberto II reigned for less than a month, "the May King."

Among his many dreams, though it is not very clear in all its aspects, one is worth recounting. It was May 30, 1862 and Bosco told his youth: "Imagine that you are on the beach near the sea, or better, on an isolated rock and that around, you can see nothing but ocean. Over the vast surface of the water you can see a countless multitude of ships ready for battle; their bows ending in a sharp iron point like that of an arrow. These ships are armed with cannons and are loaded with rifles, weapons of all kinds, flammable materials and also books. They advance toward a much bigger ship, the tallest, and try to strike into it with their ram, set it on fire and cause it all possible damage. That fully furnished majestic ship is escorted by many small ships which take orders from her and execute maneuvers to defend themselves from the enemy fleet. But the wind is blowing against them and the rocky sea seems to favor the enemies.

Amidst the immense open sea, two robust, very high columns rise from the waves very close to each other. On top of one there is the statue of the Immaculate Virgin at whose feet hangs a large sign with the writing: "*Auxilium Christianorum*"; on the other, which is much taller and ticker there is a bread host, proportional in size to the column and beneath it another sign with the words: "*Salus Credentium*". The supreme commander of the big ship, the Roman Pontiff, seeing the enemy fury and the evil circumstances in which his faithful lay, called his pilots from the secondary ships to gather around him to have a council and decide on the course of action. All pilots boarded and gathered around the Pope. They began the meeting but the since the storm lashed out in fury, they were sent back to govern their ships.

After the sea calmed a bit, the Pope gathered the pilots around him a second time while the captain ship followed its course. But the storm returned, and it was terrifying. The Pope was at the helm and all his efforts were aimed at sailing the ship in between those two columns. From the top of the column, all around them, many anchors and big hooks hung down with chains. The enemy ships tried to assault and sink it: some with writings, with books, with flammable material which they try to throw on board; others with cannons, rifles and rams. The fighting was increasingly adamant, but their efforts were vain: the great ship proceeded securely and frankly on its way. Sometimes, struck by formidable blows, large and gaping holes appeared on its sides, but immediately, a wind blew from the two columns and the breach closed up and the holes were plugged.

In the meanwhile, the assaulting cannon fire, the rifles and all other sorts of weapons broke in their hands, many ships shattered and sunk into the sea. The enemies, now furious, took up fighting hand to hand: with their hands, with their fists, and with their blaspheming. Suddenly, the Pope, gravely wounded, fell. He was immediately aided, but he fell a second time and died. A shout of victory and joy resounded among the enemies; on their ship there was an indescribable jubilation.

So, as soon as the Pope died, another Pope took his place. The pilots gathered together elected him so quickly that news of the Pope's death arrived in tandem with news of his successor's election. The enemies began to lose heart. The new Pope, surpassing all obstacles, sailed the ship straight in between the two columns. There, with a small chain hanging at the bow, he tied the ship to an anchor of the column on which the Host lay; and with another small chain hanging on the stern, tied it on the opposite side to another anchor hanging from the column on which stood the Immaculate Virgin. Then a great upheaval took place: all enemy ships fled, dispersed, smashed into each other, and shattered. Some sink and tried to sink others with them, while the ships that bravely fought with the Pope were also tied to the two columns. Now, a great calm reigned over the sea."

Bosco explained: "The enemy ships are persecutions. The gravest of trials are coming against the Church. What has happened until now is almost nothing compared with what is to happen. There are only two means to save oneself in such disarray: Devotion to the Most Holy Mary and frequent Communion."

In the Name of Liberty of Conscience

The Vatican Council I in 1870 closed an era lasting over fifteen hundred years. It began with the Council of Nicea called by Constantine: for the first time in history, an ecumenical council had nothing to do with political power especially because officially, the nations had severed their ties to Catholicism starting with the first born daughter of the Church, France. After the carnages perpetrated by the Commune, in 1875, France inaugurated the Third Republic. The Republic was born of freemasonic inspiration and aimed to complete what was started by the revolution. In 1877, the Grand Orient de France removed the requirement for admission into the lodge to believe in God and instead of God, faith was directed towards the lay republican state. In order to eradicate Catholic religion, still the majority of the French, the republic withdrew education from the parents' control, made primary education mandatory and free, and forbad religious and priests from having any contact with adolescents: "The sect of the Freemasons aimed to take control of adolescents' education. In fact, the Freemasons felt that they could easily form and bend that feeble and flexible age to their will; therefore, there was nothing better suited for this than to hand the children of citizens over to a State which they admire. That is why they gave ministers of the Church no part in teaching or watching over the education of youth." This was written by Leo XIII (1878-1903) to describe the state of affairs in the *Humanus Genus*, the most complete and analytically written encyclical by a Pope about Freemasonry.

The persecution started with the Jesuits again. In 1880 the Third Republic decreed: "The unauthorized Society of Jesus, within three months, must dissolve and vacate the institutes it occupies in the territory of the Republic" The institutes were vacated by the police which began its work at four in the morning and put on the streets 500 fathers and 9,000 students. The other congregations followed one by one: "Each unauthorized congregation or community needed to ask within the following three months for authorization." At the start of the 20th century, diplomatic relations with the Holy See were broken off and in 1905 the law separating state and Church was approved. All catholic goods were seized – including churches, objects for worship, furnishings and libraries – and assigned to "associations" expressly made to handle their management.

The first article in the constitution of French Freemasonry, composed in 1877 clarified that the order, "Has as its founding principles, absolute liberty of conscience and human solidarity"; in 1905, the first article in the law of separation between Church and State declared: "The Republic guarantees liberty of conscience." How could it be possible that Catholics saw their liberty of conscience denied in the name of liberty of conscience, and on top of that, were robbed of all their goods? The blatant contradiction may be understood only by considering that when Freemasons speak of liberty of conscience, they refer to truly free conscience, which only they incarnated. They believed that the conscience of Catholics was enslaved to dogma and therefore, since it is not free, it must not be taken into account. On the contrary, it must be fought.

Leo XIII was crystal clear in his analysis of Freemasonry, its objectives, its strategy and the tactics adopted to reach power and keep it, giving life to an actual state within the state. In his last encyclical *Annum ingressi*, written in 1902, he wrote: "It [Freemasonry] is the permanent embodiment of the revolution and constituted a kind of upside down society whose aim is to control accepted society, as it were, in secret and whose reason to exist is the waging of war against God and his Church"; "This sect, which includes almost all nations in its immense network and is connected with other sects, which it manipulates with hidden strings by alluring their members with the bait of many advantages, bending their leaders to its will with promises or threats, has successfully infiltrated all social orders and practically formed an invisible and irresponsible state within the legitimate State."

The dynamics of the Third Republic's religious policies and its relentless hatred for the Church were not hard to understand or even foresee. Pope Pecci especially saw through them and described the main features of freemasonic power in many encyclicals. However, the *ralliement* policy, enacted by Leo XIII and his secretary Mariano Rampolla in 1890 and made official in his 1892 letter *Au milieu des sollicitudes* to come to terms with the Third Republic, although we keep the utterly delicate situation of the Holy See in mind, its international isolation and the Pope's *status* as "prisoner" in the Vatican, it is yet quite hard to understand.

In the meantime, a real cultural explosion took place in England: John Henry Newman (1801-1890) adhered to the Catholic Church. He was a leading figure of the Anglican Church's religious and university life. The Church in England had great privileges and was enormously influential. Maybe, it was the first and foremost among the quite spectacular conversions to Rome which began at the turn of the century. In fact, despite all negative financial implications, many world renowned personalities converted, such as John Ronald Tolkien's mother and the firm adhesion to the Church of Rome of Tolkien himself or even the conversion in the first years of the 20th century writer, debater, journalist and poet, Gilbert Chesterton.

Besides, for quite some time already, England was the place of choice for believers of Gnosticism. They continued producing new theories, passing them off as scientific and inflicting desolation and death on many peoples forced to accept them. For instance, Sir Francis Galton (1822-1911), Darwin's cousin and father of eugenics. Galton noticed that among the people cited in *The Dictionary of Men of the Time*, many were part of high society and many were of the same family. This realization served as the inspiration to come up with the theory that intelligence must be hereditary. Sharing Darwin's belief that species evolved casually and passed from lower to higher complexity casually, Galton suggested that the evolution of the human species should be accelerated by selecting individuals suitable to reproduce and eliminating those who instead were not. In the latter group were all the poor, the mentally sick and all difficult individuals. The leading intellectuals and politicians of the Anglo-Saxon world, mainly American and Scandinavian, numbered among those who subscribed to eugenics. As a consequence, tens of thousands were sterilized. Hitler, who also was a firm believer in eugenics, provided a much faster and cheaper solution: death.

Spes contra Spem

A time of luxury, lack of restraint, financial scandals, entertainment and balls: La Belle Époque was the name given to the first years of the 20th century. It was a time of irresponsibility and injustice during which the world was divided based solely on the sole criteria of inhuman exploitation in order to benefit a laughable minority of people and states. It was a time which prepared ruin for millions of people: the explosion of the first and then second world wars, the envisaged and long anticipated rise of Communism, and disintegration of the Habsburg empire. It was a time, which also redeemed the secular House of Habsburg through the rise of a blessed emperor, Charles I of Austria (1887-1922) and his wife, the servant of God Zita of the House of Bourbon and Parma.

Upon Leo XIII's death, the pontifical magistery on Freemasonry came to an end: everything which could and should have been said on the freemasonic phenomenon was said and explained. Pius X (1903-1914), the first Pope to become saint in the 20th century, turned the magisterium's attention not outwards, but inside the Church. The true danger, the deathly threat to the faith in Jesus Christ is heresy. What Paul VI bemoaned as the smoke of Satan which tries to introduce itself in the body of the Church, sometimes succeeds. On September 8, 1907, Pius X wrote *Pascendi Dominici Gregis*, the encyclical which confronted the smoke of Satan, that is, the infiltration of categories belonging to sectarian thought into the world of the clergy and faithful.

In his battle with no quarters against Gnosis, Pius IX, in the *Syllabus* listed and condemned the errors of modern society and at the same time proclaimed the dogma of the Pope's infallibility. Following the same guideline, in 1905, Pius X published the Catechism, a bulwark to defend the faith of the people by "clearly explaining the rudiments of the holy faith" so that, through simple questions and answers, everyone could learn the "divine truths on which the life of every Christian must be based." After having clarified the doctrine, in 1907 he published the decree *Lamentabili* which condemned 65 distinctive errors of the times and then the *Pascendi* confronted the *cupio dissolvi* which had taken hold of the Church through Modernism, defined as the "synthesis of all heresies." The Pope's diagnosis was precise: "The sowers of error are not only amongst the declared enemies anymore, but rather – something which is cause for terrible distress and much pain – they hide in the same bosom of the Church; more hidden they are, that much more dangerous."

Rome had fallen, the Pope was prisoner, and modernity seemed to have ignited seemingly unstoppable scientific and cultural progress that apparently was irreconcilable with Christian truth. Many thought the moment had arrived to come to terms with the world as it was. Under these circumstances, some, mainly intellectuals, mainly priests or religious, but also novelists and journalists, thought that the time had come for the Church to open up to the world meaning, first of all, to update dogma by ceasing once and for all to defend some revealed, immutable and fixed truth.

Modernism was a ghastly danger also because as a heresy, besides going straight to the heart of faith and revelation, it did not show itself for what it was. It feigned its true intentions. It denied its ambitions. It was very shrewd in its lies. In Italy, the leading figure of modernism was the priest, who was later excommunicated, Ernesto Buonaiuti. He wrote: "Until today, we have wanted to reform Rome without Rome, or maybe even against Rome. We must reform Rome with Rome: make the reform pass through the hands of the very people who must be reformed"; we must open the road to Protestantism, "but it must be an orthodox and gradual Protestantism and not a violent, aggressive, revolutionary and insubordinate one." Modernism aimed to have the Church die a slow, gradual, almost unnoticed death. Why were modernists so obstinate about staying inside the Church by professing to be catholic? Because "they needed to remain inside the Church in order to slowly alter the collective conscience." This was the recurring ambition of those who believed Gnosticism. Since they claimed to be the only champions of truth, they tried by all means, beginning with deceit and simulation, to bring people to their side. They despised the Church and found ways to make their loathing spread to others so that once again, history became "a conspiracy against truth": "They wrote history essays and feigning to search for truth, they highlighted – with much care and a clumsily hidden pleasure – everything that seemed to blemish the Church"; "Basically, they are taken up with the vain greed to have the world speak about them; and they are certain that this cannot happen if they continue saying only what has been always said by all." The danger is that much greater because "the good name and reputation of the writers [supported by a hammering campaign in the press, author's note] guaranteed that these books were read without any fear and so they were even more dangerous because, little by little, they led to modernism." To defend the faithful against modernist Gnosticism, on September 1, 1910, Pius X approved the *Motu proprio* with title *Sacrorum Antistitum*, which required the clergy, the superiors of religious orders as well as philosophy and theology teachers in seminaries, to make an oath against modernism.

Despite the differences, *Pascendi* can be compared to Augustine's *City of God* because they have analogous goals: to defend the faith from cultural questions and doubts which may arise from the analysis of facts. Cultural doubts induced by anti-Christian philosophical thought. Facts which, just like the takeover of Rome in 410, or the fall of Rome in 1870, may cause one to doubt trusting divine Providence as it guides history.

It is the undying problem of success and victory versus defeat and failure. It is the scandal of the cross which cannot be eliminated. The Christian view of history is opposed to that of Islam and Freemasonry which hold in common the belief that their creed will triumph everywhere as an absolute certainty. Radically opposed to the way of the world, the triumph of Christ comes about with his climbing on the cross. Christians are called to follow the footsteps left by Jesus and to not be scandalized by persecution. Sure, it's not easy. Certainly, doubts, moments of discouragement and an interior sigh are daily companions. But certainly, as two thousand years of history show, with all its atrocities and persecutions, God is stronger and wins.

Christians have received the prophecy not of attaining victory on earth but of victory over the world in view of heaven. "When the Son of man comes, will he find faith on earth?" The question Jesus posed in the Gospel of Luke was not rhetorical. In the *Book of Revelation*, John wrote that history is not proceeding towards the victory of the Gospel: the beast "was allowed to make war on the saints and to conquer them. And authority was given it over every tribe and people and tongue and nation." Certainly, God "loves life." Also Christians do. Certainly we cannot stop praying for peace and that all may live peacefully and without persecution. Pope Sarto defended the flock entrusted to him with the difficult labor of his magisterium in order to preserve the faithful from greater suffering. Expectation for the coming of the Kingdom of God doesn't remove the need to make all efforts in directing things on earth as best as possible. It does not remove hope against hope: *spes contra spem* of Paul to the Romans.

The Brief Century

The whole of the 20th century, and especially its first half, saw an unending series of crimes and cruelties on a global scale committed in the name of science, equality, progress and happiness. It began with the untiring activity of a nun in the area of Bergamo. She was unknown to most, but to the poor Italians who immigrated by the millions to the United States because liberal governments left them nothing on which to live on, she was famous. Francesca Cabrini (1850-1917), was the first saint of United States, the teacher who was in love with the Sacred Heart of Jesus and who after founding many schools in Italy, in 1889 arrived in the USA Pius XII canonized her in 1946 and said about her that "she was a heroine of modern times", "a strong woman, a conqueror who took daring and heroic steps"; "nineteen times she crossed the ocean," she faced storms, crossed the Andes mountains through places where "the same guides" trembled, and with a zeal the Pope compared to that of Saint Paul, "she bought furniture, furnished hospitals, colleges, houses for charitable works, hotels, castles," she established "all kinds of schools for all levels of teaching"; "all turned to her because they admired her Christian genius of goodness and almsgiving: all kinds of callings need responding with all kinds of works.", "On top of the poor schools and schools for higher education, standing before the colonies that Italian immigrants formed in which she saw many 'little Italys', she added festive oratories, orphanages, later also hospitals and clinics, the apostolate in prisons and the apostolate in Alaska", "the care of soldiers and the wounded whose daughters she took in." A woman, one single woman, on top of the Missionary Sisters of the Sacred Heart of Jesus, gave life to all kinds of charitable institutions throughout the western hemisphere. These were geared towards the good of the poor but also towards the education of the rich. It was out of love for the Gospel that she went to preach to the "mosquitos of Central America's Indian reservations." What governments did not do, the Church did. It was a woman who did all this. She was orphan of mother and father. Her father and mother were the Spirit of God. She is the patron saint of immigrants. Francesca added Xavier to her name because he is the patron saint of missions. Frances Xavier Cabrini.

Outside the Church, charity is unknown. The Gnosis that was in power imposed on everyone an idea of happiness which it believed could be obtained through the theories it elaborated. It did not care for the numberless sufferings it inflicted along the way. The story began in 1915. The dying Ottoman Empire had fallen in the hands of enlightened nationalists. The Young Turks, as they were called, with disastrous fury launched a systematic plan meticulously designed to exterminate the still Christian Armenian population. The crimes committed were so horrendous that still today, the Turkish government refuses to acknowledge them for what they were: genocide. It continued in Russia. Moscow rose from the ashes of Byzantium and thus was called the 'Third Rome.' In 1917 it fell under the blows inflicted by a conspiracy devised and organized abroad: Communism. The Bolsheviks held that, to achieve a kingdom with equality, freedom and justice here on earth, they needed to eliminate belief in God among the common people. God needed to be expelled from man's universe as the primary responsible of their unhappiness. In 1917 the Cheka was formed, the ill-famed secret police. In 1918, a Decree from the Council of People's Commissars began persecuting the Church in the name of liberty of conscience (just like in France) and the same year, terror broke out. Immediately the first concentration camps appeared and in 1932, the anti-religious five-year plan was enacted. The plan decreed the shutdown of all places of worship and "banned the idea of God."

The abolition of private property and the ensuing civil war led the country to widespread starvation. Because of the desperate famine, fairly often the population turned to cannibalism in order to survive. Under these circumstances Lenin and Trotsky conceived a diabolical plan to destroy the Orthodox Church and all its *lavre*, its monasteries, its churches, icons and relics: they meant to exploit the famine and Christian charity for those who were starving in order to rob the

Church of all its goods. On March 19, 1922, Lenin wrote to the *Politburo*: "As quickly and radically as possible, we must absolutely confiscate all precious objects of the Church so as to guarantee ourselves a few thousand rubles in gold." Only now can we do this successfully. All calculations show that, later we shall not have the chance to act. There is no better occasion than this desperate famine because it allows us to play on the feelings of vast multitudes of farmers."

The Bolsheviks in the meantime financed the birth of Communist parties throughout the world while journalists and intellectuals – all paid by the Soviet Communist party – told of the economic, cultural and moral advancement taking place in Communist Russia. In 1937, Pius XI published the encyclical *Divini Redemptoris*, a very harsh censure of Communism which anticipated by decades the results later revealed by historical research: the soviets – he wrote – "boast that they obtained a certain economic progress which, when it is real, is explainable by many other causes such as the intensification of industrial production in countries which did not have any factories, taking advantage also of Russia's enormous natural resources by means of brutal methods to accomplish colossal works with minimal expense." "Brutal methods," the Pope wrote. Much time passed before historians noted that the USSR's economic achievements were made possible by the forced labor of over 20 million people working in inhuman conditions. In Asia, America, Africa and Europe, everywhere Communism arrived it produced bloodshed, injustice, and immeasurable suffering.

Starting in 1846, Pius IX had warned against the communist abomination. The Virgin Mary, on her part, when communism was not in power, appeared in Fatima on May 13, 1917. She appeared to Lucia, Jacinta and Francisco, three young shepherds raised to the altars, so as to avoid Russia from divulging its errors to the world. Our Lady confided the recipe to stop the First World War (the "useless carnage" according to Benedict XV) to the three children: "I would like that you recite the Rosary every day to obtain peace in the world and the end of the war." The recipe to stop the march of Communism and the explosion of another World War, more terrible than the first, was to consecrate Russia to her Immaculate Heart: "Otherwise [Russia] will spread her errors throughout the world and promote wars and persecutions against the Church. Good Samaritans will be martyred, the Holy Father will suffer much, and many nations will be destroyed."

Poland is Ready

One hundred twenty-three years after its division, when the First World War finished in 1918, Poland was reborn as a state. Poland had remained firmly catholic and in 1920 was able to stop the red army. Looking down on the newly reconstituted polish army and confident with two million soldiers, Russia was convinced it could export the revolution with arms and reach Paris easily after conquering Warsaw and Berlin: the conquest of Europe was viewed as the platform from which to conquer the rest of the world.

It was not so. Just like the Polish King Sobiesky saved Wien and Europe from Islam in 1683, in the same way the Commander in Chief of Polish forces Jozef Piłsudski and the polish nation, in August of 1920, not only saved Warsaw, but also the rest of Europe from Communism: the miracle of the battle on the Vistula river. In absence of anyone to do it, the bishops, the Church promoted opposition to the Soviet invasion. The polish episcopate mobilized the nation to prayer and implored help from the Pope and the universal Church. In a letter addressed to bishops from all nations, polish bishops said: "Poland had no intention of fighting but it was forced to do so"; "A swarm of locusts in one place destroys all signs of life and then by its own destructive action is forced to move elsewhere. Likewise, Bolshevism, after having 'poisoned' and looted Russia, nowadays turns threatening towards Poland"; "To the enemy fighting against us, Poland is not the ultimate goal of its march. It is rather a phase, a platform from where it can launch to conquer the world." The Communist International had already penetrated everywhere and in every nation, uprisings were prepared to open the doors for the liberating army: "Poland is the last obstacle on Bolshevism's road to world conquest: if it should fall, Bolshevism would spread to the entire world with all its destructive power. The wave that today is threatening the whole world is truly terrible"; "Besides doctrine and action, Bolshevism bears within it a heart full of hatred. This hatred is directed above all towards Christianity, of which it is decidedly a denial. It is against the cross of Christ and against His Church." The Pope mobilized. He solemnly called upon God to protect Poland while standing in the Church of the Gesù in Rome and invited bishops from all over the world to do the same. In the letter written on August 5 to his cardinal vicar, Benedict XV recalled how the Holy See had always defended Poland ("When all civil Nations silently bowed down in front of brute force overpowering justice, the Holy See was the only one to protest against the evil division of Poland and against the no less evil oppression of the polish people"). At the same time, he warned about the true proportion of the confrontation at hand: "It is not only the national existence of Poland which is in jeopardy, but all of Europe is threatened by the horror of new wars." The Pope concluded by appealing for "the intercession of the Most Holy Virgin, the protector of Poland."

While the whole civilized world laughed at the invocation of heaven's intervention, the cardinal of Warsaw ordered an appeal to national mobilization read in all churches. The polish people answered and enrolled in mass. Piłsudski's military genius did the rest and the Communist march for the moment came to a halt.

Poland was the main character in Catholic history of the 20th century. It gave the world a series of great saints and a Pope who changed history: Faustina Kowalska (1905-1938), Maximillian Kolbe (1894-1941), Karol Wojtyla (1920-2005).

The Brief Century was full of horrors. Countless. Immeasurable. Everywhere. And hate was what seemed to decide the fate of the world. But it was not so (though it may seem so). What does a world destroyed by sin need? A world in which sin eats up hope and the gloomy oppression of the evil committed produces disgust with oneself and desperation? All sin in the world, confided Jesus to Sister Faustina, is like a drop in the infinite sea of God's love. The whole of the bottomless and enormous abyss of evil in the world is nothing. It is only a speck compared to the all-powerful and eternal love of God: "My Love and Mercy know no limits." It was the feast of Divine Mercy which Jesus wanted instituted on the first Sunday after Easter, Sunday *in albis*, the solemn Sunday on which the baptized depose the white robes received in baptism during the Paschal vigil. John Paul II fulfilled Jesus' desire ("The feast of Mercy comes from my Heart: I want it to be solemnly celebrated on the first Sunday after Easter") and starting from the year 2000, the first Sunday after Easter was dedicated to the celebration of Divine Mercy. Pope Wojtila died on April 2, 2005, on the vigil of Divine Mercy.

In 1939, Polish independence came to an end when Poland was invaded and divided by the German and Russian armies according to the Molotov-Ribbentrop Pact. Polish lands became filled with concentration camps – the so-called Lager which Hitler modified from the gulag. Maximillian Kolbe was interned in Auschwitz, one of these camps. He was a Franciscan who had been sent to Rome to study[31]. There, in 1917, he founded the Militia of the Immaculata to promote the conversion of Freemasons and sinners through the radio and the press. Kolbe's apostolate was extraordinarily successful: a magazine, a newspaper, a convent called City of the Immaculate Mother of God, which gathered a thousand people with a seminary and a printing press. In 1941 he was interned in Auschwitz. When the Nazis randomly chose 10 prisoners and condemned them to a slow death by starvation and dehydration as punishment for the escape of a prisoner, Kolbe was there. One of those selected for the starvation bunker begged for mercy in the name of his family which needed his care. Kolbe offered himself as a substitute. After fourteen days of agony, only four of the ten were left, persevering as they could by praying and singing. The Nazis chose to finish them off. It was

---

[31] Kolbe celebrated his first mass in the Church of Sant'Andrea delle Fratte in Rome. There, on January 29, 1842, the anti-Christian Jewish lawyer Alphonse Marie Ratisbonne suddenly converted. After walking into a church with a friend, a beautiful woman appeared to Ratisbonne. She had the same bearing as the one portrayed in the miraculous medal revealed in 1830 to Caterina Labouré in the monastery of Rue de Bac in Paris (this was the first of the great Marian apparitions which took place in France during the 19th century. Ratisbonne fell to his knees before Mary which in an instant revealed to him all the truths of Christianity: "I have been asked how I came to know these truths because I never opened a book of religion in my life, I never read one single page from the Bible: all I know is that, walking into the church I was ignorant of everything and leaving I clearly understood everything"; My prejudices against Christianity were gone, the love of my God had taken the place of any other love." This is the witness left by Ratisbonne who six years later joined the Society of Jesus.

August 14, 1941. Kolbe told the person who made the fatal injection: "You have not understood anything of life"; "hate is useless"; "only love is able to create."

The Church is the sole cause of all of Mexico's misfortunes

Anti-Catholic persecutions in Latin America began immediately after the Spanish were expelled. As always, it was the hatred which precedes and follows the rise of sects to power. Such blind violence was directed especially to Mexico, the heart of Catholic faith in the new world and where the icon of the Virgin of Guadalupe, patron of America, was preserved. Mexico also borders on the continent's imperial power, namely the United States of America, protestant in faith and influenced pervasively by Freemasonry.

War on God was unleashed to eradicate faith from the continent which four centuries earlier had so impetuously received and welcomed it. From the second half of the 19th century, Mexico witnessed multiple coups d'état and revolutions: these were the result of a ruthless battle for power so violent and so unfair, that Socialist propaganda spread with great ease[32]. "The Church was the sole cause of all of Mexico's misfortunes." Thus spoke Elias Calles (1877-1945), in 1926. He was the president of Catholic Mexico who put forth his will to remake Mexicans in the image and likeness of his own thirst for power.

The government elite wanted to deprive Mexican people of their religious, spiritual and cultural identity: "While during the first centuries of the Church and in the times that followed Christians were more brutally treated, perhaps never before in no other place did a small group of men so trample and violate the rights of God and of the Church. Without any care for the values handed down to them, without any feelings of pity towards their own fellow citizens, they

---

[32] In *Humanum genus*, Leo XIII connected Freemasonry to Communism: "The sect of Freemasonry does not at all seem foreign to their aims [of Socialists and Communists]. It welcomes their opinions with approval and the most important principles are common to both." Probably, it was not by chance that Leon Trotstky escaped from Stalin and took refuge in Mexico where he was assassinated in 1940.

suffocated the liberty of the majority in every way by means of such premeditated art and issuing what appeared to be legislation but was in reality a ruse to masquerade their arbitrary acts.", this was written by Pius XI in the encyclical *Iniquis afflictisque* published in 1926. The semblance of legislation the Pope referred to be the constitution president Carranza had approved in 1917 which took as model the Third French Republic. It proclaimed the separation between Church and State in the sense that it robbed the Church of all its properties and transferred these to the State (art. 27); it forbade religious vows and dissolved congregations (art. 5); it made lay education mandatory (art. 3); it deprived the clergy of the right to vote (art. 130). The Carranza Constitution was applied with determination by Calles who also added further vexating rules such as those prohibiting the sign of the cross in public, prohibiting priests from wearing their habits, specifying the permissible number of candles in front of the altar, forbidding baptism without sterilized water, forbidding the saying, "if God wants," or "God-willing," and forcing priests to marry civilly.

Pius XI described and commented on the government's new laws: priests are deprived of their civil rights, "and thus treated as evildoers and delinquents"; "It is affirmed that there is freedom to teach, yet with the following restrictions: priests and religious are forbidden to open and run elementary schools; absolute ban on the teaching of religion to children even when this is done privately"; "insult is added to persecution; it is now common use to present the Church in a negative light to the people: by some, in public committees saying impudent lies while our friends are prevented from retorting through hooting and insults, by others, using newspapers that are professed enemies of the truth"; "In almost all states, the number of priests allowed to exercise their ministry was limited and fixed at a minimum. Even that was not allowed, if they were not registered with the magistrates or if they had not obtained their explicit permission"; "all Mexicans assigned to teaching infants or youth or occupying other public offices, were asked to answer if they were with the President of the Republic and if they approved the war on Catholic Religion; moreover, if they wanted to avoid losing their office, they were required with soldiers and workers to participate in a march organized by the Socialist league called Regional Workers' League of Mexico."

Furthermore, "government leaders had ordered that churches everywhere were to be entrusted to the care of lay people chosen by the head of the municipality. Under no circumstances were they to be handed over to anyone appointed or designated by bishops or priests (thus ownership of churches passed from ecclesial to civil authorities). Bishops almost everywhere forbade the faithful from accepting any appointments made by civil authorities and from entering those temples that were not held by the Church": the Interdict, that is, generalized suspension of worship. Mexicans promoted passive resistance by withdrawing their full accounts in banks, boycotting the purchase of any products that were subject to state owned monopolies like tobacco the consumption of which decreased by 74%, dressing in black, sending the government a petition signed by 2 million people, of a total 15 million. All this had no effect and while the bishops, starting from August 1, 1926, promoted the Interdict, the general population organized itself spontaneously in the League to Defend Religious Freedom: the *Cristiada* had begun, the war fought in the name of Christ the King. Despite the government's use of concentration camps and many martyrs, the *cristeros*, supported by the population and by women enrolled in the paramilitary brigades of Saint Joan of Arc, continued to rise in number even to the point of passing from guerrilla style warfare to head confrontation with the professional army.

By 1929, a good part of Mexico was controlled by the *cristeros* who went into battle shouting "Viva Cristo Rey!" (Hurray for Christ the King). They waved flags with the image of Our Lady of Guadalupe, lived an intense prayer life by reciting the rosary daily, Eucharistic adoration, confession and mass whenever it was possible. Catholics fought for the possibility of existing as Catholics. When the government saw how hard it was to win despite the help afforded by the United States, they offered peace treaties and as soon as the bishops agreed to the *arreglos*, the pacts, the faithful obeyed and surrendered their weapons. Those who were not killed in battle were killed after the signing of the *arreglos* which did not gave back religious freedom and included no guarantees for the protection of the *cristeros*. A real carnage.

The first pastoral trip abroad of John Paul II was to Mexico. While the farmers crowded around him, he shouted: "The Pope wants to be your voice, the voice of those who cannot speak or of those who have been silenced, wants to be the conscience of the consciences, an invitation to action in order to recover lost time which often is a time of prolonged suffering and unfulfilled hopes." In 1979, the Carranza Constitution was still in force and public religious functions were still not allowed. But Wojtyla ignored it and went to console, encourage, and fortify the faith of Mexican Catholics who had been oppressed for over one hundred years suffering wrongdoing and violence. In 1990, the Pope went back to Mexico and his welcoming was triumphant. Eight years after the United States, despite the Freemasonry's official opposition, also catholic Mexico recognized the Vatican State and in 1992 established diplomatic relations.

Lateran Pacts, Church and Fascism

In 1929, Mussolini put an end to the scandal of an Italian State that did not acknowledge the Holy See and was its proud enemy. Just think that when King Vittorio Emanuele III decided to go to war with the Alliance in May of 1915 (despite the fact that Italy was allied with the central empires and though the majority of parliament was contrary to war), article 14 of the Treaty of London which quite comprehensibly was secret, established: "France, Great Britain and Russia commit themselves to support Italy on the issue of admitting representatives of the Holy See to any diplomatic initiatives, to anything having to do with the peace conference or any provisions about issues that have to do with the present war."

Benito Mussolini (1883-1945) was well aware that to make Italy come out of the disaster wrought by liberal politics and the war's aftermath, he needed the support of the people who were entirely catholic, and he also needed a new leading class. A good part of Freemasonry, however, was contrary to any reconciliation with the Holy See. This produced a quite ridiculous and self-destructive situation wherein they ignored that for almost two thousand years, Rome hosted the universal heart of the Catholic Church. In 1925, the Duce outlawed Freemasonry and thus paved the way to an agreement with the Holy See.

In the nineteen twenties, Christians were persecuted everywhere: from Russia to Mexico to Spain. In this context, the Italian situation was a positive exception because though Mussolini initially was connected to very strong anti-Catholic positions, he changed direction and adopted a reconciliatory tone towards the Church. After the Pope's "prison time" in the Vatican which lasted fifty-nine years, on February 11, 1929, the Secretary of State cardinal Gasparri of the Holy See and the Duce, on behalf of the Italian state, signed the Lateran Accords. Two days later, on February 13, addressing members of the Catholic University of the Sacred Heart in Milan, Pope Ratti recalled the intricate legal knot which needed to be undone in order to reach an accord and he jokingly remarked: "In order to resolve the issue, maybe an alpinist Pope is exactly what was needed, a mountaineer who had no fear of heights and who was used to confronting the hardest climbs; just like sometimes we have thought that what was needed was a librarian Pope, somebody accustomed to get to the bottom of historical and documentary research, because obviously a lot of books and documents had to be consulted."[33] At this point, Pius XI added: "We also have to say that the other party has very nobly seconded our motions. And maybe, we needed also a man like that set there by Providence, a man who had none of the liberal school's worries. For these men, all laws, all ordinances or rather disordinances, let's say all those laws and regulations were fetishes and just like fetishes, the more intangible and venerable, the uglier and more deformed they are." The Pope concluded: "It is with profound pleasure that we believe to have given back God to Italy and Italy to God."

The Lateran Accords are made up of a Treaty of conciliation which recognizes the state of Vatican City thus guaranteeing the Pontiff's sovereignty, a Concordat to regulate civil and religious relations between Italy and the Holy See, and a Financial Convention to give back 750 million Lire to the Church in reparation of all the goods (including the same Pontifical State) stolen. Without a doubt, the Lateran Accords is a fact of historic proportions both for the

---

[33] Pio XI, Prefect of the Biblioteca Ambrosiana and of the Biblioteca Vaticana was a skilled mountaineer who dedicated to him a road he opened on Mont Blanc.

Church and Italy. Nevertheless, just two years later, Fascism broke the concordat by dissolving Catholic Action associations of youth and of university students, and doing so with "violence even unto bloody blows." This was ignored by the party press, "the only free" one. Moreover, the press spewed "lies and slander" against members of Catholic Action and attributed to them inexistent political aims: "It is with inexpressible pain – wrote Pius XI in the encyclical *Non abbiamo bisogno* (*We do not need*) of June 29, 1931 – that we are witnessing a true and real persecution unleashed throughout this Our Italy and in this Our very own Rome."

Pope Ratti lamented the ingratitude "shown to the Holy See by a party and a regime which, in the eyes of the whole world, through its friendly relationship to the Holy See, increased in prestige and trust both in Italy and abroad. Many in Italy and abroad deemed this favor and all this trust on Our part excessive." The Pope identified the cause for the new start of anti-Catholic hostilities in the strengthening of the lodges: "We, the Church, Religion, catholic faithful (and not only Us) cannot be grateful to those who after having expelled Socialism and Freemasonry, our avowed enemies (and not only Ours), have so magnanimously readmitted them, as all can see and deplore, and to those who aided to make them more powerful, dangerous and harmful by their increased dissimulation and their new uniform."

The main point of the challenge, wrote Pope Ratti, is cultural: the regime aimed to control the youth according to the dictates of "a pagan idolatry of the state," through "a conception of the state which makes the young generation belong to it," according to a view of the world which is unacceptable for a Catholic and unacceptable even for the natural rights of the family. "Let no one say – the Pope highlighted – that Italy is Catholic, but rather anticlerical" because it is well known "that anticlericalism in Italy has as much power and importance as was given to it by Freemasonry and Liberalism which created it." Despite the firm condemnation of the ethical state following its actions towards Catholic Action, Pius XI clarified: "We did not want to condemn the party and the regime per se."

In the following years, yearning to give Italy "a place in the sun," Mussolini conquered Ethiopia and after producing a not very credible indignation on the part of England (at the time, the most powerful colonial nation) was condemned by the United Nations. Forced to turn to Hitler for an alliance, on September 18, 1938, he pronounced ratial law also in Italy. The Church's condemnation was firm: on November 4, Pius XI wrote the Duce a letter which received no reply and then another to Vittorio Emanuele III, lamenting, among other things, the violation of the Concordat with respect to marriage norms between Catholics and different races (Jewish and not) which from that point on were outlawed.

Ildefonso Schuster, bishop of Milan made a homily in the Duomo on November 13, 1938 which was very articulate and interesting from a cultural point of view. Schuster juxtaposed Roman tradition (Mussolini's inspiration) to "Nordic philosophy which was both a theosophical and a political view." Roman imperial tradition was "truly universal and cosmopolitan." Therefore, if there is "an anti-imperial and anti-Roman concept, undoubtedly, it is the ratial myth of the 20th century, which violently turned the history of the world back two thousand years!" Also Dante would agree, Schuster recalled, as he exalted the glories "of that Rome where Christ is a Roman."

"Christ can't be dismembered": The Church does not admit ratial distinctions.

A Worshipper of Satan in Power

In 1945, when the Russians arrived in Berlin, they carried many pictures of Hitler's studio, designed in detail and then photographed by Albert Speer, the Führer's architect, to Moscow. The relief on the entrance door depicts a knight (Hitler) with a skeleton gripping his left hand and the devil clutching his left shoulder – always the left, the side which is traditionally attributed to the devil – where he supports his indefinite animal head. It is an interesting image because it expresses in a nutshell the Führer's government program.

Hitler's *Table Talks* are equally interesting, as they were for Luther. They were transcribed with great care because nothing having to do with the Führer was to go lost. We will report here some considerations made with regard to science and Christianity, noting how the tradition Hitler referred to when he spoke about science was the English scientific tradition – Bacon-Darwin-Galton – while his ideas about Christianity suffered Nietzsche's influence:

- Science: "Time will flow until the science will be able to answer all questions"; a movement such as ours "must keep faith to the spirit of exact science"; "Science can never lie"; "When it errs, it errs in good faith. Instead, Christianity lies"; "Nature is the best pedagogue even with regard to selection. It is impossible to imagine that nature would occupy itself with a more fruitful activity than that of determining the rise of beings through perpetual battle";
- Christianity: "It is the worst regress humanity could undergo"; "it proclaims its inconsistent dogmas and imposes them with force. A similar religion bears within it intolerance and persecution. There is not a bloodier one"; "Any man gifted with a minimum dose of reason," "cannot believe in the resurrection of bodies"; "Christian religion is an enemy of beauty"; "Our age will undoubtedly see the end of the Christian disease"; "We are entering into an age of the world which will be a sunny, an era of tolerance"; "Judeo-Christians have systematically destroyed the monuments of Greco-Roman civilization. They are also responsible for the destruction of the library in Alexandria."

This was the program for after the war: "After this war, I shall adopt the necessary measures so that recruiting priests may become extremely difficult"; "I avoid publicly confronting religious issues, but the shrewd in the Church are not deceived about my motives. It is easy for me to imagine that Bishop von Galen[34] knows perfectly well that once the war is over, I will settle my accounts with him until the last penny"; "After the war, each of our prefects must make it

---

[34] A few examples of von Galen's preaching. In the homily of July 20, 1941, he said: "Be strong and steadfast, just like the anvil under the raging blows which are raining down upon us, in your boundless and faithful devotion to the people and to the homeland. We must obey God over men." In the homily of August 3, he went on a rampage against euthanasia: "It's a matter of being human, of those like us, of our brothers and our sisters. They may be poor people, sick people, and unproductive people: but have they lost their right to life simply for this?"

unequivocally clear that he treats the Church just like any other association and will not allow interference from any third party. Then the Nuncio can calmly take the road back to Rome."

Hitler rose to power in 1933. In 1934, the Night of the Long Knives took place in which all leaders of the SA, until that point allied to Hitler, were killed. In 1935 the *Anschluss* (annexation) of Austria was completed. In 1938, the Munich Conference joined the chief European powers in Bavaria: Great Britain, France, Italy and Germany. Hitler, as shown by the choice of the place to host the meeting, was the most influential person in Europe.

In 1933, Hitler obtained the signing of a concordat with the Holy See: the Führer wanted to oppose himself against the Bolsheviks' anti-Catholic hatred and make a show to reassure the faithful in order to gain their support. In 1937, Pius XI published the encyclical *Mit brennender Sorge* (*With burning concern*), an attack of the most violent and resolute kind against National-Socialist ideology: the Holy See was the only state, the only authoritative voice in the entire world, heard in defense of the Jews. It would be worthwhile to analyze the Pope's considerations here:

- "by request of the government of the Reich," in view of the "dutiful need to safeguard freedom and the saving mission of the Church in Germany," "not without effort," "we have accepted to take up talks again for a Concordat";
- anyone with any love for the truth must "recognize with awe and intimate revulsion, how the opposite party [the Germans] has made it an ordinary rule for itself to arbitrarily and more or less openly bend, elude, empty and finally violate all pacts";
- the "purpose" of this encyclical is the right of all catholic faithful "to receive a word of truth and moral encouragement" from the Pope in a moment when "the impossibility of obtaining truthful information and of defending oneself by normal means is cause for much oppression";
- *Gott mit uns*: "He who uses the name of God rhetorically cannot be considered a believer in God"; "He who with pantheistic indetermination identifies God with the universe by materializing God in the world and deifying the world in God, does not belong among true believers"; be very careful [he

addresses the bishops] "about the growing abuse which manifests itself in speech and writing, of using the thrice holy name of God as an empty name tag," "make every effort so that this aberration may find the watchful revulsion it deserves among your faithful";

- "Only superficial spirits can fall in the error of speaking about a national God, of a national religion, and undergo the crazy attempt to imprison [God] in one sole people, in the tight ethnic space of one sole race";

- "The Holy Books of the Old Testament are all Word of God, an organic part of His Revelation"; "Only blindness and stubbornness can cause one to close their eyes in front of the saving teachings hidden in the Old Testament. Whoever wants biblical history and the wise teachings of the Old Testament banished from Churches and schools is blaspheming against the Word of God, is blaspheming the all-powerful plan of salvation and erects a narrow and restricted human thought as judge of divine plans";

- "religious notions are emptied of their genuine content and applied to profane meanings." The Pope gave various example of the deceiving and distorted use of language: "Revelation, in the Christian sense, means the Word of God to men. To use this same term for any allusions to blood and race," means to "cause disorientation"; "immortality": "Those who use the word immortality to indicate nothing more than the collective survival of the continuity of one's own people", "perverts and falsifies one of the fundamental truths of Christian faith"; "humility": "By describing Christian humility foolishly, as if it were a sort of debasement or pettiness, it is only the revolting pride of these innovators which is made to look ridiculous"; "Grace": "The denial of this supernatural elevation to grace because of some supposed peculiar German character is a mistake, it is an open declaration of war against a fundamental truth of Christianity. To place supernatural grace and the gifts granted by nature on the same level means to pervert the language created and sanctified by Religion";

- "Productions in the press and the radio flood your attention daily with content adverse to Faith and the Church"; "If the

State were to organize all youth in mandatory national associations," then the youth and their parents have the right to "demand this association to be cleaned of all tendencies hostile to the Christian Faith and the Church." Parents "cannot give the State what is being required of them in the name of the State without taking away from God what belongs to him." "Through hidden and blatant pressure, by intimidating, by promising financial, professional, civil or other kinds of advantages, the attachment to faith of Catholics, and especially of certain classes of catholic officials, is put under violence which is both illegal and inhuman." "But we have reached such a situation that the ultimate and highest end, salvation or perdition, is in jeopardy. Therefore, the only way of salvation left for the believer is the path to generous heroism."

Hitler's private cabinet

Hitler's private cabinet, particular

Incredibly, the Church managed to elude the Gestapo's surveillance and the encyclical *Mit Brennender Sorge* was read at the same time in all churches of Germany on March 21, 1937. It was Palm Sunday. The bitter condemnation of National-Socialism is greatly owed to the pen of the Secretary of State Eugenio Pacelli, the nunzio in Germany for many years.

Civil War in Spain

Throughout the 19th century, anti-Catholic hatred in Spain spread by the lodges favorable to France exploded in phases. It became the cause for a general war which lasted from 1936 to 1939, exactly ten years after the *Cristeros* war in Mexico. The Spanish Civil War was a European war. On the side of the revolution fought Bolsheviks, Anarchists, and Communists from all the world and they aimed to export the conquest of Russian communism to Spain. On the opposite side of the Communists stood Mussolini and Hitler (in 1942, the Führer said: "If there had not been the risk that the red danger could have submerged Europe, I would not have obstacled the revolution in Spain. The clergy would have been exterminated").

In Spain, the 20th century began with the tragic week of Barcellona in 1909. Following was the advent of the republic in 1931 and the Spanish first minister who proclaimed: *España ha dejado de ser católica* (Spain has stopped being Catholic). On May 11, 12 and 13, over one hundred churches and convents were burnt down and looted, while cardinal Segura, the archbishop of Toledo and primate of Spain was sent in exile. To grasp the exaltation which possessed the revolutionary, one need only read what was written in "El socialista" on August 20, 1931 about anti-Catholic vandalism committed during the month of May: "Back then, harmless convents were the target of the people's fury; now, let their inhabitants be the victims of its fury." The political program of Anarchists, Communists, Freemasons and Republicans, who owed obedience to different parties, were clear: the Church was to be annihilated and all means were valid to reach that objective. In 1932, more than three thousand Jesuits were expelled and in 1933, the *Ley de Confesiones y Congregaciones* forbade religious orders teaching and any other kind of activity and decreed that the seizing of their assets was quite possible.

In 1933, the election was won by the party on the right. But the radical Left did not accept the result and tried to enact the revolution. It was the Red October in Asturias. It marked the beginning of violent persecution which had been prepared for some time already. In ten days, 12 priests, 7 seminarians, and 18 religious were killed, while 58 churches were burnt down. This is the tragic picture which results when hatred prevails. In such desperate circumstances, there were many martyrs. Besides any political battle, those guilty of the crime of being Catholics were immolated and tortured in the most revolting ways. They were killed in *odium fidei*. After the victory of the Popular Front in 1936 and after the *alzamiento* of Franco on July 18, the persecution was generalized. The Frankist insurrection offered a perfect occasion to intensify the much planned campaign to annihilate the Church: "Documents show that the PSOE (Spanish Socialist Workers' Party) wanted civil war: it desired it, it prepared for it and was sure of winning," wrote the historian Pio Moa who came from the ranks of the extreme Left.

From 1931 to 1939, 4,080 priests, 2,365 religious, 283 nuns were killed: 13% of the diocesan priests and 23% of the religious. This percentage however is not emblematic because it refers to only half of the Spanish territory (the socialist-anarchists-communist party). In fact, in some regions, the annihilation of the clergy reached extreme cruelty: in Barbastro, for example, 87% of priest were exterminated, together with the Bishop Florentino Barroso, who was executed by firing squad after being evirated in public, his testicles wrapped in a page of the newspaper *Solidaridad Obrera* and then carried in triumph to all cafes in the city. The minister Manuel de Irujo wrote a government memorandum in which he described the Spanish situation: "A. All altars, images and objects used for worship, with few rare exceptions, were destroyed"; "B. All churches were closed for worship; worship was universally suppressed"; "E. The churches have been transformed into warehouses of all kinds, markets, garages"; "G. Priests and religious were incarcerated and shot by a firing squad by the thousands and without any formal accusation. There was no other reason except their distinctive feature, they were priests or religious." The destruction of Spanish artistic treasure went hand in hand with profaning the tombs containing bodies of religious exhumed and exposed to public shame.

The number of civilian massacres cannot be counted. Among them was the first gypsy beatified by John Paul II on May 4, 1997, Ceferino Giménez Malla. He was killed because he opposed himself to the pastor's arrest and because he refused to separate himself from his rosary crown which he clenched when executed. Love for Jesus Christ in Catholic Spain had not disappeared: the many martyrs, the many helpless people, the youth, the mothers, all killed because they were Catholic, gave witness in their blood and through the forgiveness offered to their butchers to the faith and the hope that supported them. A few testimonies from their beatification process: Bartolomé Blanco, a 21-year-old worker, near death wrote to his family members: "I know all my accusers. The moment will arrive when you also will get to know them. You must behave as I did not because my example is worth anything but because being so close to death, I feel also very close to God our Lord and my behavior towards those who accuse me is one of mercy and forgiveness. Let this be my last will: forgiveness, forgiveness, forgiveness"; Bance Brissac wrote to her son: "I ask you only to be good always, very good. Love everyone and never bear rancor towards those who killed your parents; never. Good people do not bear grudges and you must be a good man"; the discalced Carmelite Tirso de Jesus Maria wrote: "All of you be very good. Forgive, bless and love everyone as I love, forgive and bless them."

While decades of dark times tried to undermine Spain's grounding in faith and family, Antoni Gaudì's (1852-1926) artistic genius and faith, which always moves mountains when it is really there, conceived a grandiose project dedicated to the Holy Family: the Tempio espiatorio de la Sagrada Familia (Expiatory temple of the Holy Family) in Barcelona. To build it, one hundred years were not enough, almost two hundred were needed. Time and money were no problem for Gaudì: the Spirit takes care of everything. Just as in the Middle Ages, collections made among the poor allowed for the building of a new cathedral, the "cathedral of the poor." The building is a synthesis of many styles and uses all possible materials: enchanting forms, stain glass, stones, ceramic, squiggles, spires, flowers and fruit, statues, trees and columns, which exalt heaven, celebrate the light of God, of his angels and of his saints, of the apostles and evangelists, of the Virgin and Saint Joseph, growing in splendor up to the apex, the irradiation of the Holy Spirit. Men want to distance themselves from heaven by denying its existence. But heaven descends upon earth and makes beauty visible, the strength and glory of God's city who overcomes death and prepares the heavenly Jerusalem.

On June 28, 2003, John Paul II wrote the Apostolic Exortation *Ecclesia in Europa* about the host of European martyrs: witnesses to faith, "are an eloquent and grandiose sign which we are asked to contemplate and imitate. They attest to the liveliness of the Church. They appear to us as a light for the Church and for humanity because they have the light of Christ shine forth into darkness." John Paul II went to Spain five times to strengthen the faith of *España evangelizadora* (Spain, the evangelizer) and to recall the identity of the nation who resisted to Islam in the name of faith and who converted a continent in the name of faith.

Virgin, Mother, Daughter of your Son

"Vergine Madre, figlia del tuo figlio,
umile e alta più che creatura,
termine fisso d'etterno consiglio,
tu se' colei che l'umana natura
nobilitasti sì, che 'l suo Fattore

non disdegnò di farsi sua fattura";
"Donna, se' tanto grande e tanto vali,
che qual vuol grazia ed a te non ricorre,
sua disianza vuol volar sanz'ali";

> The thirty-third canto of Dante's *Paradiso*.

Upon his death, Jesus entrusted a new son to his mother, John: "Woman, Behold your son"; at the foot of the cross, John was invited to welcome Mary as his mother: "Behold your mother! And from that hour the disciple took her to his own home." Over time, the Church, moved by the Spirit, by miracles and by Marian apparitions elaborated the great mystery of the Mother whose heart was pierced by seven swords and who accepted to take as adoptive children, the same killers of her only son. Over the last two centuries, the great Marian apparitions that were approved by the Church occurred in tandem to the dogmatic definition of the wonderful nature of the mediatrix of all graces, described in many litanies with an infinite variety of sublime images. On December 8, 1854, Pius IX proclaimed the Immaculate Conception. On November 1, 1950, Pius XII (1939-1958) published the Apostolic Constitution *Munificentissimus Deus* which proclaimed Mary's assumption, body and soul, into heaven: "We pronounce, declare and define as a dogma revealed by God that: the Immaculate ever Virgin Mary Mother of God, having finished the course of her earthly life was assumed into the heavenly glory both body and soul."

Pius XII composed a hymn of praise to Mary: "While the Most Holy Virgin fulfilled her office with inordinate love of the mother for all those redeemed by the blood of Christ, the mind and heart of her children were moved with greater commitment to a more loving contemplation of her privileges"; "We, who have placed Our pontificate under the special protection of the Most Holy Virgin to whom we have turned in so many overly sad circumstances, We, who by a public rite have consecrated all mankind to her Immaculate Heart and have repeatedly experienced her most valuable protection, we firmly believe that this solemn proclamation and definition of the assumption will bring great benefit to all mankind because it will give glory to the Most Holy Trinity, to whom the Virgin Mother of God is tied in a singular way."

Pius XII had been Pope 11 years when he proclaimed the dogma of the Assumption. During those years, he witnessed the desolation brought by war, the tragedy of the holocaust, the fall of fascism, the threat and then the presence of communism throughout Europe. Pacelli did all he could to avoid these tragedies: on April 24, 1940, he wrote Mussolini a letter to avoid throwing Italy headlong into the horror of war; he pleaded to the French and English governments so that they would not bombard Rome "in view of her sacred character"; though he was pressured on all sides to leave Rome, although the Nazis' threats to deport him were real, he did not budge from Rome; on July 19, 1943, when Rome was bombarded causing thousands of dead, he was the first to aid, bless, and comfort. When the war came to a close on June 2, 1945, in his address to the cardinals, *Nell'accogliere*, he called upon all to recognize the chasm all those who rebel against God fall into: "You may clearly see the outcome of a certain conception and activity of the state which takes no account of the most sacred feelings of humanity and which tramples over the inviolable principles of Christian faith. Today, the entire world contemplates in awe the ruin which it caused." Before the "satanic specter" of Nazism, continued Pius XII, "no one could ever reprove the Church for failing to denounce and point out in advance the true character of the National-Socialist movement and the danger to which it exposed Christian civilization."

Pius XII recalled how the encyclical *Mit brenneder Sorge*, issued with a lot of courage amidst total silence from the whole world, led to an aggravation of anti-Catholic persecution: "The year 1937, was a year of unspeakable bitterness and raging storm for the Catholic Church in Germany." The hostility showed by Nazism towards the Church, the Pope continued, "Was visible even until these last few months, when its followers flattered themselves by thinking that they could still annihilate the Church once and for all as soon as they obtained military victory." Pius XII never heard Hitler's *Table talks* but the facts spoke for themselves: "By repeated and increasingly hostile actions against the Catholic Church in Austria, in Alsace-Lorraine and above all, in those regions of Poland which during the war had been incorporated to the ancient Reich, everything was struck, annihilated; that is, everything which by means of external violence could be reached."

At the end of the war, Pius XII was overtaken by a furious conspiracy promoted by Moscow, the center for world communism, which aimed to destroy his character and his papacy. Radio Moscow welcomed the address to the cardinals with the following comment: "No atrocity perpetrated by the followers of Hitler ever aroused the Vatican's contempt and indignation. The Vatican was silent when the German machines of death were at work, when the chimneys of cremation furnaces were smoking," "when Hitler's doctrine about the elimination and extermination of nations and peoples was becoming a hard reality." Stalin, who accused Pius XII of not speaking out against Nazi crimes, in 1939 made an agreement with Hitler, just two years after the public and detailed papal condemnation of National-Socialism.

After *Mit brenneder Sorge*, Pius XII did not issue other condemnations because to do so would have meant to place many human lives in jeopardy: "Precisely the failures and retaliations which followed as a direct consequence of public protest convinced Pius XII to concentrate the Church's efforts on projects for secret assistance to the persecuted." "It is enough to think of what happened when the bishops from Holland protested against anti-Semite persecution: well over 40 thousand Jews were killed," wrote the Jesuit Father Gumpel who acted as the reporting witness in Pius XII's cause of beatification. Giovanni Battista Montini, a month before becoming Paul VI (1963-1978), on "The Tablet" edition of May 11, 1963 declared: "An attitude of condemnation and protest [...] besides being useless would have been harmful; that is all." Here, we want to recall only two facts. Eugenio Pacelli ordered convents to break their rule of enclosure in order to hide thousands of Italian Jews who were doomed to be exterminated in convents – risking the lives of the religious. The Chief Rabbi of Rome, Israel Zolli, an educated and pious man, at the end of the war converted to Catholicism and chose Eugenio Pio as his baptismal name.

If Italy did not plunge into a chasm of communist tyranny, it is owed to Pacelli and the widespread mobilization of the Church under his guidance. Pius XII, without any hesitation, clearly pointed out the deadly dangers that their adhesion to Communism entailed. This is the succinct text of the decree issued by the Holy See on July 1, 1949: "This Supreme and Sacred Congregation was asked 1. If it were legitimate to join or support the communist party; 2. If it were legitimate to print, divulge or read books, magazines, newspapers or pamphlets which support the doctrine or work of Communists or if it were legitimate to write for them; 3. If Christians who consciously and freely did what is in points 1 and 2 may be admitted to the Sacraments; 4. If Christians who profess the communist materialist and anti-Christian doctrine, and, above all, those who work to defend and spread it, *ipso facto* shall incur excommunication reserved to the Holy See, as apostates of the Catholic faith." For point 1, 2, 3, the answer was negative. For point 4, it was affirmative.

Humanity Heads towards a New Order

Thanks to Vatican Council II (1962-1965) "the whole Church became once again aware that it is the People of God, a People who participate to the mission of Christ, a People who goes through history with this mission, a People 'on pilgrimage.'" This was pronounced by John Paul II in the speech made in Warsaw on June 2, 1979, during his first apostolic trip to Poland. The council which gave back an extraordinary missionary impulse to the Church was called on December 25, 1961, by John XXIII through the Apostolic Constitution *Humanae Salutis* in which he also said: "In these times we are living, the Church sees the gravely perturbed human community aspire to a total renewal. And while humanity walks towards a new order, tasks of enormous proportions await the Church, as we know has occurred in each of the most tragic circumstances. This is what is now asked of the Church: to insert the perennial, vivifying, divine energy of the Gospel into the veins of today's human community. Though it is elated because of its conquests in the fields of technology and science, it suffers the consequences of a temporal order some have tried to re-organize by excluding God."

Which "some have tried to re-organize by excluding God": while Communism destroyed the life and culture not only of Russia and Eastern Europe, but also of such great nations as China, devastated Indochina, Cuba, many African nations and infiltrated the Church of Latin America with Liberation Theology; while western gnostic elites, once the mythologies tied to class and race came to an end, directed their distinctive thirst for freedom towards the body thus preparing the sexual revolution of '68; in the meantime, John XXIII had an intuition about the momentous implications of the times and about the need to prepare the Church in order to withstand the impact of post-modernity by convoking a council.

In those years, the Catholic world was overwhelmed by a kind of anxiety for radical renewal. Benedict XVI, in the speech made to the Roman clergy right before he stepped down from office on February 14, 2013, said: "We were hoping everything would be renewed"; "The common feeling was that the Church was not moving forwards but rather was shrinking. It seemed to be more a reality of the past a not the bearer of the future." Yet we hoped, "that the Church could become once again the strength of tomorrow and the strength of today"; we hoped that the Church could once again begin on a new path together with the modern world; we thought to be able "to find a new union between the Church and best powers of the world, in order to open up the future to humanity, to open up the way to true progress." In his "chat" with the priests of Rome, after having recalled the main points of the council's discussion (liturgical reform, Ecclesiology, Word of God), Benedict XVI recalled also the drama surrounding the media's attempt to engineer a parallel council to damage the Church: "There was the Council of the Fathers – the true Council – but there was also the Council of the media. It was almost its own council, and the world perceived the Council through the media. And from the media's perspective, the council was nothing more than a political struggle, a power struggle between different currents in the Church," the power of the Pope, the power of the bishops and the power of all, "popular sovereignty." Naturally, for the media "the latter is the party which should have been approved, promoted, favored. The same for the liturgy: the liturgy itself as an act of faith was uninteresting; it was interesting however as a place where comprehensible things are done, as a thing of the community's activity, as something profane." Similar "banalization of the idea of council" created "many calamities, many problems, truly many miseries: closed seminaries, closed convents, the liturgy turned into something banal." What happened was that "the virtual Council was stronger than the real Council."

Some years before, on December 22, 2005, in his first Christmas address to the Roman curia, Benedict XVI, as the young protagonist of the synodal assembly, had felt the need to clarify the reasons for the difficulties which arose within the Church in the years following the Council: "No one can deny that in vast areas of the Church the implementation of the Council has been somewhat difficult, even without wishing to apply the description that Saint Basil, the great Doctor of the Church, made of the Church's situation after the Council of Nicea to what occurred in these years: he compared her situation to a naval battle in the darkness of the storm, saying among other things: 'the raucous shouting of those who through disagreement rise up against one another, incomprehensible chatter, the confused din of uninterrupted clamoring, has now filled almost the whole of the Church falsifying through excess or failure the right doctrine of the faith.'" Why so much clamor, Pope Ratzinger asked himself? "It all depends on the correct interpretation of the Council or – as we would say today – on its proper hermeneutics, the correct key to its interpretation and application. The problems in its implementation arose from the fact that two contrary hermeneutics came face to face and quarreled with each other. One caused confusion, the other, silently but more and more visibly, bore and is bearing fruit. On the one hand, there is an interpretation that I would call a 'hermeneutic of discontinuity and rupture'; it has frequently availed itself of the sympathies of the mass media, and also one trend of modern theology. On the other, there is the "hermeneutic of reform", of renewal in the continuity of the one subject-Church which the Lord has given to us. She is a subject which increases in time and develops, yet always remaining the same, the one subject of the journeying People of God." There is not a Church that is pre-conciliar and a Church that is post-conciliar. There are no texts of the Council which were the fruit of compromise and which are opposed to some supposed 'spirit' of the Council: "The Church, both before and after the Council, was and is the same Church, one, holy, catholic and apostolic, journeying on through time."

The Council, the Pope continued, had to "determine in a new way the relationship between the Church and the modern era," which had a stormy beginning with the Galileo case. Among the pressing issues that needed to be addressed: "The relationship between faith and modern science had to be redefined," including historical science, challenging the supposed incontestable "historical-critical method"; "it was necessary to give a new definition to the relationship between the Church and the modern State," and offer "a new definition of the relationship between the Christian faith and the world religions, [...] "between the Church and the faith of Israel." By making its own "an essential principle of the modern State with the Decree on Religious Freedom," the Church did nothing more than take up the teaching of Jesus and the martyrs who "died for freedom of conscience and the freedom to profess one's own faith – a profession that no State can impose but which, instead, can only be claimed with God's grace in freedom of conscience." In the document *Nostra Aetate*, "a text about interreligious dialogue," starting from "faith in the uniqueness of Christ, who is one, and that it is not impossible for a believer to think that all religions are variations on one theme" (these were the expressions used in the speech to the roman clergy of 2013), the Church reaffirmed the Pauline magisterium with regards to the Jews: "The Church cannot forget that it received the Old Testament Revelation by means of the people with whom God, in his ineffable mercy, deigned himself to stipulate the old covenant and that the Church nourishes itself at the root of the good olive tree on which the wild olive shoots, that is the pagans, were grafted."

Be holy, for I, the Lord Your God, am holy

Paul set forth the model of Christian married life when he wrote to the Ephesians – we have recalled already – that marriage is the sacrament of the absolute, of eternity and of perfection in the love of Christ for his Church. Christians are called to be holy, heavenly men, just as Jesus Christ, whose body they form, is holy. In the *First Letter to the Corinthians*, he wrote: "Do you not know that your bodies are members of Christ?" And further: "Do you not know that your body is a temple of the Holy Spirit?" And concluded: "So glorify God in your body!"

After the end of the Second World War, a gnostic storm was unleashed upon the whole western world. It rejected revelation and the goodness of creation, it considered the body too narrow a limit for the liberty of the spirit, it decreed the need to reduce births, and it disjointed sexuality from spousal love open to life. Just like a media campaign is able to artfully create a fake council, a media campaign can artfully create a desire for happiness based on the spouses' liberty of conscience and now, it seemed, these may reject the plan of God over their bodies and yet remain catholic. So now the body was not the temple of the Holy Spirit anymore but the temple of free love. Love that is free to manifest itself in the times and modes chosen by the single husbands or single wives: union and procreation, the distinctive features of marriage life, were place on parallel tracks which rarely intersect.

The Church was overwhelmed by a amazing pressure in the media pushing it to accept the conquests of modernity by welcoming the newly marketed birth-control pill as a liberation. At the same time, abortion was made legal – with time it was also included among the rights of the human person – and while towards the end of the seventies the highest French intellectuals (starting from Jean Paul Sartre, Louis Althusser, Gilles Deleuze, Jacques Derrida, Michel Foucault, André Glucksmann, Roland Barthes, Alain Robbe-Grillet) launched a media campaign to make sexual relationships between different generations legal – pedophilia – Simone de Beauvoir separated sexual identity from biological datum and tied it instead to free cultural choices (the belief "one is not born, but rather becomes, a woman," which over the years was transformed into Gender Theory).

Within the Church, those who advocated the need to update the norms of sexual ethics were many and authoritative. Cardinal Leo Suenens, archbishop of the diocese of Malines-Brussels claimed: "We follow the progress of science. I beg you, Fathers, let us avoid another Galileo case." In these circumstances, on July 25, 1968, going against the majority opinion of a commission convoked for this reason, against the opinion of many bishops, against the opinion of the media, basically against the whole of world, Paul VI reaffirmed in the encyclical *Humanae Vitae* that Catholic doctrine, anchored to revelation, does not change with the changing times and does not follow the "progress" of the world. In response to the questions: "Granted the conditions of life today and taking into account the relevance of married love to the harmony and mutual fidelity of husband and wife, would it not be right to review the moral norms in force till now, especially when it is felt that these can be observed only with the gravest difficulty, sometimes only through heroic efforts"; and the question about whether the "procreative finality applies to the totality of married life rather than to each single act"; and the question about whether, considering that "people are more conscious today of their responsibilities, the time has not come when the transmission of life should be regulated by their intelligence and will rather than through the specific rhythms of their own bodies"; the Pope answered: "The exercise of responsible parenthood requires that husband and wife, keeping a right hierarchy of values, recognize their own duties toward God, themselves, their families and human society. From this it follows that they are not free to act as they choose in the service of transmitting life, as if it were wholly up to them to decide what the right course to follow is. On the contrary, they are bound to ensure that what they do corresponds to the will of God the Creator. The very nature of marriage and its use makes His will clear, while the constant teaching of the Church spells it out." And further: "Unless we are willing that the responsibility of procreating life should be left to the arbitrary decision of men, we must accept that there are certain limits, beyond which it is wrong to go, to the power of man over his own body and its natural functions"; "each and every marital act must of necessity remain open to the transmission of human life."

Paul VI reminded priests how important it was that "all should obey the magisterium of the Church and should use the same language," and warned bishops "to devote [themselves] with all zeal and without stop to the defense and holiness of marriage." He did not achieve the desired effect. In many cases, priests gave spiritual counsel that was inspired to couples' freedom of conscience and to responsible parenthood (in the sense that parents can decide on their own how many children to have), while entire episcopal conferences opposed themselves to the Pope's encyclical. When Paul VI took a firm stance on human sexuality, a real storm unleashed in the media.

Peter's boat took in a lot of water polluted by love of the world. In the following decades, the consequences were drastic: the life of families formed by parents, grandparents, siblings, cousins and uncles was almost extinguished; the progressive aging of the population; the desperate solitude of old people and of entire generations. The Pope was accused of issuing abstract laws and of neglecting to address the concrete needs and hardships of couples. This accusation turned out to be false and the exact contrary proved to be true: it was Paul VI who defended life in its most concrete dimension with its needs and hardships. The road to the kingdom of heaven is narrow but it is the only one that brings human existence to its fullness.

Humanae Vitae marked a divide. Its refusal by European nation that were still catholic caused a drastic fall in the birth rate as well as the spread of sexual practices that are clearly condemned in the Bible: onanism and homosexuality, among others. The legitimization of sexuality conceived as separate from reproduction offered members of the clergy with homosexual tendencies a mitigating argument in the evaluation of their behavior, thus minimizing its moral gravity. The plague of homosexuality among the clergy and of pedophilia, with which it sometimes goes hand in hand, represents a grave and deviating phenomenon which deeply pollutes the priestly ministry. The refusal to accept the guidelines contained in an albeit short yet precious encyclical, by rebelling to the pontifical magisterium and to the requisites of holiness in the body, in the name of science, of progress, and even of the same will of God, has had catastrophic consequences.

A New Evangelization

On June 29, 1972, in the homily delivered for the feast of Saints Peter and Paul, Paul VI made a dramatic statement: I have the sensation, he said, that "from some fissure the smoke of Satan has entered the temple of God." A few months before his death, on September 8, 1977, the Pope confided to his friend, the philosopher Jean Guitton (1901-1999): "What strikes me, when I consider the catholic world, is that sometimes within Catholicism, a kind of non-Catholic thinking seems to prevail, and it may occur, that tomorrow, this non-Catholic thinking within Catholicism, may become stronger. But it will never reflect the Church's thinking. A small flock must survive, no matter how small it may be."

Karol Wojtyla took control at the helm of the Peter's boat in a time of doubt, of confusion, of loss of trust in the existence of truth, of surrender to communism viewed as a kind of calamity unavoidably destined to spread everywhere, of a weary reproposing pastoral models which failed to stop the hemorrhage of faithful, who in Latin America were moving towards protestant sects financed and supported in large part by the cultural and religious imperialism of the United States, and which in Europe were not up to the challenge posed by liberal-freemasonic relativism.

John Paul II's (1978-2005) course of action covered three hundred and sixty degrees. After three decades at the helm, Peter's boat overcame aimless drifting and sailed decidedly towards it natural destination, heaven, firmly anchored in the two columns prophesied by Don Bosco: the Eucharist and the Immaculate Virgin. Communism, taken head on in battle, crumbled in the seat of its own choice, Russia and its European satellite states; relativism was shown for what it was, that is, a form of totalitarianism masquerading in nice words; the truth of Jesus Christ was solemnly reaffirmed in the *Dominus Jesus*, the rational capacities of the human mind were acknowledged to have the capacity to reach for truth and recognize it (*Veritatis splendor*).

In the apostolic letter written in 1989 for the fiftieth anniversary since the beginning of the Second World War, after having listed the unspeakable sufferings, injustices and carnages leading to the death of fifty-five million deaths, after having warned government leaders that "respect for God and respect for man go hand in hand," Wojtyla called to mind that war exploded on the Christian continent by antonomasia: "Such an observation cannot but incite us to make an exam of conscience about the quality of evangelization in Europe. The freefall of Christian values which favored yesterday's mistakes, must make us watchful about the ways in which today the Gospel is announced and lived." Four years earlier, during the symposium of the Council of European Episcopal Conferences, Wojtyla stated: "The Europe we have been sent to, has been the subject of so many and such profound cultural, political, social and economic transformations that the problem of evangelization is now posed on completely new terms." In this context, John Paul II invited the

Church to return to "the founding and paradigmatic model" of the evangelization enacted in the "very first apostolic model."

The greatest evangelizers of Europe were the saints": "We need new saints." We need credible people who may witness with their lives the truth of what they preach: "Just like the very first evangelization – also the new age of evangelization will be able to count on authentically missionary lay people." Cardinal Wojtyla began a new model of evangelization by blessing the erection of a great cross by workers of Nowa Huta, the neighborhood model designed by the communist regime without churches of religious symbols. Upon his return to Nowa Huta as Pope on June 9, 1979, Wojtyla affirmed: with the cross "we have received a sign; at the threshold of the new millennium – in these new times, in these new life circumstances – the Gospel is announced again. A new evangelization has begun as if it were a second announcement." John Paul II blessed the new evangelization again in 1986, when he sent on mission one hundred families, all members of the Neocatechumenal Way[35]. These are families open to life and therefore overflowing with children who left all securities, work, relatives, and friends and made themselves available to announce the Gospel wherever there is need; that is, wherever a bishop should request them to establish or re-establish the Church in areas that are completely dechristianized. To accompany the missionary families, priests were needed and so in 1987, John Paul II established in Rome the first international missionary seminary *Redemptoris Mater*.

"The individual, from his own autonomous reason, wants to receive the ends, the values, the meaning of his life and activity. But he often finds himself amidst the darkness of metaphysical certainties, of ultimate ends and of certain ethical points of reference. This man, who in this way wants to be adult, mature, free, is also a man who flees from freedom to search for comfort in conformism, a man who suffers solitude, is threatened by various discomforts of the soul, tries to remove death and is in a state of fearful loss of hope" (John Paul

---

[35] The Neocatechumenal Way was born in 1964 in the shantytowns of Palomeras Altas in the outskirts of Madrid by the initiative of Kiko Argüello and Carmen Hernandez. In 1990, John Paul II defined this community life experience as: "An itinerary of Catholic formation, valid for our society and for our times." Today, the families sent by the Popes in mission are 1600.

II to European bishops): the missionary families, priests and their socii who accompany them, and some sisters, form a community and the Christian community is the answer to modern man's desperate loneliness.

For five hundred years, starting from Luther's doctrine about the free interpretation of scripture which exalted the individual relationship of man with God at the expense of the community, modernity targeted the central nature of the individual and his desires, his needs and wants. The upshot is that man is alone. "It is not good for man to be alone," is written in Genesis: the Christian community is the jewel thought by God to give hope and consolation to the world. And the Church took off again. Year after year, the Pope's steering shakes her up, the certainty of truth moves it and the Holy Spirit grants it courage once again.

Do not be Afraid

In *Mein Kampf*, Hitler identified terror and force as the most effective means to achieve victory over the opposition of the human soul: "The one means that wins the easiest victory over reason: terror and force." Karol Wojtila knew the weight of terror and force by experience because he lived in Poland during the Nazi and then Communist occupations. But Wojtyla was an athlete of God. Actor, philosopher, poet, and worker. An orphan, consecrated to Mary, witness to Jesus. A Globetrotter, a magnet for youth, intrepid, open towards all, cordial with all, inflexible towards members of the mafia and phony defenders of mankind. Erudite, brave, suffering, heroic in his forbearing evil, great in his old age, a giant in his sickness. During the first years of his pontificate he was slandered, persecuted, mocked, derided, scorned. Calumnies could do nothing against the holiness of his life and his enemies, and the enemies of the Church changed their tactics and provoked a muddy river of public debates about the suitability of abdicating for excessive sickness. For excessive old age. For manifest incapacity to govern the Church. For the good of the Church. It was useless. The Pope resisted to bear witness that the Master of History and life is God, not man.

Karol Wojtyla was a danger to many. He was a danger to the Communist regimes of Europe: he was Pope, the first Slave Pope and the Communist regime could not stop him from visiting his homeland as a Pope. Nine times John Paul II went to Poland and there repeated: "Do not be afraid"; "Open wide the doors to Christ." Behind the force of the Wojtyla cyclone, the polish people were given back faith and hope, they stopped bowing their heads low terrorized by Communist spies hidden everywhere. From resurrected Poland, a small pebble began rolling and crumbled the *Moloch* of Soviet Communism. The Soviet Union fell without shedding a drop of blood. A miraculous event; just as miraculous as the survival of the Pope after the attempt on his life made on May 13, 1978. A "professional assassin," the Turk Ali Agca shot him from a few yards in Saint Peter's square while he greeted the faithful on the Popemobile: "Agca knew how to shoot, and he certainly shot to kill. Nevertheless, it was as if someone guided the bullet to stray off course," recalled John Paul II in his last book *Memory and Identity*. May 13 was no ordinary day: it was the first day of Mary's apparitions in Fatima. The Pope connected the two days: "Again I am in debt towards the Most Holy Virgin and towards all Patron Saints. Could I ever forget that the event in Saint Peter's square took place on the very same day and hour in which for over sixty years, the first apparition of the Mother of Christ to the poor shepherds in Fatima, Portugal, is remembered? In everything that happened to me on that day, I felt an extraordinary protection and maternal care. It proved to be stronger than the deadly bullet."

After the attempt, John Paul II had the sealed envelope handed over to him containing the third secret revealed to the children in Fatima but not yet divulged. Mary – we already mentioned this – revealed to the little shepherds the way to avoid that God's wrath would unleash itself again against mankind: "I shall come to ask for the consecration of Russia to My Immaculate Heart and the Communion of reparation on the First Saturdays. If my requests are heeded, Russia will be converted, and there will be peace; if not, she will spread her errors throughout the world, causing wars and persecutions of the Church. The good will be martyred; the Holy Father will have much to suffer; various nations will be annihilated. In the end, my Immaculate Heart will triumph. The Holy Father will consecrate Russia to me, and she shall be converted, and a period of peace will be granted to the world."

Pope Wojtyla wrote an *Act of Entrustment* to Mary which was to be celebrated in the Basilica of Saint Mary Major on June 7, 1981, the Solemnity of Pentecost and anniversary of the Council of Ephesus in which the Church proclaimed Mary *Theotokos* (Mother of God). The Pope repeated the consecration on May 13, 1982 from Fatima where he went to personally thank the Virigin for the protection she gave him and then again in Saint Peter's square on March 25, 1984, in communion with all the bishops of the world. This time, sister Lucia, the last living seer of Fatima, in a letter dated December 8, 1989, confirmed that the consecration took place "as our Lady had asked." On Christmas day of 1991, the Soviet Union dissolved.

"I know that I am not alone in what I do as the Successor of Peter. Let us take the Communist system as an example," recalled Wojtyla in *Memory and Identity*: "I am well aware that it would be ridiculous to claim that it was the Pope who knocked down Communism with his own hands. I think the explanation is to be found in the Gospel. When the first disciples, after being sent on mission came back to their Teacher, they said: 'Lord, even the demons are subject to us in your name!' Christ answered them: 'do not rejoice in this, that the demons submit to you; but rejoice that your names are written in heaven.' And in another occasion, he added: 'Say, we are useless servants; we have only done what was our duty.' Useless servants... The awareness of the 'useless servant' grows in me amidst everything occurring around me – and I think to be happy with this."

Angioli, Keep these Letters

In 1948, the priest Karol Wojtyla went to San Giovanni Rotondo to meet with Padre Pio (1887-1968): "With Padre, all we spoke about were the stigmata," John Paul II retold to cardinal Deskur. "The only question I asked: which stigmata hurt him the most. I was convinced it was that of the heart. Padre Pio surprised me by saying: 'No, the one on the shoulder hurts most, which no one knows about and is not ever cared for.'" Fifteen years later, on November 17, 1962, bishop Wojtyla, from Rome where he was working on the council, wrote an urgent letter to Padre Pio: "Venerable Father, I ask you to pray for a mother of four girls who is fourty years old and lives in Krakow, Poland. During the last war, she spent five years in a German concentration camp and now her health is in grave danger, rather her life is, because of a cancer. Pray so that God, with the intervention of the Most Blessed Virign, may show her and her family mercy." "Angiolì, we can't say no to this one," was the comment Padre Pio made to Angelo Battisti who read him the letter. On November 28, Battisti read a second letter to Padre Pio. This one was also urgent: "Venerable Father, the woman who lives in Krakow, Poland, mother of four girls, on November 21, before the operation suddenly healed. Let us give thanks to God, and also to you venerable Father I offer the greatest thanks in the name of the same woman, her husband and the whole family." Padre Pio addressed Battisti as follows: "Angiolì, keep these letters. One day they'll be important."

Pope Wojtyla returned to San Giovanni Rotondo on May 23, 1987 for the hundredth anniversary of Padre Pio's birth. These were some of the words he said in the church: "An essential aspect of the sacred ministry, which can be found in the life of Padre Pio, was the offer the priest makes of himself to Christ and with Christ as victim of expiation and reparation for the sins of men." The Pope was speaking of the Capuchin friar, but his words were the faithful description of his life. During the Angelus of May 29, 1994, after a month of convalescence in the hospital, Karol Wojtyla addressed the faithful with the following words: "I would like that, through Mary, today, my gratitude may be expressed for this gift of suffering newly tied to the Marian month of May. I want to give thanks for this gift. I have understood that is was a necessary gift. The Pope needed to be at the Gemelli Polyclinic, he needed to be absent from this window for four weeks, four Sundays, he had to suffer: just like he had to suffer thirteen years ago, so also this year"; "I understood that I must introduce the Church of Christ into this Third Millennium with prayer, with various initiative, but I saw that it was not enough: I needed to introduce her with suffering, with the assassination attempt of thirteen years ago and with this new sacrifice. Why now, why this year, why this Year of the Family? Exactly because the family is threatened, the family is assaulted. The Pope must be assaulted, the Pope must suffer, so that every family and the world may see that there is a Gospel, I would say, that is superior: the Gospel of suffering, by which the future must be prepared, the third millennium of the families, of every family, of all families."

Upon the death of John Paul II, Rome became Rome again, the City, that is, the world. While Romans, Polish and Italians got in line for hours, if not for a whole day, in order to see only for an instant, the Pope who devoted every moment of his life to them, three presidents of the United States of America – George Bush, Bill Clinton and George W. Bush – stopped on their knees before the body of the Pope while powerful men throughout all continents, of all faiths and of all political beliefs watched the funeral ceremony on the steps of Saint Peter.

Mark 16,15-20

"Jesus said to them: 'Go into all the world and preach the gospel to the whole creation. He who believes and is baptized will be saved; but he who does not believe will be condemned. And these signs will accompany those who believe: in my name they will cast out demons; they will speak in new tongues; they will pick up serpents, and if they drink any deadly thing, it will not hurt them; they will lay their hands on the sick, and they will recover.

So then the Lord Jesus, after he had spoken to them, was taken up into heaven, and sat down at the right hand of God.

And they went forth and preached everywhere, while the Lord worked with them and confirmed the message by the signs that attended it."

Table of Contents

Foreword 7
Jerusalem 10
Rome 11
The Virigin gives birth to a Child 13
The drunken woman 14
You, follow Me 16
The Age of Paul 18
Strive for perfection 19
The primitive Church 22
If they persecuted me, they will persecute you 23
Tolerant paganism? 25
They slander tou as evildoers 27
He went off to make war on the rest of her offspring 28
Many Antichrists have appeared 30
They will forbid marriage 32
Truth is in Rome 34
Come over to Macedonia and help us 36
Anthony the Great 38
Flavius Valerius Aurelius Constantinus 39
What does Constantine say of himself? 41
Is the Pope infallible? 43
Christianity, official religion 45
Barbarians 47
The *Katéchon* 49
Augustine of Hippo 51
Compelle intrare 53
Leo the Great 55
The Last shall be First 58
A First-born Daughter 60
Western monasticism: Benedict 62
A New Civilization 64
Flavius Petrus Sabbatius Iustinianus 66
Gregory the Great 68
The blind gods roar for Rome fallen 70
Mohammed 72
I am who I am 75
An agreement conceded 77
From Britain to Germany 79
Heretical Byzantium 82
The Pope King 84

Charlemagne 87
Translatio Imperii 90
Cyril and Methodius 93
Constitutio Romana and *Privilegium Othonis* 95
Once Again 12 97
A New Millennium 99
In defense of the *Libertas Ecclesiae* 102
The investiture controversy 105
Hermits, Patarini and New Orders 107
A Conspiracy against Truth 109
Deus vult 111
A Sun upon the World 114
Altissimu, onnipotente, bon Signore – Most High, all powerful, good Lord 117
Cathars in Languedoc 120
The Inquisition 122
Beauty by analogy 125
Faith and Reason are in agreement 128
Pontifical hierocracy 130
Between Pope and Emperor, a king emerged 132
The Pope is not in Rome anymore 137
Twenty-fourth daughter 140
Western schism 142
Renaissance papacy 145
Spain is ready 148
Inter Caetera 151
Do Indios have a soul? 156
Martin Luther 158
The greatest revolutionary of the Second Millennium 162
An abominable sin 165
Charles V, Holy Roman Emperor 167
Contemplatives in action 170
Anglican England 172
John Calvin 175
The Jewish Question 179
The Age of Mannerism and Baroque 182
A horrendous crime 185
The Galileo Case 187
To understand history one must keep philosophy in mind 190
1648 Westphalia: A revolutionary peace 193
De Propaganda Fide 197
Wien, September 11, 1683 200
A Presbyterian Pastor at Work 202
Go, set a Watchman, let him announce what he sees 205
Dominus ac Redemptor 208
"Quanno nascette Ninno" – When the little Child was born 211
From Enlightened Despots to Terror 215

Slaughtered lambs...... 218
A New Empire...... 221
The Age of Restoration...... 224
Caritas Christi Urget Nos...... 227
Liberal Catholics...... 230
In Rome against Rome...... 233
Acherò...... 236
A Pope to defend liberty and truth...... 239
A priest acrobat, prophet and saint...... 242
In the Name of Liberty of Conscience...... 246
Spes contra Spem...... 249
The Brief Century...... 252
Poland is Ready...... 255
The Church is the sole cause of all of Mexico's misfortunes...... 258
Lateran Pacts, Church and Fascism...... 261
A Worshipper of Satan in Power...... 264
Civil War in Spain...... 269
Virgin, Mother, Daughter of your Son...... 272
Humanity Heads towards a New Order...... 276
Be holy, for I, the Lord Your God, am holy...... 279
A New Evangelization...... 282
Do not be Afraid...... 285
Angiolì, Keep these Letters...... 287
Mark 16,15-20...... 289
Table of Contents...... 290

www.ingramcontent.com/pod-product-compliance
Lightning Source LLC
Chambersburg PA
CBHW030239170426
43202CB00007B/53